THE THEORY OF SPEECH AND LANGUAGE

Oxford University Press, Amen House, London E.C.4

GLASGOW NEW YORK TORONTO MELBOURNE WELLINGTON
BOMBAY CALCUTTA MADRAS KARACHI LAHORE DACCA
CAPE TOWN SALISBURY NAIROBI IBADAN ACCRA
KUALA LUMPUR HONG KONG

FIRST EDITION 1932
SECOND EDITION REPRINTED LITHOGRAPHICALLY
AT THE UNIVERSITY PRESS, OXFORD, 1951
FROM CORRECTED SHEETS OF THE FIRST EDITION
REPRINTED 1960, 1963

THE THEORY OF SPEECH AND LANGUAGE

By

SIR ALAN GARDINER
FELLOW OF THE BRITISH ACADEMY

SECOND EDITION

OXFORD
AT THE CLARENDON PRESS

401
G168t
1951

PRINTED IN GREAT BRITAIN

THIS BOOK
IS DEDICATED TO THE MEMORY OF
GEHEIMRAT PROFESSOR DR.
PHILIPP WEGENER
A PIONEER OF LINGUISTIC
THEORY

PREFACE TO
THE SECOND EDITION

THIS book having been out of print for several years, it was gratifying to learn that the Delegates of the Clarendon Press considered the demand still sufficient to justify them in undertaking a second edition. The question then arose as to the form the new edition should take. Aware of how, too often, an author will spoil his work in revision, I decided that a reprint, with alteration of only a very few words and phrases,[1] would be the wisest plan—a decision that also fitted in well with the economic aspect of the matter; the original text could then be reproduced lithographically and costly re-setting avoided.

However, in the twenty years that have elapsed since my typescript was sent to Press, much has been written upon the same theme; Professor W. E. Collinson's article entitled 'Some Recent Developments of Syntactical Theory' in *Transactions of the Philological Society*, 1941, gives an admirable conspectus of what had appeared up to ten years ago, and if one adds all that has seen the light since, it might well seem that my own contribution must be hopelessly out of date. Whether it is so or not must be left to my readers to decide. Occupied with many other tasks in the interval, I certainly cannot undertake to survey the entire field anew, and must content myself with

---

[1] Apart from some minor typographical details, the only changes in the main text of the book are a slight modification in the definition of word-form on p. 138, the substitution of 'detachment' for 'intellectuality' p. 225, l. 17, and the replacement of 'a proposition' by 'something asserted', p. 297, n. 1, l. 5. Here and there, however, a small reference letter has been added to a word (e.g. 'proper names^e', p. 41, l. 6) in order to indicate a correction or further discussion in the Retrospect at the end of the book.

appending a Retrospect of which the purpose is a few necessary repairs and some, as I hope, strictly unnecessary underpinning. Reference will there be made to a paper I read before the Congress of Linguists at Rome in 1935, to a reply to critics which was printed in 1937, and to an essay on Proper Names that followed in 1940. These are the main, though not quite the sole, writings I have devoted to the subject, of which I now take leave with regret.

Unfortunately this Preface cannot be concluded without an apology. In 1932, when my book first appeared, I was still young enough and optimistic enough to believe it would in due course be followed by a second volume dealing with the theory of the Word. Allusions to this projected second volume will be found scattered up and down the present pages. Alas, I have to admit that the writing of such a sequel is now altogether beyond my powers. Knowledge of more languages than I have at my command would be indispensable for the satisfactory treatment of the so-called Parts of Speech; nor could I, at my time of life, acquire sufficient familiarity with the vast literature which others have devoted to the subject. But I must not repine at a failure that belongs to the common lot, and I conclude with the hope that some younger man will supply this much needed book in a form with which I could not have competed, even in my more vigorous days.

ACKNOWLEDGEMENTS

SOME fifteen years ago it became my habit, whenever occasion offered, to discuss questions of grammar and linguistics with such of my friends as were interested, and it is under the influence of conversations with Miss Paget (Vernon Lee), Dr. Malinowski, and my former assistant, Mr. Battiscombe Gunn, that the first outlines of my linguistic theory were conceived. At a subsequent date I had various opportunities of discussion with the late Professor Sonnenschein and with Professor Rolf Pipping. The real impulse to the writing of this book was, however, given by Dr. Bertrand Russell, as he then was. A somewhat crude attempt to describe and analyse a single act of speech had been made in a paper of mine which failed to find acceptance when offered for publication. On my appealing to Dr. Russell he was good enough to express the opinion that the contents might fitly form the nucleus of a book. In another quarter, also, I received valuable encouragement, namely from my friend and Egyptological colleague, Professor H. Grapow. Spurred on in this manner, I finally decided to embark upon the present adventure. A number of unsuccessful efforts were consigned to the wastepaper-basket. At last, in 1928, the first chapter was written to my satisfaction, and the second was added in the following year. Both of these have been read by many friends, among them Dr. Ludlow Bull, Dr. A. de Buck, Dr. E. Classen, Professor Peet and Mr. Leonard Woolley, and to each and all I owe comments of interest. Later on, Mr. Gunn read the first four chapters with great care and sent me a number of notes which have proved very helpful. He considered that I had understressed the mechanization of speech as usually practised, and in revising I have endeavoured to bear this criticism in mind. To Professor Peet I am especially indebted for the knowledge of Samuel Butler's witty essay. Until last autumn I imagined that some years of work still lay ahead of me. Two stimulating conversations with Professor Karl Bühler of Vienna convinced me, however, that it would be better to publish a first instalment without further delay, so I set to work on the final revision. When the book was complete, Professor Morris Ginsberg had the kindness to read it through in its entirety, and to him I owe some valuable observations. I cannot sufficiently thank Mr. K. Sisam, of the Clarendon Press, for his interest and help.

My old friends the Printers have expended their wonted skill upon the external appearance of my book, and I am correspondingly grateful. To Mr. Paul Jones I am indebted for the care bestowed on the drawings, and to my assistant, Mr. R. O. Faulkner, for much secretarial help and vigilance in reading the proofs. I am particularly happy to acknowledge important aid from two members of my own family. As in the case of my Egyptian Grammar, my father has backed my work with the necessary financial subsidy. To my daughter Margaret my debt is particularly great. She has revised my typescript with me from beginning to end, and there is hardly a page but has benefited by her sensitive and acute criticism. To my many helpers I tender my sincerest thanks.

A. H. G.

CONTENTS

FOREWORD 1

The crisis of grammar, § 1; the problem stated, § 2; the method to be employed, § 3; the practical results anticipated, § 4; the present volume and remoter prospects, § 5.

PART I. GENERAL THEORY

I. SPEECH AND THE FACTORS INVOLVED THEREIN . 17

The usual definition criticized, § 6; the social origin of speech; the listener, § 7; the things spoken about, § 8; words, § 9; meaning and thing-meant, § 10; the function of word-meaning, § 11; a preliminary account of word-meaning, § 12; the relation of words to the things referred to in speech, § 13; the mechanized elements in speech, § 14; selective attention, § 15; the situation, § 16; depth of intention, § 17; word-consciousness, § 18; style, § 19.

ADDITIONAL NOTE A. *Is the listener a necessary factor of speech?*
ADDITIONAL NOTE B. *Has the distinction between 'meaning' and 'thing-meant' really been ignored hitherto?*

II. THE ACT OF SPEECH. THE SENTENCE AND THE WORD. SPEECH AND LANGUAGE . . . 62

Summary of the argument, § 20; silence and speech, § 21; the act of speech at once social and individual, § 22; the ultimate basis of speech, § 23; the superiority of spoken language to all other systems of signs, § 24; words not really objects of sense, but psychical entities, § 25; the *modus operandi* of a simple act of speech, § 26; once again the thing-meant, § 27; the material and the standpoint of the theorist of speech, § 28; how language enters into speech, § 29; the nature of the sentence, § 30; the ambiguity of the word 'meaning', § 31; summary and conclusion, § 32.

ADDITIONAL NOTE C. *Extract from S. Butler, 'Essays on Life, Art, and Science',* pp. 201–4.

THE MUTUAL RELATIONS OF LANGUAGE AND SPEECH 106

The antithesis of language and speech, § 33; secondary forms of speech, § 34; language as the product of speech. § 35; is all use of language of the type here already described? § 36; the undifferentiated word-sentence of pre-human times, § 37; the word as a linguistic entity distinct from the sentence, § 38; the emergence of words in the many-word sentence, § 39; the many-word sentence as a whole, § 40; word-form, § 41; word-form and word-function as correlated linguistic facts, § 42; the application of words, § 43; form and function become grammatical, § 44; syntactic and intonational form and function, § 45; final remarks on incongruent word-function, § 46; metaphor, § 47; correct and faulty speech, § 48; conclusion, § 49.

ADDITIONAL NOTE D, *on my statement (p. 119) that 'the variety of possible things which the speaker may intend is always far greater than the variety of the expressional means contained in his vocabulary'.*

PART II. THEORY OF THE SENTENCE

IV. THE SENTENCE AND ITS FORM 181

Function as the criterion of the sentence, § 50; general and special sentence-quality; the four kinds of sentence, § 51; the specific purpose of the speaker as a new kind of overtone; description and implication the two methods of speech, § 52; sentence-quality, sentence-function and sentence-form, § 53; locutional and elocutional sentence-form; intonation, § 54; utterance the principal quantitative criterion of the sentence, § 55; sentences without locutional sentence-form, § 56; sentence-form in the main elocutional, § 57; the claim that every sentence must consist of subject and predicate, § 58; the claim that every sentence must contain a finite verb, § 59; other words suggesting special sentence-form; word-order, § 60; locutional sentence-form in incongruent function, § 61; quoted words, § 62; conclusion, § 63.

ADDITIONAL NOTE E. *Remarks on some definitions of the sentence, mostly recent.*

V. THE SENTENCE AND ITS LOCUTIONAL CONTENT 240

The content of the sentence, § 64; the origination of sentences, § 65; concessions to the expressionistic hypothesis, § 66; predication as a process involved in all speech, § 67; subject and predicate, § 68; grammatical and logical subject and predicate, § 69; the subject becomes a matter of choice, § 70; the predicative use of words, § 71; statements, § 72; questions, § 73; requests, § 74; exclamations, § 75; quantitative classifications of the sentence, § 76; conclusion, § 77.

RETROSPECT 1951 328
   ADDITIONAL NOTE F. *'Tweak' or 'Twinge'?* 342
INDEX 345

FOREWORD

§ 1. **The crisis of grammar.** It is in periods of transition like the present that the never-ending struggle between authority on the one hand, and the spirit of reform on the other, becomes most insistent and vocal. Belief in the established order being weakened, the number of those who advocate a wholesale clearance of what they regard as clogging traditional rubbish is correspondingly increased, while a party of opposition automatically arises among those who feel that the achievements of the past are being jeopardized. This state of affairs, familiar in the contemporary world of politics, repeats itself in the smaller domains of science and art, so that the latter appear as veritable microcosms. The uninformed might be excused for assuming that so apparently tranquil a backwater as that of grammatical lore would be exempt from any such violent antithesis. In this assumption they would be wrong, however, for the science of language is, at the present moment, more than ever a storm-centre of conflicting theories and opposing cross-currents. Nothing could be more apparent to those for whom, during no inconsiderable part of their working lives, the supposed backwater is their actual world. On the one side we see the revolutionaries, as those scholars must be called who regard conventional grammar as a tissue of absurdities. Theirs is at least the merit of having recognized how inadequate, or on occasion positively false, are many of the definitions and explanations propagated in even the best of our school-books. Their weakness is an excessive readiness to throw overboard such time-honoured grammatical categories as verb and noun, subject and predicate, adverb and conjunction, sometimes substituting a terminology of their own to the defects of which they are completely blind. On the other side we find the traditionalists, the most open-minded of whom admit, perhaps somewhat grudgingly, the strictures of their opponents, and who seek to remedy the situation by more acute, more carefully reasoned, logical analysis of the facts. As exponents of the forward movement may be named Brunot[1] and Jespersen,[2] while equally distinguished champions of the conservative party are the late Professor Sonnenschein[3] and the German grammarian John Ries.[4] It would seem that the differences between these eminent scholars could be reconciled, if at all, only by appeal to general linguistic theory. But although Brunot entitles his great work *La pensée et la langue*, and though Jespersen is author of a *Philosophy of Grammar*, neither is in truth a systematizer or a theorist. Both are scientific investigators and exponents of linguistic facts; the same is true of Sonnenschein, who would have claimed nothing different for himself. Ries is a theoretician less of speech or language than of grammar. Now it is quite in accordance with the present writer's outlook that the practical grammarians should be regarded as the protagonists in this controversy rather than the psychologists, logicians, and other more philosophically minded adepts of grammar. My own approach to linguistic theory

---

[1] F. Brunot, *La pensée et la langue*, Paris, 1922.

[2] O. Jespersen, *Language, its Nature, Development, and Origin*, London, 1922; *The Philosophy of Grammar*, London, 1924.

[3] E. A. Sonnenschein, *A New English Grammar*, Oxford, 1916; *The Soul of Grammar*, Cambridge, 1927. The latter work bears on its title-page the motto, 'Evolution, not Revolution'.

[4] John Ries, *Beiträge zur Grundlegung der Syntax*, Prague, 1927-31, Part 1, *Was ist Syntax?*, 2nd edition, 1927 (first published in 1894); Part 2, *Zur Wortgruppenlehre*, 1928; Part 3, *Was ist ein Satz?*, 1931.

is from the side of specific grammatical problems, and I could wish that such a theory should be constructed purely on the basis of empiric observations. Unfortunately, most professional grammarians are too deeply absorbed in particular problems to be willing or able to look at the mechanism of speech as a whole. Their attitude is not unlike that of Delbrück, who, writing concerning the opposing schools of *Sprachpsychologie* represented by Paul[1] and Wundt[2] respectively, declared that it was possible for the practical grammarian to live at peace with either.[3] Within its limits this standpoint cannot be disputed. The fact is that important progress in detail may still be made without reference to general theory. But it is another question whether all philological work would not be strengthened and deepened by the possession of a systematic and comprehensive theory of speech acceptable, at least in its main lines, to all. The prevailing disharmony leads one to suspect that the absence of such a wide theoretic view is the real root of the trouble.

It is not to be denied that linguistic theory is nowadays attracting more and more attention. Every few months some new book dealing with the topic makes its appearance,[4] and the problem of the nature of speech seems to be slowly but surely nearing solution. But with a few honourable exceptions—and here the names of Wegener,[5] de

---

[1] H. Paul, *Prinzipien der Sprachgeschichte*, 4th edition, Halle, 1909.
[2] W. Wundt, *Völkerpsychologie*, vol. i, *Die Sprache*, Parts I–II, 2nd edition, Leipzig, 1904.
[3] B. Delbrück, *Grundfragen der Sprachforschung*, Strasbourg, 1901, p. 44.
[4] For a brief survey, with bibliography, see G. Ipsen, *Sprachphilosophie der Gegenwart*, Berlin, 1930, being *Philosophische Forschungsberichte*, Heft 6.
[5] Ph. Wegener, *Untersuchungen über die Grundfragen des Sprachlebens*, Halle, 1885. Philipp Wegener was born at Neuhaldensleben in 1848, and died in 1916 as Director of the Gymnasium in Greifswald. A sympathetic

Saussure,[1] Erdmann,[2] Sheffield,[3] and Kalepky[4] may be specially mentioned—the theorists of speech are mainly recruited from the ranks of psychologists and logicians. Among the psychologists Karl Bühler[5] is the writer on linguistic theory with whose views I find myself most in sympathy. Many of his conclusions, reached along quite different channels from my own, coincide almost completely with those to be expounded in the present book.

§ 2. **The problem stated.** What then is this 'linguistic theory' to which the foregoing section repeatedly made allusion, and which has given the present book its title? Let me disclaim, without further delay, any intention of writing about origins. It has been found difficult, or at least inexpedient, to exclude all speculation with regard to the origin of speech, but the main argument neither depends thereon, nor yet is seriously affected thereby. Less than anyone else can a competent student of Egyptian hieroglyphics believe that the language of his predilection will teach him anything of value concerning the origins of speech. The old Egyptian language, like Sanskrit and Chinese, is a highly developed and sophisticated tongue, on a long view little less modern than French or English. Such information as Egyptian can yield to throw light upon the nature of speech is due not so much to its

account of the man and of his career as a teacher is given by A. Leitzmann in *Indogermanisches Jahrbuch*, vol. iv, Strasbourg, 1917, pp. 246 foll.

[1] F. de Saussure, *Cours de linguistique générale*, Lausanne and Paris, 1916. Posthumous work published by C. Bally and A. Sechehaye.
[2] K. O. Erdmann, *Die Bedeutung des Wortes*, 3rd edition, Leipzig, 1922.
[3] A. D. Sheffield, *Grammar and Thinking*, New York and London, 1912.
[4] Th. Kalepky, *Neuaufbau der Grammatik*, Leipzig, 1928.
[5] Various articles summarized and criticized by H. Dempe, *Was ist Sprache?*, Weimar, 1930. See especially K. Bühler, 'Kritische Musterung der neuern Theorien des Satzes', in *Indogermanisches Jahrbuch*, vol. vi for 1918, Berlin and Leipzig, 1920.

antiquity as to the difference of its structure from that of the languages most frequently studied by writers on general linguistics. At all events it is not the main source from which I have drawn my arguments. That source is English, my mother-tongue. It is my conviction that every adult human being is the living repository of a profound knowledge of language. Not only does he possess a vast store of words, but even the veriest yokel is something of an artist in the matter of their employment. Here, then, existent in the consciousness of everyone, is an immense treasure of evidence available for the construction of a solid fabric of linguistic theory.

The problem which I am setting before myself may best be indicated by a comparison. Suppose an intelligent boy to be inquiring how the telephone or the wireless works. If the question were rightly addressed, the answer would doubtless supply a clear account of the mechanism—an account which, without penetrating very deeply into the laws of physics, would satisfy the inquirer and carry with it immediate conviction. Could a like question be profitably put to the ordinary philologist? Could he be trusted to give a sensible reply to the inquiry what language is and how speech works? A fairly wide acquaintance with the literature of linguistics has convinced me of the contrary, and indeed I have searched high and low without finding the problem either stated or systematically handled in this way.

§ 3. **The method to be employed.** The problem here to be studied is, accordingly: How does speech work? And if now we ask ourselves by what method this problem should be tackled, the procedure of other sciences at once affords the answer: By the study of concrete, particular examples. Here, however, the practical grammarian will intervene and object that his own way of approach is no other. On this point I cannot altogether agree with him, for though the grammarian certainly treats of specific words and types of sentences, it is only when he assumes the role of commentator that he is really concerned with particular occasions of speech. In what manner, then, does the method which I am advocating differ from that of the orthodox grammarian? The botanist may be called upon to point the road. Words being so constituted as to be used over and over again, they are comparable, not to individual plants, but to the botanical species of which those individual plants are specimens. Similarly, syntactic forms and rules correspond, not so much to observed conditions appertaining to particular flowers or trees, as to the general inferences based on much observation of such conditions. But what botanist would think of attacking his problems otherwise than by a minute examination of individual specimens, considered in relation to the soil in which they have grown, to the climate, in fact to their total environment? So far as the philologist is concerned, this way of procedure is, unless I am mistaken, nearly an untrodden path. Kalepky[1] and others have, it is true, devoted some attention to individual samples of speech observed in their natural surroundings, but I am aware of no attempt, except my own, to analyse a single act of speech with fullness or exactitude.

This, then, is my method: to put back single acts of speech into their original setting of real life, and thence to discover what processes are employed, what factors involved. For controversial reasons it seemed desirable to precede the analysis of a simple act of speech (Ch. II) by some discussion of its essential factors (Ch. I), and I have

[1] *Neuaufbau der Grammatik*, p. 21.

found surprising and encouraging confirmation of my views at a lecture recently given in London. On that occasion Professor Karl Bühler, of Vienna, wrote upon the blackboard the four factors, (1) the speaker, (2) the listener, (3) the things referred to, and (4) the linguistic material, the interrelations of which I had declared, nearly ten years ago, to constitute the whole mechanism of speech.[1] No more welcome indication that I have been upon the right track could have been desired than this independent testimony of one who is primarily not a grammarian, but a psychologist.

On the view here advocated, speech is a human activity demanding at least two persons possessing a common language and finding themselves in a common situation. The science to which linguistic theory thus ultimately owes allegiance is neither logic nor psychology, but sociology.[2] Logic is concerned with the relations of propositions to facts, and psychology with subjective states, observed or inferred. Sociology, on the other hand, has at least as a large part of its field intersubjective phenomena, the dealings of man with man, among which speech is one of the most important techniques. This formulation of the status of speech is not, of course, intended as a denial of the claim of the logician or the psychologist to regard certain aspects of linguistics as his own peculiar sphere. Much more questionable is, indeed, the claim of the philologist to construct a linguistic theory without the help of experts in those abstract fields. My own feeling is that the philologist not only has the right to form a general

[1] A. H. Gardiner, 'The Definition of the Word and the Sentence', in *Brit. Journ. Psychol.*, vol. xii, pp. 354–5.

[2] This has, of course, been recognized by many, but by none more clearly than Durkheim and his school, with Meillet as the leading philological exponent. See, too, J. Ward, *Psychological Principles*, p. 287.

conception of the nature of the material with which he deals, but that it is also his duty. To penetrate deeply into the psychological processes or philosophical truths which underlie the mechanism of speech is no doubt as much beyond his powers as to explain the ultimate mysteries of the telephone or the wireless is beyond the powers of the practical engineer. But surely every intelligent workman in any of these branches should possess a shrewd idea how the mechanism with which he is particularly concerned achieves its ends. His views will be based on elementary technical knowledge combined with common-sense observation, and will be expressed not in philosophical jargon, but in the language, and from the standpoint, of everyday life. Such, then, are the subject and the method of my book.

§ 4. **The practical results anticipated.** The first benefit that may be expected from a sound general linguistic theory, if attainable, is that it will teach us which of the old-accepted grammatical categories should be retained and which of them are really in need of modification or rejection. On the whole, I believe it will be found that most of the traditional terms, though often badly named, correspond to real facts and distinctions in the linguistic material. It may be reasonably doubted whether a serviceable grammar which dispenses entirely with such terms as noun or verb will ever be written. The second benefit which I anticipate is, however, that the current accounts given of such categories will be substantially changed; to my mind it is not so much the traditional terms that are unacceptable as the explanations of them which are usually given. Common sense favours this view. It is *a priori* hardly likely that practical grammarians should have continued, generation after generation, to use terms utterly unsuited to the facts. In writing my

Egyptian Grammar,[1] I found no difficulty in fitting the material into the framework of the grammar which I learned at school. On the other hand, I derived considerable benefit from the revised terms and even from the definitions provided by the Joint Committee on Grammatical Terminology. Nevertheless the commonly accepted definitions do, in very many cases, stand in need of serious revision. Even so great a scholar as Meillet could state, not many years ago, that the noun is a means of indicating things, while the verb is an indicator of processes (*procès*).[2] Though these definitions are clearly approximations to the truth, as they stand they are either ambiguous or else definitely false. The second of them is rendered nugatory by the fact that *assassination*, *flight*, *pressure* are undoubtedly names of actions or processes, but nevertheless are nouns, not verbs. And as regards the first, denominative verbs like to *cage*, to *motor*, and to *censure*, at the very least render the formulation inadequate. The linguistic theory set forth in this book will, I think, not only throw some light upon the reasons why these definitions are open to objection, but will also show how they may be ameliorated. All words whatsoever will be seen to be names of 'things', that term being understood in the very widest sense as covering material objects, persons, actions, relations, concepts, and figments of the imagination. The so-called parts of speech are distinctions among words based not upon the nature of the objects to

---

[1] A. H. Gardiner, *Egyptian Grammar*, Oxford, 1927. [2nd ed., 1950.]
[2] 'Le nom indique les "choses", qu'il s'agisse d'objets concrets ou de notions abstraites, d'êtres réels ou d'espèces: *Pierre, table, vert, verdeur, bonté, cheval*, sont également des noms. Le verbe indique les "procès", qu'il s'agisse d'actions, d'états ou de passages d'un état à un autre: *il marche, il dort, il brille, il bleuit* sont également des verbes.' A. Meillet, *Linguistique historique et linguistique générale*, Paris, 1921, p. 175.

which they refer, but upon the mode of their presentation. Thus the name of anything presented *as* a thing is a 'noun', and the name of anything presented *as* an action, or, if Meillet's expression be preferred, *as* a process, is a 'verb'. In the verb to *cage*, reference is made to the thing called a *cage*, but it is not presented as a thing but as an action. In the noun *assassination* reference is made to an action, but it is not presented as an action but as a thing. The details of this topic belong to my second volume; here it need be added only that the terms 'verb' and 'noun' are not really incompatible, but that one and the same thing may be presented simultaneously as an action and as a thing, though possibly never with exactly equal emphasis. Thus grammar rightly distinguishes between verbal nouns, e.g. (*the*) *murder*, and nominal parts of the verb, e.g. (*the*) *murdering*.

To some philologists the acquisition of a satisfactory linguistic theory will appear a worthy aspiration in itself. But it is not to be denied that many regard the quest upon which I am engaged as idle and nebulous. Before the eyes of such I must dangle a few more enticements not to throw my book in a corner even at this early stage. Every schoolboy is familiar with the phrases 'a noun used as an adjective' or 'an adjective used as a noun'. If these terms refer to function, why, our schoolboy may well ask, does his master not call the former an adjective, and the latter a noun, and have done with it? The reasons why the accepted mode of expression is not merely legitimate, but even imperative, are among the things which I pledge myself to explain. Enticement the second. Wundt tells us that the boundary between the word and the sentence is shifting and uncertain.[1] This standpoint is utterly false.

[1] *Die Sprache*, vol. i, pp. 599 foll. See, too, L. Sütterlin, *Das Wesen der*

I shall prove that one and the same verbal expression may be simultaneously both a word and a sentence, but that there is no more difficulty about this than there is about a rat being simultaneously both a rodent and a nuisance. Enticement the third. Is it not something of a puzzle that especially in letters and in ancient documents of different kinds the meaning of the component individual sentences should often be perfectly clear, but that the reader should nevertheless be left in almost complete darkness as to what the document is really about? At first sight this state of affairs seems almost a contradiction in terms. The position is one which the argument of my book will, I hope, completely elucidate.[1]

§ 5. **The present volume and remoter prospects.** Critics acquainted with the treatises on general linguistics by Steinthal,[2] Paul,[3] von der Gabelentz,[4] Marty,[5] Wundt,[6] and a host of others will possibly be indignant at my implied pretension that the search for a comprehensive linguistic theory is something new. Far be it from me to decry or underestimate the very real merits of these learned and admirable works. Nevertheless the method here advocated is relatively untried, and I believe that it holds out promise of greater success than previous efforts on account

---

sprachlichen Gebilde, Heidelberg, 1902, p. 59: 'Zwischen Wort und Satz sind nach Wundt die Grenzen fliessend. Das ist nicht zu bezweifeln, und darum vielleicht stellt Wundt auch nirgends begrifflich fest, was das Wort eigentlich sei.'

[1] See below, p. 61, the last paragraph of Additional Note B.

[2] H. Steinthal, *Abriss der Sprachwissenschaft*, Part I, *Die Sprache im Allgemeinen*, 2nd edition, Berlin, 1881.

[3] See above, p. 3, n. 1.

[4] G. von der Gabelentz, *Die Sprachwissenschaft*, Leipzig, 1901.

[5] A. Marty, *Untersuchungen zur Grundlegung der allgemeinen Grammatik und Sprachphilosophie*, vol. i, Halle, 1906.

[6] See above, p. 3, n. 2.

of its superior concreteness and its regard for all the factors of speech. The pioneer along this road was Philipp Wegener, a scholar whom I never had the honour of meeting, but to whose memory I venture to dedicate my book. Wegener[1] was the first, so far as I know, to emphasize the importance of the 'situation', and to determine the true reason for the dichotomy of 'subject' and 'predicate'. His analysis of the 'verb' is equally valuable, and interspersed throughout his meagre and perhaps hastily written volume are illuminating remarks which reveal him as having possessed a linguistic outlook far in advance of his contemporaries. None, if I judge rightly, would have been fitter to expound a systematic and comprehensive theory of speech. In a sense, perhaps, he did expound such a theory, though I miss in his writings that analysis of a particular act of speech which to me seems the necessary point of departure.

My own previous contributions to this topic have been confined to some general observations published in *Man*[2] and an article on the 'sentence' contributed to the *British Journal of Psychology*.[3] My duties as an Egyptologist have, indeed, left but little time for any wider field of research. In a very literal sense the present volume is a parergon, having been written at the rate of about one chapter a year mainly during my summer holidays. At times I have been frightened at my temerity in making this incursion into a domain where I confess to being a mere adventurer. A number of colleagues and friends have encouraged me to persist. This first instalment outlines a general theory of speech and language, and deals with the sentence, both

[1] In the book quoted above, p. 3, n. 5.
[2] A. H. Gardiner, 'Some Thoughts on the Subject of Language', in *Man*, 1919, No. 2.   [3] See above, p. 7, n. 1.

form and substance, in some detail. The projected second volume, which at all events cannot appear for several years to come, will deal mainly with the word and its kinds, as well as with the various extensions of the word, in particular the phrase and the clause. I am, of course, well aware that there are important aspects of speech and language which I have as good as completely ignored. My interest being primarily semasiological, i.e. concerned with the function of speech as an instrument for conveying meaning, I have paid but small attention to either its sounds or its aesthetic bearings.

Whatever the defects of the present work, I am confident that its method is sound and marks a real advance in the manner of regarding linguistic problems. It lay in the nature of the case that the treatment should be controversial and tentative. My theory holding that all writing (written speech) implies an author addressing his public, I was less persuaded than are some of the virtue of an impersonal tone. But I have the vision of three other books,[a] more objective in their manner, to be written from a similar standpoint at perhaps no very remote date. The first of these will be an elementary grammar for children, free from the usual taint of abstraction and unreality which those hardest and sanest of critics are so quick to detect and condemn. The opening lesson will explain what men seek to achieve by speech, and how this is to be distinguished from language. Word and sentence will be contrasted as things fundamentally different, and the pupil will be made to recognize both of them as facts of daily experience; thus they will cease to be felt as figments expressly invented to torment the juvenile mind. In the hands of a good teacher, even such grim entities as nouns and adjectives may possibly come to be tolerated, or at least no longer regarded with hostility. The second book I have in view will be a brief introductory treatise for young philologists, inculcating the right attitude towards speech and language generally, and anticipating many of those illusions and fallacies which disfigure much of the technical linguistic literature of to-day. The last book of the future for which I look is far more ambitious in theme, and I hardly know how to foretell its trend. Its author will be, not only a consummate grammarian, but also a man of great intellect and wide humanity. His work will be addressed to all men of science, philosophers, and seekers after Truth impartially, and will have as its starting-point a very simple argument. No science or philosophy exists which is not presented in terms of written language. But the sentences and words used for this purpose are no more identical with that philosophy or science than a landscape framed and hung upon the wall is identical with the landscape seen from yonder hill. Every painter is well aware of the differences between his picture and what he set out to depict, and has at least some familiarity with the laws of perspective. Surely translation into another medium must involve much alteration and subjective bias. Is not a distortion similar to that of pictorial art inherent in all verbal description, and should not a solidly grounded linguistic theory be the recognized prolegomena to all serious thinking? The position amounts to this: Does the present-day logician already possess a sound linguistic theory or does he not? If not, the project on which I am now bent may well prove the seed-sowing for a new Logic.

PART I
GENERAL THEORY

I
SPEECH AND THE FACTORS INVOLVED THEREIN

§ 6. **The usual definition criticized.** The objection to formal definitions is that, while they are seldom positively wrong, they are so often unhelpful, if not actually misleading. Such is characteristically the case with the common definition of speech as the use of articulate sound-symbols for the expression of thought. With slight verbal variations, this definition is found throughout the whole range of general treatises on language, old and new alike.[1] And indeed, if the term 'thought' be interpreted widely enough, there is little here to which one can take serious exception. Everything that is spoken of must, at all events in a metaphorical way, pass through the mind of the speaker before it is put into words. In this sense speech does really subserve the expression of thought. The main objection to the current definition is then, not that it is untrue, but rather that it leads nowhere, that it contains no fructifying principle. As applied to many samples of speech, the description is even grotesque. Consider a mother anxiously asking for news of her son, or a tradesman driving a hard bargain. Or again, imagine an angry traveller hurling words of abuse at an uncomprehending porter, or a judge pronouncing sentence of death upon a murderer. Shall we say that these persons are expressing thought? We may do so, of course, without departing from the strict truth, but such a statement would be, to

[1] See the definitions by Paul, Sapir, Sweet, Whitney, Wissler, and Wundt collected in G. de Laguna, *Speech, its Function and Development*, New Haven: Yale University Press, 1927, pp. 12 foll.

say the least, singularly inept. There are, however, cases where this description is both natural and appropriate, as when, for example, a lecturer is explaining some scientific discovery or analysing some philosophic subtlety. This gives us the clue to the source of the definition here impugned. Its academic origin is only too apparent, reflecting as it does the habits of the teacher, so different from those of the man in the street. The dislike of the ordinary mortal for serious thinking is proverbial, and yet speech is one of his commonest occupations. If any normal, semi-educated person could be brought to discuss the why and the wherefore of speech, he would probably say that it gives people the opportunity of talking about the things they are interested in, though he would admit that a good deal of conversation is about nothing in particular. He would assuredly scoff at the notion that speech serves mainly to effect the expression of thought. In order, therefore, to elicit the true nature of speech, we must survey the facts from a position more central and more commonplace than that of the philosopher or man of science. As a first approximation let us define speech as the use, between man and man, of articulate sound-signs for the communication of their wishes and their views about things. Note that I do not attempt to deny the thought-element in speech, but the emphasis of my definition does not lie on that element. The points which I wish to stress are, firstly, the co-operative character of speech, and, secondly, the fact that it is always concerned with things, that is to say with the realities both of the external world and of man's inner experience.

§ 7. **The social origin of speech: the listener.** We are often warned, and wisely, against basing far-reaching conclusions on theories of origin. These are bound to be conjectural in a high degree, and nowhere more so than in the cases of language and speech. Still, the philologist can barely escape from some working hypothesis regarding the genesis of speech, and it may be well here to point out that its origin cannot be conceived of otherwise than as the result of social conditions. True, the ultimate basis must be the involuntary cry of the individual animal. This was, I suppose, at the outset little more than the audible result of muscular movements due to the incidence of some external stimulus. The squeal of the trapped rabbit provides the type. But such emotional monologue is very far removed from speech, nor could any amount of variety either in the stimuli or in the reactions ever have given rise to anything resembling a real language. For the development of a language we are bound to assume a purposeful use of articulate utterances in order to influence the conduct of others. Speech of a kind undoubtedly exists among many species of animals. Naturalists have observed and recorded the warning or courting cries of birds and monkeys, besides other cries connected with food or with the building of the home. It is by means of such signals that one member of the flock or family helps another or in turn profits by his companion's aid. Recent research becomes more and more unwilling to admit, or at least to assume, the purposive character of these signals. But it is generally recognized that they mark a stage in the evolution of speech, and that they do, in fact, perform the functions ascribed to them.[1] Thus, the utility of animal cries as a means of communication is not in doubt, though their purposiveness is unproved. Apart from this, the chief difference between animal speech and human speech

---

[1] See the careful formulation of the problem in J. Ward, *Psychological Principles*, Cambridge, 1920, pp. 287-8.

consists in the extreme poverty and vagueness of the former. The warning cry, for example, affirms the presence of a danger without specifying it, and at the same time serves as an exhortation to resist it. Such human utterances as the cry of *Fire!* still resemble the animal cry in the latter point, but are far more explicit as regards the former. Without indulging in any questionable speculations, we may be sure that the gradual building up of a well-stocked vocabulary, such as even the most primitive man possesses, advanced *pari passu* with the ever-increasing complexity of tribal life, and was the outcome of the growing demand for more precise information as to the exact facts perceived, as to the exact emotions felt, and as to the exact responses desired.

Thus at every stage the mutual interaction of speaker and listener is presupposed. We see how futile it is to describe the purpose of speech as the expression of thought. Why, after all, should men go about expressing their thoughts? For their intellectual needs the mere thinking is enough. For the satisfaction of such desires as they can achieve unaided they have at their disposal muscles and limbs. And if the emotions should require some vocal outlet, they can shout or laugh or shriek or groan. But speech, with its deliberate and calculated pointing at things, is emphatically not explained by self-expression. It is, on the other hand, easily accounted for by recognizing that mankind is gregarious and dependent upon co-operation. The impulse to seek the help of our fellow men is both powerful and universal. Nor will anyone deny that speech is the principal means whereby, in fact, that help is obtained. The problem, then, must necessarily take the form: Is the co-operative employment of speech primary and original, or is it only secondary and derivative? A school of philosophy fashionable at the present time equates aesthetics and linguistics, or in other terms asserts the identity of speech and self-expression. But it is significant that the protagonist of this view (Croce) undertakes no careful investigations into the nature of the word and the sentence, but is content with dogmatic and, if the truth be told, very slap-dash assertions.[1] At a later stage (§ 66) I shall find it necessary to make important concessions to the expressionistic standpoint, but this must not be allowed to eclipse the fact that speech is fundamentally a social activity. Those who have the patience to read my book to the end will have to admit, further, that language is no personal creation, but a codified science built up by a myriad minds with a view to mutual understandings. If language has proved necessary for thought of an abstract kind and for intellectual self-expression, that function is secondary and a by-product, so to speak; surely the primary function of speech was to facilitate co-operation in such matters as could not be indicated by mere pointing or gesticulation. Its vocal character is decisive: Why express oneself aloud, unless it be that inner thoughts are inaccessible to other individuals, while uttered sound-signs are accessible to them?[2] Upon those who refuse to accept this view lies the onus of explaining how, if language arose out of the individual urge to self-expression, it came to be employed later and secondarily for co-operative ends. To cut short this discussion, let it be noted that the expressionistic theory fails to account for either questions or commands. In asking for information the speaker tries to make use of the listener's knowledge, and in giving an order he exerts his authority over the listener to make him

[1] See B. Croce, *Aesthetic*, Engl. translation, London, 1922, especially pp. 142 foll.   [2] See below, § 23.

perform some action desired by himself. The necessity of the sociological attitude to speech seems herewith to be finally vindicated, and the listener stands forth as an essential factor in its normal occurrence.[1]

§ 8. **The things spoken about.** A still graver defect of the current definition of speech is that it makes no allusion to 'things'. Yet common sense and English idiom alike tell us that we can talk about 'things', and indeed that utterances which do not refer to 'something' are not speech at all. The statement that speech serves to express thought simply ignores the fact that I can speak about this pen with which I am writing, about my house, my books, my family, and, in short, about everything else in the world. If linguistic theory is ever to make a wide appeal, it must clearly be placed upon a more realistic basis than at present. The rudest villager knows that he can talk about all the various things which he can see or touch. Why, then, should that truth be hidden from the theorist of language? Let us, however, be just. The writers responsible for the definition here criticized are scholars whose acumen and ability have been proved by admirable researches. We must try to understand the reasons for which they have omitted to mention 'things'. I shall reserve for the next section my discussion of what I believe to have been the principal reason. Here I shall deal only with some of the more obvious lines of defence that might be adopted. In the first place it is true, as pointed out above, that everything that is spoken about must, in a sense, pass through the speaker's mind; must, as one might say, be previously transmuted into thought. In the second place, material objects and sensible phenomena are not the only things to which we can refer; we can talk equally well about abstractions,

[1] See Additional Note A at the end of this chapter, p. 57.

about feelings, or about creations of the imagination. Thus the term 'thought' might seem required to cover the entire field of the subject-matter of speech. And, lastly, it must not be forgotten that all schools of grammarians are now agreed that the unit of speech is not the word, but the sentence. Consequently, when we inquire what a certain utterance is about, our question refers not merely to the nouns in the sentence, but is concerned with the signification of the sentence as a whole; and this can never be just a concrete object. Take, for example, the sentence *Pussy is beautiful*. From the standpoint just mentioned, what is spoken about is not merely Pussy, but the beauty of Pussy. Thus, even if it be admitted that speech may refer to concrete things, it will at least be said that speech always refers to them in a certain aspect. And aspects can (so the argument might run) better be described as 'thoughts' or 'thoughts about things' than actually as 'things'.

I shall discuss these three possible lines of defence in inverse order. (1) The general truth of the argument about 'aspects' is undeniable, but it is irrelevant. To say that Pussy is beautiful may indeed be to express a thought about something, but there is no reason to deny that a thought about something is in itself a thing. For to describe the reference of a complete sentence as a 'thing' is not only in accord with common linguistic usage, but is also vital and fundamental for a satisfactory theory of speech. English permits us to say: *That Pussy is beautiful is a* THING *which can be expressed in many different ways*. Or again: *Pussy beautiful? I never heard of such a* THING! *You said some*THING *quite different a few minutes ago*. Commands and questions may also be taken as 'things', e.g. *The question 'how much did he spend?' is a* THING *you* *are not entitled to ask; The order to start work at 6.0 a.m. was a* THING *unparalleled.* . . . With a little contriving it could be shown that the gist of any sentence could be described as a 'thing' without departing from the general usage of our native tongue and thought. But a much more cogent argument in favour of my contention is the fact that, as explained at the beginning of this section, a sample of genuine speech which does not deal with some 'thing' is impossible to conceive.[1]

Now the 'thing' which is referred to in speech is as much outside it as are the 'speaker' and the 'listener'. These three are, indeed, factors of speech, though not parts of it. Being such, it is no positive duty of the theorist of language to prove their existence or explain their nature, except in so far as they affect, or are affected by, speech. Those factors of speech which are not speech lie outside the philologist's province, and in seeking to determine their characters he incurs the risk of trespassing upon the domains of other sciences. Nevertheless, in the present case that risk must be run, since the very existence of 'things' as the object of linguistic activity seems to be in dispute. That 'things' to be spoken about are not simply illusory, and that, furthermore, they are extra-verbal (i.e. outside the words) is indicated by the two complementary facts that (*a*) one and the same 'thing' can be expressed

---

[1] This book having been written in English, and primarily addressed to an English-speaking public, it has been impossible to take into account the difficulties which might arise in foreign languages over this wide concept of 'things'. German might make shift with *Gegenstand*, a general term covering both *Sache* and *Ding*. I fancy that French *chose* will serve in most cases. In English itself a strain is felt only through the inclusion of persons in the category of 'things'. That inclusion is necessary for my linguistic theory, and such a terminological awkwardness does not, of course, affect the substance of my argument.

(i.e. referred to) in various different ways (i.e. by several different sentences), and (*b*) that one and the same sentence*b* may, on separate occasions, refer to various different 'things'. (*a*) Instead of *Pussy is beautiful* there might be substituted *Your cat is very lovely*; *Minette est bien belle*; *Ihre Katze ist von einer fabelhaften Schönheit*, &c., &c. If it be argued that these four sentences express, or refer to, four different things, it may quite fairly be retorted that they express one and the same thing, only this thing has been slightly diversified, or differently decked out, in the course of alluding to it.[1] The argument is like that which asserts that Philip drunk is not the same person as Philip sober. It is, indeed, a true and lamentable fact that, in ultimate analysis, one cannot speak about anything without altering it to some extent.[2] In the present instance, at all events, I have had before my mind one particular 'thing', and I feel satisfied that this 'thing' is adequately represented to my readers in each of the four sentences given above. (*b*) Again, the single sentence *Pussy is beautiful* might refer to many different 'things'. The word *Pussy* might refer to a variety of cats, black, tabby, grey, Persian, &c.; and the quality of beauty intended might vary in like manner. In the context where I first employed this example *Pussy* served merely as substitute for anything X denoted by a noun, and *beautiful* as substitute for anything Y denoted by an adjective. No real cat and no real beauty were involved.

(2) I now turn to possible defence No. 2. It must first be pointed out that, though the unit of speech is the sentence and hence the 'thing' signified by every such unit

---

[1] Here the principle which I have named 'Depth of Intention' comes into view. For this see below, §§ 17, 27, and p. 257.

[2] This theme is developed at some length in my fifth chapter; see §§ 65-7.

is always of complex kind—a state of things, as we might say, or a *Sachverhalt*, if we prefer to use the convenient German equivalent[1]—yet that 'thing' may involve or contain a number of other 'things'. Just as the 'thing' called a house comprises other things such as doors, windows, curtains, floors, so too the thing denoted by a sentence comprises as many things as there are words in it. When the sentence *Pussy is beautiful* is used of a real cat of flesh and blood, both the single word *Pussy* and also the sentence as a whole may be said to refer to the 'thing' which is that cat. In similar fashion all material concrete objects can undoubtedly be talked about, and any theory of speech which glosses over this important truth is likely to suffer in consequence. At the present moment the contention which we are required to meet is that it would be better to substitute 'thoughts' for 'things' in conformity with the usual definition of speech, seeing that abstractions, feelings, and purely imaginary entities can all be spoken about no less easily than concrete objects, and that the former belong to the mental, not to the physical, world. Otherwise said, the term 'thoughts' is preferred to 'things' on the ground that it is more comprehensive. To this I reply (*a*) that the term 'thoughts' is not really more comprehensive, and (*b*) that the term 'thoughts' presents a serious ambiguity. As regards the first point (*a*), note that English very often does employ the term 'thing' in reference to abstractions, as in the sentence: *Religion is a* THING *of great value*; in reference to feelings, as in *What a wonderful* THING *is enthusiasm!*; and in reference to pure fictions, as in *Centaurs are not real* THINGS. There is,

---

[1] The term usually employed in English for *Sachverhalt* is 'content', but that term implies the very fallacy which I am attempting to controvert, namely that the signification of a sentence is 'contained' in its words.

indeed, absolutely no ground for affirming that 'thoughts' is a wider term than 'things'. (*b*) In the second place, the word 'thought' shows a bifurcation in its meaning, on the one hand in the direction of '*that which* is thought', on the other hand in the direction of '*processes* or *acts* of thinking'. Now in distinguishing things like 'religion' or 'enthusiasm' or 'centaurs' from concrete objects like 'cats' or 'houses', and in qualifying the former as 'thoughts' instead of 'things', there seems to be some confusion between these two employments of the word 'thought'. It appears to be implied that abstractions, feelings, and fictions, just because they are not objects of perception, are instantaneous, personal creations out of the void. Nothing could be further from the truth. That 'religion' is a real thing, independent of any one individual mind that experiences it, is vouched for by the millions to whom it is an all-pervading influence. That 'enthusiasm' can be shared is a sign that it is no individual emanation. And 'centaurs' have amused and inspired generations of artists. 'Religion' and 'enthusiasm' and 'centaurs' are 'things' at least in the sense that they are elements in man's existence which have their appointed place and possibility of recurrence.

(3) I come now to the argument that everything that is spoken about must first be transmuted into thought. But it is clear that this is only an inaccurate and figurative way of emphasizing the fact that speech cannot take place without some previous presentations in the speaker's mind. What is 'presented' is not for that reason 'transmuted'. There is no hocus-pocus in speech which can transform Pussy into a psychical entity; there she remains in her basket, purring quite unconcernedly. Instead of 'transmutation', we might possibly use the term 'reflection', since man seems to be in the position of a being condemned

to look at the external world solely through the medium of mirrors. When a speaker refers to anything, he has first to see it mirrored in his mind, and similarly when a listener apprehends anything, he has first to see it mirrored in his mind.[1] But perhaps it will be argued that abstractions and the like are not mirrored in the mind, but were there to start with. At this point in the controversy, however, the philologist will realize that he has been beguiled into a discussion which is outside his province. He will repeat that both common sense and our ineradicable habits of thought make it necessary to regard whatever is talked of as a 'thing'. He may perhaps hazard the doubt whether in this connexion 'thing' means much more than 'terminus', a goal or ending behind which we do not look. But he will also submit that, even though a debate might turn upon whether or not the moon is made of green cheese, the fact that several persons can simultaneously direct their attentions to this topic gives it something of the appearance of fixity and externality which we are accustomed to associate with 'things'. And here he will surrender the issue to the tender mercies of the metaphysicians.

§ 9. **Words.** Thus the speaker, the listener, and the things spoken about are three essential factors of normal speech. To these must now be added the actual words themselves. There has never, of course, been any risk that philologists would overlook this fourth factor. On the contrary, words have assumed such importance in the eyes of all who have dealt with speech and language that time and time again they have totally eclipsed the three other factors. This I believe to be the hidden fallacy lurking in the common definition of speech as the use of articulate sound-symbols for the expression of thought. The error arises

[1] For further discussion of this fact see below, pp. 142–3.

from the two-sidedness of words, from the fact that they indeed are, as speech in the current definition is supposed to be, sound on the one face, and thought on the other. And is it not, at first sight, a plausible view that words constitute the whole truth of speech? A word or sequence of words is uttered, its sound is heard, and its sense apprehended. The transaction might seem as simple as the giving of a cheque in the place of cash. The scholar's habit of attending too exclusively to books has probably done much to encourage this illusion. In books speaker, listener, and things are well out of the way. Words alone are seen on the printed page, and they carry their meaning apparently without recourse to the three factors which I would fain add to them. Gradually, however, writers on the theory of language have come to realize that actual speech is the source from which healthier views on the subject can alone be obtained. Speaker and listener have thus, in recent treatises, recovered much of the importance due to them. Things, on the other hand, are almost completely ignored, and to all but a few the doctrine of the distinction between the meaning of words and the things meant by them will come as a revolutionary thesis, if not as a damnable heresy.

§ 10. **Meaning and thing-meant.** Yet the distinction is really incontestable, and seems to me essential for any true understanding of the nature of speech. In the case of material objects my contention will be quickly conceded. When I say to a friend *Cake?* holding out the plate, the thing meant by the word is eatable, while the meaning of the word is not. When I say *Oxygen is an element*, the thing meant by *oxygen* can be isolated in a test-tube, while the meaning of the word *oxygen* cannot. Take again the pronoun *I*. This has as its meaning the speaker in every case; but when you are speaking, the thing meant by the word *I* is you. My point is perhaps less obvious in the case of abstractions, but there, too, it is not open to doubt. In the section dealing with 'things' (§ 8, p. 27) reasons have been given why religion should be regarded as a thing. But it is not the meaning of the word *religion* which stirs such emotions, which can create saints and inquisitors; only the thing meant by *religion* can do that.

Let us look at the matter from another angle. We are here discussing speech and language, and are agreed, I suppose, that these are not ends in themselves, but methods of attaining certain ends. But the meaning of a word is something inherent in it, something inseparable from it. Word-meaning is, in fact, a purely philological affair. If speech is not to remain suspended in mid-air as indeed a means to an end, but without any visible end, then we must recognize the existence of things for speech to refer to. Nor are things factors of speech only; they are factors of our universe, of our life, of our whole being.

The distinction between 'meaning' and 'thing-meant' runs through speech in all its manifestations, and applies equally to whole sentences and to the separate words which enter into their composition. Since it is impossible to expound a thesis of such wide application in all its bearings at once, my illustrations have hitherto been confined to nouns. However, we shall soon see that the distinction holds good, not only of spoken nouns, but also of spoken verbs and adjectives, and indeed even of those minor elements in our vocabulary which we somewhat contemptuously lump together under the heading of 'particles' (see below, § 13). The applicability of the same distinction to whole sentences is obscured by the fact that 'meaning' in the sense here intended is customarily restricted to words, and not extended to the total 'expression' of a sentence. Substituting 'expression' for 'meaning' we find ourselves on familiar ground. No difficulty is felt in contrasting the opinion or sentiment which is the gist of a sentence with the manner in which it is expressed. This opinion or that sentiment is extra-verbal in the sense that its expression may differ on different occasions, and that it may be entertained without being expressed at all. Such an opinion or sentiment is the 'thing-meant' underlying the sentence which serves as its expression; and the expression is simply a sequence of words or purveyors of 'meaning' strung together in the appropriate arrangement known, as we shall later learn (§ 50), as 'sentence-form'. Thus the distinction between 'meaning' and 'thing-meant' applies no less to sentences than to single words.[1]

The analysis of word-meaning will be the topic of the next few sections. Here we may profitably dwell a little longer on the 'thing-meant'. In describing this as extra-verbal, I do not declare it to be real or materially existent. It is existent, or accepted, merely for the purpose of speech. The world in which speech moves and has its being is a curious conglomerate of fact and fiction. When I untruthfully say *The centaur is an animal found in Greece*, the gist of my sentence is false, i.e. not in conformity with reality. But my listener accepts my 'thing-meant' as something existent, not only for me, but also for himself. This is hinted by the form he gives to his words when he contradicts me. He then says, *The centaur is not an animal found in Greece*. Similarly as regards the component words of these sentences. The 'centaur' is a creature of the imagination, while 'Greece' is a fact of the external world. For speaker and listener the centaur and Greece both

[1] See Additional Note B at the end of this chapter, p. 58.

exist as possible subjects of conversation. This in-and-out-of-reality is characteristic of all speech. Speakers and listeners treat the things with which they deal on the same level of reality. Or rather, the question of their existence or non-existence is ignored; if raised at all, it is raised, not during the act of speaking or understanding, but only at a later stage.

There is nothing mystical, disputable, or recondite about the distinction here made when once it has been firmly grasped. Nor is it new, indeed; I am only trying to revive the old scholastic doctrine of *suppositio*, while keeping it clear of the sophistries and hair-splitting to which it was subjected in medieval times.[1] In plain English, all I am maintaining is that the things we talk about are to be distinguished from the words with which we talk about them. Things must occur to our minds before they can be clothed in words. This correlation of 'thing-meant' and 'meaning' is itself variously described by the various scientific disciplines on whose territory linguistic science borders. The biologist will regard the thing-meant as the 'stimulus' to which the meaning is the 'reaction'. Consider, for example, the warning cry of the chamois. This has the constant and inseparable meaning of 'Danger!' with which the chamois 'reacts' when 'stimulated' thereto by the approach of a huntsman or aeroplane. The term 'thing-meant' can be properly employed only when the purposive plane of speech has been reached (§ 7); but in so far as the cry of the chamois calls the attention of other

---

[1] Of this doctrine a brief but luminous account is given in K. O. Erdmann, *Die Bedeutung des Wortes*, Leipzig, 1922, pp. 66 foll. The author of that admirable book is among the few who have recognized how necessary the scholastic doctrine, at least in its broad outlines, is for the theory of speech, as well as for its practical interpretation.

animals to the huntsman or aeroplane, to that extent the one or the other is, on its own particular occasion, the thing-meant.[1] The psychologist will insist upon the 'subjective' character of meaning, and upon the 'objective', or at least relatively 'objective', character of the thing-meant. The logician who discerns predication at the root of all use of words will discover a 'predicate' in my 'meaning', and a 'subject' in my 'thing-meant'. Lastly, the grammarian has his own metaphors for picturing to himself the correlation of 'meaning' and 'thing-meant'. As he sees it, the meaning of a word or sentence qualifies the thing meant by it in the way that a predicatival adjective qualifies a noun. In the jargon of grammar speech is adjectival, and the universe to which it refers is substantival.

§ 11. **The function of word-meaning.** I now return to 'words' and 'word-meaning'. My argument having deprived words of some of their importance by denying the self-sufficiency of their meanings, it will naturally be asked what value I do attribute to them. My answer is that they are primarily instrumental, that their function is to force or cajole the listener into looking at certain things. The speaker may be compared to a commercial traveller who is unable to show the actual wares in which he traffics, but who carries in his bag various samples and books of patterns. Another comparison which will answer my purpose equally well is the familiar game of animal, vegetable, or mineral. One of the party is sent out of the room, while the remainder decide upon something which he is to guess. The guesser, on his return, puts a series of questions which may be answered only by *Yes* or *No*. *Is it animal? Is it vegetable? Is it mineral?* And so forth, until the

[1] See the remarks on the technical meaning of the words *sign, symbol, symptom*, below, p. 101, n. 1.

field of possibilities is so narrowed that the guesser sees what is meant.

In exactly the same way the function of words is to make the listener 'see what is meant'. They are, in fact, 'clues'. The thing-meant is itself never shown, but has to be identified by the listener on the basis of the word-meanings submitted to him for that purpose. It is true that most of the sentences to which we daily give utterance are much more complex than the simple operations evoked by me to illustrate the process. Still, the general truth of the account given above emerges from the consideration of such a phrase as *your old brown hat*. The word *your* indicates the possessor of the thing meant by the speaker but as yet unknown to the listener. *Old* and *brown* successively indicate qualities of that thing which will assist in its identification. *Hat* affords the final clue; it is not a suit or a hand-bag of the type described by *old* and *brown* that is meant, though the listener possesses both. The thing-meant is an object belonging to the category of *hats*. The listener now has in his mind's eye the real article intended.

§ 12. **A preliminary account of word-meaning.** No amount of pedantic advice is going to cure anyone of loose speech, for which it is a good defence that, so long as we can make our audience understand what is intended, the language employed is a secondary consideration. An observatory chronometer need not be used to keep an appointment for tea. I do not imagine for a moment that the distinction established in the last two sections will prevent even scholars from employing the term 'meaning' in the sense of 'thing-meant'. They will continue, as before, to designate both word-meaning and thing-meant by the same ambiguous term, and also to speak of the various 'meanings' of a single word. Such approximate statements are, in my opinion, no very serious offence, so long as the real facts of the matter are clearly grasped and are remembered when the problems of grammar come up for discussion.

Can a word have more than one meaning? This question may be answered both affirmatively and negatively, according to the point of view. There is a very real and important sense in which each word has only one meaning, as I shall proceed to show. Every word is a heritage from the past, and has derived its meaning from application to a countless number of particulars differing among themselves either much or little. When now I utter such a word, I throw at the listener's head the entire residue of all its previous applications. Indeed, how could I do otherwise? Most words are pronounced in a trice, and how should I be able, within so brief a space, to pick out from a multitude of meanings just that one which will suit the present occasion? In uttering a word, the speaker necessarily offers to the listener the whole range of its meaning. So far as that one word is concerned he has no alternative, though he may, and often does, add other words which indicate what part of the meaning he had in view. To take an example: if I say *ball*, this word comes to my listener charged with the possibilities of cannon-ball, football, tennis-ball, as well as a dance, and much else. It remains for the listener to select from the whole range of meaning offered that aspect or part of it which suits the context or situation. If the words *Help yourselves!* are heard in a sermon, a very different interpretation will be given to the verb *help* than if the same words are heard at a tea-party.

The meaning of any word may be looked at in two

different ways, either subjectively or objectively. The subjective or introspective way of looking at word-meaning is often very complex. Involved in the meaning of a noun like *horse*, apart from all the variations enumerated in the dictionary, are such grammatical implications as substantiality and singularity.[1] The way of introspection is the only way in which the *quality* of word-meaning can be felt and appraised. The external or objective way consists in noting all the different things-meant to which the word can be applied, for example, this brown cab-horse, that grey race-horse, the nursery rocking-horse, the horse of Troy, horse as a kind of meat, the gymnasium horse, the towel-horse. In point of fact the two methods of regarding word-meaning are inseparable. Introspection alone can discern the identities and similarities which make possible a general survey, while a reference to the things-meant is necessary if introspection is to perform its part adequately.

We can perhaps best picture to ourselves the meaning of a word such as *horse* by considering it as a territory or area over which the various possibilities of correct application are mapped out.[2] Consequently, I shall often make use of the expression 'area of meaning'.[d] If a short-sighted person points at a cow in the distance, and says *Look at that horse!* he will perhaps be understood, but no cow is among the things accepted as meant by the word *horse*. Cows are, in fact, 'off the map' so far as the word-meaning *horse* is concerned, or, otherwise put, the meanings of *cow* and of *horse* do not overlap.[3] But within the legitimate

[1] These implications of meaning will later be described as 'word-form', see below, § 41.

[2] I do not know from what source I derived the notion of an 'area of meaning', but that the same comparison has occurred to others is clear from Erdmann, *Bedeutung*, pp. 4–5.   [3] See below, p. 173.

range of the word-meaning *horse* the various things meant will be differently grouped, some rather near the borderline, and others distinctly central. An eminent physiologist told me that the mention of the word *horse* always conjured up for him the image of a prancing white steed. To myself as a poor visualizer such a visual image would appear an obstacle to comprehension rather than a help, particularly when towel-horses or gymnasium horses are the subject of conversation.[1] At all events such an image shows that, for that particular *sujet parlant*, prancing white horses were right in the centre of the word-meaning *horse*. Doubtless for most of us live horses of one kind and another are pretty central. A slight strain is felt when *horse* is applied to toy horses, a greater strain when it is applied to the gymnasium horse, and a still greater strain when it is applied to a towel-horse. In terms of our map, these applications grow increasingly peripheral.

§ 13. **The relation of words to the things referred to in speech.** The relation of word to thing-meant may be defined in two ways: either the word expresses the class of the thing-meant, or else it qualifies the thing-meant in the manner that a predicative adjective might qualify it.[2] Both descriptions amount to the same in reality, but

---

[1] For the different kinds of images under which words are conceived by different individuals see Th. Ribot, *L'évolution des idées générales*, Paris, 1897, ch. iv. Visual or typographic images are commoner than the purely auditory; the commonest case is where the person questioned replies that the word represents to him nothing at all. Such images appear to me to have no importance whatever for linguistic theory, though doubtless they are closely connected with their possessors' dominating interests, and are consequently not without influence upon the choice of topics.

[2] In this discussion I deliberately avoid the terms 'connotation' ('intension') and 'denotation' ('extension'), since these arise from a way of looking at speech different from my own, and accordingly bear only a superficial resemblance to my terms 'meaning' and 'thing-meant'.

it will be best to consider them separately. It belongs to the nature of a 'word', as that term is universally understood, to be utilizable over and over again in many different contexts and situations. This being the case, it is obvious that every word is susceptible of referring to many different particular things, to each of which it applies as a sort of common label. Hence every word without exception is a class-name; in uttering it the speaker is virtually saying, 'Here is a class, and the thing I mean you to understand belongs to that class'. The class is known to the listener by his *previous* experiences, the word having been applied by others or by himself to many other things falling under the same class. The thing *now* meant may or may not have been among the previous experiences associated with the word. If it has been, the listener identifies it by sheer memory; if not, he recognizes it by its resemblance to some of those previous experiences. For example: *My uncle has bought a new horse*. The thing-meant is the actual horse recently bought by my uncle; this I have not seen, but I catch my first glimpse of it, so to speak, by comparing my previous experiences of what is meant by the word *horse* with my knowledge of my uncle's preferences in horseflesh. But the sentence might have been: *My uncle has sold his old horse*. Now I know that old horse, and have heard it often alluded to by my uncle as *my horse*. Here the thing-meant has for me been long included in the class *horse*, so that, aided by the context, I have no difficulty in identifying it once again.

At the end of § 10 it was explained that every utterance is, and must of necessity be, virtually adjectival and predicatival. A word expresses the speaker's reaction to the thing spoken about. Thus when I say *my old hat* I am in substance saying to the listener: 'Think of something which I have felt, and you will feel, as being-mine, being-old, being-hat.' The listener, having the power of identifying things that are hats, and old, and mine, by their resemblance to one another as members of these classes, will find no difficulty in understanding what I mean. We must, however, forestall possible objections to this second way of describing the relation of words to the things meant by them. An objector might say: 'On your view, then, every word is an adjective; but that proposition is palpably false.' To this I should reply that the objector does not know what an adjective really is. In the Foreword (p. 9) I pointed out that the distinctions which we know by the incorrect name of the 'parts of speech' are really distinctions in the ways in which the things meant by words are presented to the listener. An adjective, on this view, is the name of a thing presented to the listener, not *as* a thing, but *as* an attribute.[1] *Beautiful*, for instance, is a word displaying 'beauty' as the attribute of something else. Here, however, we are not discussing the things meant by words, but the relation of the words themselves to the things meant by them in speech, and we say that the words, or more precisely, the word-meanings, are adjectival to, i.e. presented as attributes of, the things-meant. Thus the first objection is entirely irrelevant. A second objection that might be raised is of a similar kind, and admits of a similar answer. 'If', it might be urged, 'word-meanings are adjectival to the things-meant, then the things-meant must always be nouns, since adjectives (if understood in our ordinary grammatical sense) can only qualify nouns. But', the objector will continue, 'the

---

[1] For the present I ignore the fact that an adjective may function incongruently as a noun; see below, §§ 42-6, for incongruent function.

things meant by *in* and *is* and *very* are not nouns.' Now it is quite true that in actual speech, as in the sentence *It is very cold in this room*, the things presented to the listener by *is*, by *very*, and by *in* are not indicated by nouns. But it belongs to the very nature of a 'thing' that it can be looked at from different angles and in different aspects. As the things meant by *is*, by *very*, and by *in* are presented in the sentence *It is very cold in this room*, they are not presented as the things that they really are, but as verb, adverb, and preposition respectively. When, however, we are discussing the relation of these words to the things meant by them, we necessarily think of those things *as* things, i.e. in the substantival way which demands the use of nouns. It may help to elucidate this rather subtle point if I am able to show that the thing meant by any word in any sentence may always be described by a noun or the equivalent of a noun.[1] In our illustrative sentence the thing meant by *is* may be fairly characterized with the words 'the affirmed existence of cold in this room', the thing meant by *very* with the words 'the high degree of cold in this room', and the thing meant by *in* with the words 'position in this room of great cold'. As regards those things it is quite correct to say that the meanings of *is*, *very*, and *in* are adjectival; *is*, in the here relevant part of its meaning, signifies 'being of the nature of an affirmation', *very* has the meaning 'being of high degree', and *in* has the meaning 'being inside'. It must be admitted that it would be rather hard to describe in the form of a noun the thing meant, for instance, by *whom* in *the man*

[1] This is a good moment for remarking that all discussions about 'words' and 'things' suffer from the inherent vice that things cannot be displayed as such, i.e. in their crude substantival reality, but have to be represented by words, which deputize for them rather badly.

whom I saw, but one can at least discern the lines along which this could be attempted.[1]

I am not at all sure that my answer to these two possible objections will not obscure the issue rather than clarify it, but in that case the last paragraph may be ignored. I now turn to the problem of proper names, and shall examine the question whether they too can be considered as class-names, and whether their meaning must be conceived of as adjectival. A proper name, in so far as it remains a real proper name, is a word which refers only to one individual thing, usually a person or place. There is nothing self-contradictory in the notion of a class of one, though such a notion is naturally only of theoretical interest. But, from the standpoint adopted at the beginning of this section, a proper name is not a class of one at all. Proper names resemble all other words in the fact that they are used, not on a single occasion alone, but over and over again. Let us assume, for the sake of argument, that a given individual nickname has been used just five thousand times. Then, on its five thousand and first time of use, it is a class of five thousand members to which a new member is added. Nor indeed, if we scrutinize the matter more closely, is this member ever wholly identical, even if he is always the same person. Of necessity he is a day, an hour, or a minute older. At one moment he is calm; at another he is angry. He may be clothed or naked; moving or still; sitting or standing. To that extent the thing-meant designated by a proper name is for ever

[1] The attempt shall be made: *whom* in this phrase means 'the man referred to previously as *the man*, but here indicated by a word making possible the addition of a clause descriptive of him; in which clause the word now indicating the man serves as logical subject and also as object of the verb *saw*'. The words in inverted commas are what grammarians call a noun-equivalent.

different, even though possessing a spatial, temporal, and physiological continuity and unity which provides the meaning of the name.

Now we have it on the high authority of Mill that proper names are without meaning. It need hardly be said that in holding this view Mill was not talking sheer nonsense, but I maintain that he was using the term 'meaning' otherwise than must be done by the theorist of language. A proper name is a word, and being a word partakes of the fundamental two-sidedness of words as possessing both sound and meaning. At first blush it would seem as though here the meaning of the word really were identical with the thing-meant, but a little thought will dispel that illusion. The meaning of a word is something mental, something which leaps into the thoughts whenever the word is heard or remembered. But Goethe the person does not leap into my thoughts when I recall the word *Goethe*. The word merely tells me that I must think of something 'being Goethe', or in other terms the meaning of the name *Goethe* is adjectival to the real Goethe. The meaning of the name *Goethe* has been acquired by me as a mental possession in just the same way as other word-meanings have been acquired. I have read his life, seen his portraits, and studied his works. From these sources I have a distinct idea of Goethe. Consequently, when the name of Goethe is mentioned, I know the kind of man that is meant. I can thus concentrate my attention on the man. That a proper name is adjectival in meaning is proved, moreover, by the fact that it can be used as a predicate. The name of my daughter is Margaret. Suppose her to be playing in theatricals, and to be disguised beyond all recognition. I point to her and say *That is Margaret*. What the listener gathers is that the person yonder is the person having-the-personality-of-Margaret-Gardiner, is in fact Margaret Gardiner. Enough has been said to show that proper names are not different in essence from other words.[1]

The only real difficulty about viewing words as class-names is that we usually think of classes as assemblages of individual things which are all alike in some particular. But the meaning of words often covers applications between which it is impossible to discover any point of resemblance. Thus the word *file* is applied both to the stiff, pointed wires on which documents are run for keeping and also to front-rank men followed by other men in a line straight behind them. The resemblance comes into view only when it is realized that *file* is derived from Latin *filum* 'a thread'.[2] We must, therefore, expand the statement made at the beginning of this section by adding that the utterance of a word is equivalent to saying to the listener: 'Here is a name representing something like A, like B, like C, or like D', where A, B, C, and D are the various types or subclasses of thing covered by the same comprehensive word or class-name. We have thus seen that, as regards the things meant by them, words are (1) class-names, and (2) adjectival. As previously remarked, these ways of describing the relation are really one, for a class is an assemblage of things united by virtue of a common attribute. There is no reason why that attribute

[1] For an excellent account of proper names and the problems connected with them see Jespersen, *Philosophy*, pp. 64 foll. Another discussion, from the logical point of view, W. E. Johnson, *Logic*, Part I, Cambridge, 1921, ch. vi.

[2] Beside the Romance noun *file* another, of Teutonic origin (mod. Germ. *Feile*) indicates a metal instrument for smoothing rough surfaces. The *Oxford English Dictionary* mentions several more that are obsolete or dialectal. The topic of homophones is reserved for my second volume, but is touched upon several times below, e.g. pp. 77, 120–1.

should not take the complex form 'being of the type A or B or C or D'.

The considerations set forth in the last paragraph make it evident that the meaning of a word is not identical with an 'idea' in the Platonic sense. At first sight it might seem plausible to describe the mechanism of speech as 'the indication of things by the names of ideas'; the scholastic formula runs *Voces significant res mediantibus conceptis*. Looking closer, we see that word-meanings possess nothing of that self-consistency and homogeneity which are characteristic of 'ideas'. Ideas, if attainable at all, are the result of long and toilsome search on the part of philosophers. The metaphysician may ultimately arrive at an adequate concept of 'Truth', and the physicist may define 'Force' in a way which will stand him in good stead. But these notions are not the word-meanings with which speech operates. If we consult the *Oxford English Dictionary* we shall find the meaning of *truth* set forth under three main heads, each with numerous subdivisions. The applications of the word range from personal faithfulness or loyalty to verified facts or realities. It is not as an 'idea' that the meaning of the word *truth* must be conceived, but rather as an area upon which the various potentialities of application are plotted out.[1]

§ 14. **The mechanized elements in speech.**[2] It was hardly to be expected that in so old-inherited an art as that of speech one single explanation would account for all the instruments employed, or for all the operations

[1] The difference between word-meanings and ideas (Begriffe) is admirably treated by Erdmann (*Bedeutung*, pp. 74 foll.): 'Man sagt: Worte sind Zeichen für Begriffe. Richtiger ist es wohl zu behaupten, dass Worte auch als Zeichen für Begriffe dienen müssen', op. cit., p. 4.

[2] Jespersen has an excellent section on this topic, *Philosophy*, pp. 18 foll. For the theory see Wegener, *Grundfragen*, p. 73.

performed. To describe the words of a sentence as 'clues' is only part of the story. At this juncture it would be premature, however, to lay much stress on the other uses of words, and to do so could only distract attention from their primary function as clues. But I must anticipate one obvious objection to the previous trend of my argument; it cannot be denied that many of the words which we employ are relatively aimless and owe their place in speech mainly to historical reasons. The principle to be illustrated may be termed the **mechanization of speech**, though by another metaphor it might equally well have been characterized as the 'fossilization of words and phrases'. This topic will be considered under three heads.

(1) **Stereotyped formulas.** In the traffic of daily life situations are constantly arising so closely similar that we do not hesitate to speak of them as the 'same situation'. Every language has its own fixed ways of coping with certain recurring situations. An expression of apology is met by the Englishman with *Pray don't mention it!* or *Don't mention it!* or the less refined *Granted!* In like circumstances the Frenchman will say *Je vous en prie!* and the German *Ich bitte!* or *Bitte!* or *Bitte sehr!* In effect, these formulas all mean the same thing, and to describe their component words as separate and successive clues, cumulatively working towards a given result, is obviously inappropriate. The like holds good of countless idiosyncrasies, for example that tiresome *I mean*, or the happily nearly obsolete *Don't yer know?* with which shy or foppish youths are prone to interlard their conversation. In social intercourse formulas are frequent. So at a dinner-party: '*Have you been to the theatre lately?*' '*We were at "Bitter Sweet" a few nights ago.*' '*Rather good, isn't it?*'

'Perfectly topping!' The sentences certainly mean something, but from a shifted angle question and answer seem to follow one another like the mechanical utterances of automata. What is said is of little account. The topics are conventional, and their expression is merely a means of establishing contact.[1]

(2) **Set phrases.** Words originally separate, and still found with their own indicative force and utility in other contexts, tend to combine and to form set phrases. Such phrases are to all intents and purposes compound words, and to describe the component parts as 'clues' would clearly be beside the mark. Thus *attach importance to* or *lay store by* are phrases nearly synonymous with (*to*) *value* in one sense of the latter verb; *to hold one's tongue* or *keep silence* is equivalent to the Latin *tacere*; *to trample under foot* is *to disregard*; *to split the difference* is *to compromise*; *to set the ball rolling* is *to initiate* some action. All these expressions come to the speaker ready-made. As composite units they are 'clues' which he can choose, but their component words are not 'clues' to anything except to the phrase itself.

(3) **Idiom.** Languages differ greatly in the forms which they have adopted. No better example can be quoted than the varying extension of the definite and indefinite articles. In Latin their use is reduced to a minimum; for *Rex regiaque classis una profecti* English has *The king and the royal fleet set out together*, while *Natura inimica sunt libera civitas et rex* demands the rendering *By nature a free state and a king are hostile*. German and French agree, as against English, in using the definite article with abstract nouns, e.g. *die Wahrheit, la vérité*, but English *truth*.

---

[1] Malinowski has coined the term 'phatic communion' for converse of this kind, of which he gives a very interesting account. See C. K. Ogden and I. A. Richards, *The Meaning of Meaning*, London, 1923, pp. 477 foll.

French and English cannot employ the definite article with personal names as is often done in German, e.g. *die Maria*. It is sometimes said that such relatively insignificant words are grammatical tools. But the function of tools is to achieve some specific end. That is precisely what, in many cases, the article does not do, or at all events does only in a very slight and uncertain degree. Often it is mere useless ballast, a habit or mannerism accepted by an entire speaking community.

Do the phenomena here exemplified contradict the account hitherto given of the nature of words and their mode of functioning? I think not. The mechanization of words is a phenomenon characteristic of human activities generally. Habits grow out of acts which at the start were deliberately purposed and then possessed a real utility. In their later state such acts may become mere superfluities. In mechanized bits of language we can usually discern a rational intention at the outset. In the French *ne ... pas* the word *pas*, Latin *passum*, originally had emphasizing force; not a 'pace' further will he or she go. So, too, with the definite article; this has everywhere arisen from an identifying and locating demonstrative, while the indefinite article, originating in the numeral 'one', has now chiefly the negative function of indicating to the listener that the thing it qualifies is in no need of closer identification. The teaching afforded by these examples may be generalized. In contemporary use it cannot be maintained that every single word has deliberate significance or semantic importance, but in all cases we may be sure that the historic original was properly motivated and purposeful. The accumulation of old rubbish is so easy. As the Egyptians said in a different connexion: (*Words are but*) *the breath of the mouth, they are naught whereby one groweth weary*. Words cost little, and it was unlikely that strict economy and purposefulness would be studied in all their employments.

§ 15. **Selective attention.** It may have occurred to the reader that if an utterance is the complicated affair which it is here declared to be, involving speaker, listener, word (with sound and meaning), and thing, then it is a miracle that anything should ever be understood. And indeed it is a miracle, just as the structure of the human body is a miracle, and as everything about the constitution of man is a miracle. But proficiency both in speaking and in understanding speech is the result of hard and unremitting practice from earliest childhood. It is not for the philologist to expatiate upon the psychical equipment which enables man to perform his linguistic functions, but mention may at least be made of his power to compare and his power to select. In particular we cannot pass over in silence the most important result of the latter gift, namely the disappearance from, or great subordination in, consciousness of all that is superfluous and not essential to the effectiveness of speech. When a word is employed, both speaker and listener are able, by dint of their selective attention, to push far into the background all those potential applications of the meaning which are irrelevant to the immediate context.[1] Similarly, though through force of habit and sheer linguistic skill the speaker automatically adapts his words to suit the listener's comprehension and status, he very often forgets the listener's presence altogether by reason of his deep absorption in his theme. So, too, the listener often takes the words of the speaker, not as though they expressed merely an opinion open to

---

[1] Another, but more equivocal, name for 'selective attention' is 'abstraction'. For a simple account of this see Ribot, *Idées générales*, pp. 5 foll.

question, but as though things themselves were disclosing their own innermost nature. Perhaps the commonest phenomenon of all is that the words uttered are barely realized as such, only the things that they point at being descried. Thus on the surface speech often appears very simple—something is being said! But it needs only little change of stress to bring one or more of the underlying factors into the foreground. An incautious gesture may eclipse the things meant, and call into prominence the speaker. He almost invariably emerges into conscious presence when something false or absurd is asserted. A slightly stilted or eccentric phrase may lead to consideration of the manner of speech rather than the matter. Such swift and unpremeditated shiftings of the attention are the best testimony that the four factors of speech which I have enumerated and discussed are always present, though often only latently so.

§ 16. **The situation.** Not a factor of speech, but the setting in which speech can alone become effective, is what is here termed 'the situation'. All four factors must be in the same situation, that is to say accessible to one another in either a material or a spiritual sense. Some of the consequences of this doctrine are so trivial that they seem hardly worth mentioning. The speaker and listener must be in the same spatial and temporal situation. I in this room cannot speak to you in the country—save, of course, through the medium of writing or the telephone or the wireless. You yesterday cannot have heard what I shall be saying to-morrow. Again, the words employed must be in the situation of both speaker and listener. These two must, in fact, speak a common language.[1]

[1] See Samuel Butler, 'Thought and Language', in *Essays on Life, Art, and Science*, London, 1904, pp. 206-8.

Here the reference is not merely to the mother-tongue, but also to details of vocabulary. A Hampshire yokel will not understand if I speak French to him, but he will also fail to understand if I employ the words *psycho-analysis* or *binomial theorem*, for alike in sound and in meaning these words are unfamiliar to him.

Of far greater importance is the concept of 'situation' as applied to the things spoken about.[1] Potentially every word that is uttered might refer to the whole universe. But words are chosen with a shrewd calculation of their intelligibility; the more remote the thing spoken about, the more clues must be offered in order that it may be identified. On the other hand, if the situation is temporally and locally the same for both speaker and listener, then identification often requires but a single word or clue. The call of *Encore!* after a song in a concert-hall needs no further words for its interpretation. *Fire!* means different things when shouted aloud at dead of night and when pronounced by an officer in presence of his troops, but in both cases the single word suffices. I cannot insist too often upon the facts that words are only clues, that most words are ambiguous in their meaning, and that in every case the thing-meant has to be discovered in the situation by the listener's alert and active intelligence. The recognition of these truths disposes of the old and happily nearly obsolete view that one-word utterances like *Encore!* and *Fire!* are 'elliptic', i.e. that they need the addition of some other words 'to complete their meaning'. No amount of words will ever 'complete the meaning' of an utterance, if by 'meaning' is intended the thing-meant. The thing-meant is always outside the words, not within them. It is in the situation, but not within the utterance.

[1] See particularly Wegener, *Grundfragen*, pp. 19 foll.

Thus in the sense that the exclamation *Fire!* is elliptic, every sentence whatsoever is elliptic.[1]

It is for the philosopher rather than for the philologist to probe more deeply into the nature of the 'situation', as also of the 'things' meant by speech. For my immediate purpose these terms are sufficiently clear. It must be observed, however, that the situation of a sentence often involves several different times and several different places.[2] Consider, for example, the sentence: *I remember your telling me that your father had travelled in Spain.* Three times and at least two places are here involved, yet the thing-meant is perfectly clear. It would perhaps tend to rid the 'situation' of a certain mystical colouring if we here spoke, not of 'the situation', but of 'the situations' in the plural. To this there seems to be no serious objection.

The situation can be of many kinds. The situation of the utterances *Encore! Fire!* might be called the 'Situation of Presence'. In *Napoleon was defeated at Waterloo* we might speak of the 'Situation of Common Knowledge'. Again, there is the 'Situation of Imagination', as when an anecdote is being related. Verbal context is not in itself a situation, but together with gesture and tone of voice is the principal means of showing the situation. Each word is like a beam of light, illumining first this portion and then that portion of the field within which the thing, or rather the complex concatenation of things (*Sachverhalt*), signified by a sentence lies. Sometimes the direction of the beams remains constant, each successive word merely narrowing the area covered by its predecessor. So in the last three words of *I love my old hat*, whereas the first word points to the speaker, and the second word to an emotion

---

[1] There are, however, also legitimate uses of 'ellipse' as a grammatical term. See below, p. 270, n. 1.   [2] See below, p. 194 with Fig. 7.

of very varied quality and intensity. All five words together combine with the extra-verbal factors of speech to indicate, not the thing-meant, but its situation. The thing-meant itself is left for the intelligence of the listener to discover.

§ 17. **Depth of intention.** Under this name, which I fancy is new, reference is made to an exceedingly important aspect of the things meant by speech. As I understand 'things', no lifetime would be long, no mind penetrating enough, to comprehend the entire constitution of even the simplest of them. It belongs to the very nature of a 'thing' that the attention can dwell upon it and examine it from many different angles without ever exhausting its characters. In such a simple utterance as the vocative *Mary!* the thing-meant (always highly composite, as we shall see in the next chapter) is one upon which the mind can brood eternally. It involves both the person Mary and also the fact of, and the reasons for, my calling her. In this connexion we come across a dilemma to which the theory of speech is inevitably exposed. If we restrict our definition of the thing-meant to just so much of a thing as the speaker of the sentence intended the listener to see, then we are *ipso facto* precluded from analysing the thing-meant any further. If, on the other hand, we do analyse the thing meant, then we exceed the limits of the speaker's intention, and to that extent lose sight of the thing as so defined. For this reason it seems necessary to regard the things meant by speech as substantival and susceptible of never-ending analysis, but we must add as a rider that the theorist of speech is only concerned with so much of those things as is required to elucidate what the speaker intended the listener to see.[1]

[1] What is said here may help to dispel a difficulty which the reader may

Such is human skill in speech, and such the sympathetic responsiveness with which speech is received by the listener, that the depth of the speaker's intention is usually discerned and acquiesced in. At the end of the last section I used as an instance the sentence *I love my old hat*, which, as it happens, is a fact—one, moreover, that I had in mind while choosing this sentence as an example. I *have* an old hat, and I *love* that old hat. But my purpose in writing the sentence was to illustrate the nature and function of the words, and the reader was intended to examine the thing-meant no further. He was not called upon to speculate which of my old and shabby hats was in my mind; his concern was solely with the philological bearings of the sentence. The nature of the term 'situation' as applied to linguistic theory is herewith further elucidated. Grammars and dictionaries and books like the present one have what might be dubbed a 'Linguistic Situation'. In the sentence *I love my old hat* it matters not a jot who I am, or what hats I may possess. My depth of intention stopped short at philology.

§ 18. **Word-consciousness.** Intimately connected with the topics of the last two sections are the varying degrees in which, during the process of speech, words come to consciousness, or are thrust out of it. The instrumental character of speech ought by this time to be sufficiently apparent. But the notion ordinarily held of an instrument or tool is that of something which serves solely as a means of effecting certain results. When those results are

---

have felt in connexion with my argument in § 13 (p. 40) about *is*, *very*, and *in*. The speaker of the sentence there quoted never intended the things meant by those words to be examined as things, but the theorist of speech is forced to examine them in that way, and can do so the more readily if he labels them with words presenting them as things.

achieved, the instruments are usually removed or at least ignored. A carpenter, having completed the window-frame on which he has been working, packs up his tools and goes off to another job. Words are often instruments or tools in very much the same way. When some one asks the price of an article and is told *Six and eightpence!* he produces the money and the transaction is closed. The seller has employed the words *Six and eightpence!* merely as a contrivance to obtain his price. The words themselves are of supreme indifference; the speaker may be unconscious of uttering them, and the listener of hearing them. But not every use of language is of this simple type, though every use involves it. Frequently the word cannot be dismissed without serious injury to, or even total loss of, the vital features of the thing spoken about. Take the affirmation *He was a very stately man*. Around the word *stately* cluster memories and valuations of various and peculiar kinds, memories with which ethical and aesthetic judgements are inextricably mixed. In this region of speech words are paramount and there are no real synonyms. Substitute *dignified*, *majestic*, or *imposing*, and the thing said, though not altogether different, is modified to an appreciable extent. Here, then, we have the tool figuring as a necessary and inseparable part of the manufactured goods. If words are always instrumental, sometimes at least they are instruments of a very exceptional kind.

The fact of the matter is that many of the things about which one speaks are so intangible, so elusive, that the presence of the word itself is necessary if the thing is to be focused at all.[1] When material objects are under discussion, the names for them can be dismissed or ignored

---

[1] '*Nomina si nescis, perit et cognitio rerum*', a quotation used by Linnaeus, see Leo Spitzer, *Hugo Schuchardt-Brevier*, 2nd edition, Halle, 1928, p. 125.

without any damage to the speaker's intention. Any abstraction, however, can hardly be held in mind unless the word denoting it persists as its outward and perceptible sign. It is wholly impossible to comprehend what is meant by *religion* without the controlling and limiting consciousness of the word itself. Of great importance for the theory of speech is the fact, already noted, that the verbal formulation of all but the simplest things itself involves an alteration of them, a crystallization as it were. Everyone is familiar with the sensation of having something to say, but not knowing exactly what it is. And then the words come, and with them the feeling, not merely of expression, but even of creation. Words have thus become part of our mechanism of thinking, and remain, both for ourselves and for others, the guardians of our thought.

Let there be no mistake about it, however; even in abstract statements, the word-meaning can never be identical with the thing-meant, no matter how closely welded together the two may be. A word-meaning may crystallize in our minds a thought which has long eluded expression, but that thought is substantival in nature, and the word-meaning adjectival. The word-meaning can only describe what is meant—not *be* it. The fact of word-consciousness does not contradict the instrumental character of speech which I have been at such pains to demonstrate.

§ 19. **Style.** In every act of speech the four factors of speaker and listener, word and thing, are inevitably present, but, as we saw in § 15, selective attention usually subordinates the first three to the matter in hand. While the thing spoken about stands forth luminously and in sharp definition, the speaker, the listener, and the words themselves are discerned, if at all, only ghost-like in the surrounding penumbra. Subsequent reflection may, however, bring any one of them into prominence, witness such thoughts as 'Why did *he* say that to *me* ?' 'How beautifully he spoke!' Now the form of speech I have just described is the normal variety, but it may happen that the words employed are so cunningly chosen that they awaken in the listener, either immediately or later, distinct feelings of aesthetic admiration. The quality in a sequence of words which evokes such feelings we call 'style', and it may arise in connexion with either the sound of the words or their meaning; good style takes care of both. Here, then, we have word-consciousness in a new form; words may attain prominence not merely for their helpfulness or indispensability in focusing the thing-meant, but for their own sakes and on account of their own intrinsic worth. Style may be found in ordinary conversation no less than in an oration, but its real home is the written form of speech which we call 'literature'. In literature a distinction is made between poetry and prose, and it is generally agreed that the former is not to be equated with mere versification. To discuss the difference between prose and poetry is outside the scope of this work, but one trait must be emphasized. In poetry consciousness of the words is greater than in prose, for in poetry thought and expression are wedded in an indissoluble bond. You may change this sentence or that in prose without seriously affecting the whole. But alter a few words in poetry, and you no longer have the same poem.

ADDITIONAL NOTES TO CHAPTER I

Note A (to p. 22). *Is the listener a necessary factor of speech?*

For a very deliberate and clear statement of what seems to me exactly the wrong view I commend to my readers the following: 'What then is the essence or nature of Language, that which it is everywhere and always, and cannot not be, and therefore is, not what was or is to be, but is now? What is the true conception of it? It is that it is not a practical nor a logical, but an aesthetic fact and function. That is its present and actual nature, and by that the manner of its origin is settled and its destiny preordained. It came into existence in order that Man might express himself, might project before his inward view what moved or stirred him, so giving to it clearness and distinctness and a certain independency of being, and might furnish himself with objects to delight in; this is still the chief service it performs for us, and so it will be so long as Man's nature and world endure.' (J. A. Smith, 'Artificial Languages', in *S.P.E. Tract No. XXXIV*, 1930, p. 472.) Confronted with such assertions one can only feel as Darwin may have felt when faced by the dogma of special creation. As a counterblast to such purely academic assertions I would recommend Samuel Butler's brilliant and entertaining reply to Max Müller in his paper 'Thought and Language', in *Essays on Life, Art, and Science*, pp. 176 foll., from which I quote the following extract: 'It takes two people to say a thing—a sayee as well as a sayer. The one is as essential to any true saying as the other. A. may have spoken, but if B. has not heard, there has been nothing said, and he must speak again. True, the belief on A.'s part that he had a *bonâ fide* sayee in B. saves his speech *quâ* him, but it has been barren and left no fertile issue. It has failed to fulfil the conditions of true speech, which involve not only that A. should speak, but also that B. should hear.'

Another writer who believes that the making of sentences is performed by the speaker without regard to a listener is John Ries. His painstaking and learned book, *Was ist ein Satz?* (Prague, 1931), defends this thesis with a clarity and a vigour which leave nothing to be desired. In the course of his argument he goes so far as to say (p. 46): 'Die Eigenart keines Gegenstandes, keiner Erscheinung, keiner Tätigkeit hängt davon ab, ob und wie diese beobachtet, in welcher Weise, auf welchen psychischen Wegen sie von einem Beobachter aufgenommen oder wie weit sie von ihm erfasst werden'. Has the learned Professor ever reflected upon the nature of a sale, or upon the technique of courtship?

Note B (to p. 31). *Has the distinction between 'meaning' and 'thing-meant' really been ignored hitherto?*

Those of my readers who are here studying linguistic theory for the first time will find it barely credible that so obvious a distinction can have been overlooked. Still, it is a fact that plain statements on the subject are very hard to find. Paul's view is variable. At moments he realizes that things outside speech can be spoken about, and that the use of words consists in subsuming them under their kinds; the formulation quoted from him below, p. 256, n. 2, could hardly be bettered. No trace of this doctrine appears, however, in the sections devoted to word-meaning (*Prinzipien*, §§ 51 foll.). Here he distinguishes between *usuelle Bedeutung*, the generally accepted meaning of a word, and *okkasionelle Bedeutung*, the meaning which a speaker attaches to a word at the moment of utterance; outside these two he recognizes no objective reference. Wundt appears to lay it down as a principle that, in determining the nature of a sentence, no addition to what is expressed by the words should be assumed (*hinzugedacht*). Polemizing against this view, Paul maintains that such an assumption is 'usually' (*meistens*) necessary (op. cit., p. 130, n. 1). He should have written 'always', and it is precisely his failure to do so which proves that he has not grasped the truth. I have not succeeded in forming a clear conception of Jespersen's opinion on this matter. He evidently holds that words can refer to 'things', for, as we shall see (below, p. 286), he attempts to classify words according to the number of objects to which they can be applied. Some passages in his works seem to imply, however, a restriction of 'meaning' to the special meanings called by Paul *okkasionelle Bedeutung*, e.g., 'If I am asked to give the meaning of *jar* or *sound* or *palm* or *tract*, the only honest answer is, "Show me the context, and I will tell you the meaning." In one connexion *pipe* is understood to mean a tobacco-pipe, in another a water-pipe, in a third a boatswain's whistle, in another one of the tubes of an organ,' *Philosophy*, p. 66. A very clear case of the omission of 'things' in a general treatise by a first-rate scholar is in de Saussure's *Cours de linguistique*, pp. 28–9, where he uses the accompanying figure to illustrate the 'circuit' traced by a snatch of conversation. The process starts with a 'concept' in the speaker's mind; this disengages an 'image acoustique': 'c'est un phénomène entièrement *psychique*, suivi à son tour d'un procès *physiologique*: le cerveau

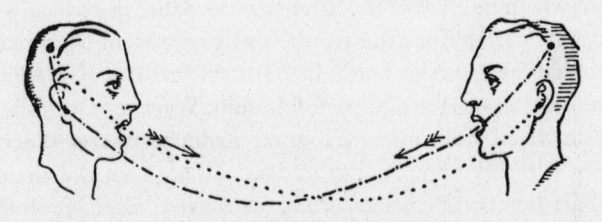

FIG. 1. A circuit of speech.
Redrawn from de Saussure, *Cours de linguistique*, p. 28.

transmet aux organes de la phonation une impulsion corrélative à l'image; puis les ondes sonores se propagent de la bouche de *A* à l'oreille de *B*: procès purement *physique*. Ensuite, le circuit se prolonge en *B* dans un ordre inverse: de l'oreille au cerveau, transmission physiologique de l'image acoustique; dans le cerveau, association psychique de cette image avec le concept correspondant. Si *B* parle à son tour, ce nouvel acte suivra—de son cerveau à celui de *A*—exactement la même marche que le premier. . . . Cette analyse ne prétend pas être complète; on pourrait distinguer encore: la sensation acoustique pure, l'identification de cette sensation avec l'image acoustique latente, l'image musculaire de la phonation, &c. Nous n'avons tenu compte que des éléments jugés essentiels; mais notre figure permet de distinguer d'emblée les parties physiques (ondes sonores) des parties physiologiques (phonation et audition) et psychiques (images verbales et concepts). Il est en effet capital de remarquer que l'image verbale ne se confond pas avec le son lui-même et qu'elle est psychique au même titre que le concept qui lui est associé.' The passage is too long to quote in its entirety, but the continuation shows beyond a doubt that de Saussure was attempting to describe a complete act of speech, or rather two complementary acts of speech, without omitting any essential features. Of 'things' referred to there is not a hint. If so acute a thinker as de Saussure has failed to note the necessity of 'things' to every linguistic act, we may be sure that the same error is widely held. It is for this reason that I have singled him out for special criticism.

Happily there are a few philologists who have diagnosed the facts more clearly. Among these Wegener, as usual, leads the way. The account which he gives of the listener's procedure in deducing what was meant, partly from the words, and partly from the situation, proves that he saw the truth in its main features (*Grundfragen*, passim, and especially pp. 19 foll.). But Wegener's terminology differs in detail from mine. How far Erdmann shares Wegener's opinions is rather obscure, but at least he has seen the virtues of the scholastic doctrine of *suppositio*, see above p. 32, n. 1. Kalepky (*Neuaufbau*, pp. 6–7) recognized, perhaps more clearly than anyone except Wegener, that speech can deal with real things and real events, and that its method of referring to them is through 'analysis' and 'subsumption'. Only unhappily he equated 'meaning' with 'ideas' (*Begriffe*), an error on which I have commented at the end of § 13. Another scholar who has not lost sight of 'things' is E. Wellander (*Studien zum Bedeutungswandel im Deutschen*, Part I, Upsala, 1917, pp. 9 foll.), but he fails to make use of it owing to his neglect of the 'situation', which alone can effectuate the reference of a word, see op. cit., p. 19, and for a mere passing mention of the 'situation', p. 21, bottom. Wellander appears to me to have been misled by the high degree of mechanization which interpretation has acquired.

I am too little familiar with the literature of logic to discuss how far modern logicians are aware of the distinction here under discussion. The contrast made between 'connotation' ('intension') and 'denotation' ('extension') has some similarity to my distinction between 'meaning' and 'thing-meant'; but to say, as logicians often do, that such-and-such a term is used in connotation, while another is used in denotation, suggests that the mechanism of speech has not been properly understood; on this point see below, §§ 67–8. Among logicians, Husserl has rightly formulated the position; in one passage (*Logische Untersuchungen*, Halle, 1913–21, vol. ii, Part 1, p. 49) he pronounces the verdict that 'der Ausdruck bezeichne (nenne) den Gegenstand mittels seiner Bedeutung'; cf. the scholastic formula quoted above, p. 44. A number of Husserl's contentions appear to me, however, either wrong or else obscurely worded. For a summary of his position, see C. K. Ogden and I. A. Richards, *The Meaning of Meaning*, London, 1923, Appendix D, § 1 (pp. 418 foll.).

Finally, commentators, literary critics, and the general public. The distinction between meaning and thing-meant is quite familiar in practice, but not having been firmly grasped as a necessary theoretic view, is frequently lost sight of at critical moments. It finds expression in statements such as, 'We have been arguing only about words' or 'His meaning (i.e. the thing meant by him) is perfectly plain, but the expression is defective'. A curious position sometimes confronts the commentator of letters or ancient texts. The sentences hang together and yield a sense which is satisfactory and certain up to a point, but no further. To the audience addressed by the author the background of fact was known, so that he could 'see what was meant'. But the interpreter is left perplexed and baffled, because for him that background is unascertainable.

II

THE ACT OF SPEECH. THE SENTENCE AND THE WORD. SPEECH AND LANGUAGE

§ 20. **Summary of the argument.** In the first chapter I sought to show that speech is no mere bilateral affair, consisting of articulate sounds on the one hand, and thought or meaning on the other, but rather that it is quadrilateral, and requires for a true comprehension of its nature the four sides, or factors, of speaker, listener, words, and things. The necessity of thus refuting, at the outset, an erroneous assumption all the more insidious because seldom categorically stated, had the disadvantage that speech could not simultaneously be depicted as the highly complex, purposeful, and individual mode of human action which it essentially is. It will be the task of the present chapter to rectify this omission. We shall see that the impulse to speech, at least in its more fundamental forms, arises in the intention of some member of the community to influence one or more of his fellows in reference to some particular thing. **Speech** is thus a universally exerted activity, having at first definitely utilitarian aims. In describing this activity, we shall discover that it consists in the application of a universally possessed science, namely the science which we call **language**. With infinite pains the human child learns language in order to exercise it as speech. These two human attributes, language the science and speech its active application, have too often been confused with one another or regarded as identical, with the result that no intelligible account could be given of their ultimate elements, the 'word' and the 'sentence'. Not the least important conclusion which will emerge from our discussion is that the 'word' is the unit of language, whereas the 'sentence' is the unit of speech.

§ 21. **Silence and speech.** In waking hours the mind of man is never at rest. His thoughts and musings flow on in unbroken sequence, showing a discontinuity only when some external event or interesting recollection stirs to greater alertness, perhaps ultimately evoking a deliberate reaction. But man is not always talking. When he is alone, the wayward reflections pursue their course in silence. Indeed, we can even say that an individual silently expresses to himself his thoughts by the mere fact of having them. In the absence of a companion it is difficult to see why speech should ever arise. And in fact, monologue is not natural to man. The mutterings of the deranged provide no argument to the contrary, and the babbling of children is not so much speech as the early private rehearsal of later conversational performances.[1] If, at moments of unusual emotional stress or intense intellectual endeavour, words spring to the lips or even come to actual utterance, this is merely for the relief they give to the feelings, or for the aid which they afford to precise thinking (§ 18). A corollary to this statement is that for normal speech the presence of some second individual is necessary. But even in that case speech does not always occur. Noticing that I am without a teaspoon, I may prefer to fetch one myself rather than trouble a companion. In

---

[1] The first articulate utterances of children are play activity, and consist simply in exercise of the organs of articulation. These utterances are without meaning, and are clearly to be distinguished from meaningful emotional cries. A few months later, however, the speech-sounds begin to share in the significant function of such cries. See Bühler, *Theorien des Satzes*, pp. 1–2. At the subsequent stage envisaged in the text, imitation of grown-ups has become a factor.

fact, the occurrence of speech depends normally upon the presence of two conditioning circumstances: (1) the perception of something interesting enough to incite to action, and (2) the desire somehow to involve another person in that perception. The commonest motives inducing speech are the desires to inform somebody of something, to ask somebody about something, to exhort somebody to do something, or to win sympathy from somebody in respect of something. In conclusion, whereas thought comprises only two factors apart from the process of thinking, namely the thinker and the thing thought of, speech comprises three factors besides the actual words, inasmuch as it adds to the thinker, now become the speaker, and to the thing thought of, now become the thing spoken of, a second person, namely the listener.

§ 22. **The act of speech at once social and individual.** The facts set forth in the last paragraph establish beyond a doubt that the act of speech is a social act, seeing that it necessarily involves two persons, and may possibly involve more, if there be a number of listeners. But it must be clearly recognized that, speaking of a social act, I do not mean a collective one. On the contrary, every act of speech is individual in the sense that it springs from an impulse or volition on the part of a single person. It is true that speech has become so easy and frequent a performance, that to describe it as the result of a volition may seem exaggerated. But at least we must admit that it is always open to the speaker to speak or to be silent. The initiative is always his. On the other hand, we must guard against the supposition that the part of the listener is wholly passive. He is a recipient rather than an initiator, no doubt, but the act of understanding is one which demands considerable mental effort. We saw in the last chapter (§ 11) that in the course of actual speech, the words serve mainly as clues. It is upon the listener that devolves the duty of interpreting those clues, of finding the thing-meant. Accordingly, also from the standpoint of the listener's activity, the act of speech is individual as well as social. Sometimes the part to be played by the listener greatly transcends the mere effort of comprehension. In questions and commands a definite responsive movement is expected of him. This responsive movement lies, it is true, outside the speaker's own linguistic act, but in a sense it belongs to it, questions and commands being otherwise inexplicable.

Speech is, of course, not the only human activity with at once a social and an individual aspect. The relations of master and servant, or those of buyer and seller, are on much the same footing as the relations of speaker and listener. The social character of speech is, however, rendered specially prominent by the ease and frequency with which the roles are there interchanged. In conversation, the person speaking at one moment becomes the listener at the next, and vice versa.

§ 23. **The ultimate basis of speech.** The activity of speech is so familiar to us that we seldom stop to consider what a remarkable type of behaviour it is. If an inhabitant of some other planet, ignorant of speech, but gifted with an intelligence resembling our own, could visit the earth and observe the conduct of its denizens, would he not be amused and puzzled by this peculiar traffic in articulate sounds, with its accompaniment of excited manual gesture, and its strange effect upon the emotions and conduct of its adepts ? Sun and stars speak not, neither do minerals and plants. Even among the higher animals speech is rudimentary and dubious. Alone for the human race speaking is a universal daily habit. How is this habit to be explained?

The growth of intelligence and the importance for conduct of conscious mental processes are evidently part of the explanation. But man can act purposively so as to influence the actions of others even without speech. When handing the apple to Adam, Eve intended that he should eat it. However, the things to which human beings seek to evoke responsive movements are seldom as simple as an apple, nor are they often so easy to present to the attention of a companion. Among concrete things in respect of which a specific course of action is desired, some may be momentarily absent or not within the individual's power to manipulate. Think of an enemy whose approach is seen by one savage but unperceived by another, or of a pair of spectacles which has been left downstairs in the dining-room. Moreover, it is often necessary to indicate exactly what kind of action is required; the man who needs the help of another may have to reveal his own feelings or the nature of his wishes.

It is difficult to find a general formula to cover all the things which desiderate speech for their communication. In rare cases words are employed to stress or enhance feelings shared at the instant of utterance by both parties; so in greetings, congratulations, and expressions of condolence. But apart from these exceptional kinds of utterance, the speaker usually assumes the listener to be ignorant of, or momentarily not concerned with, what he himself is wishing to make the object of common interest. The things meant by speech are mostly complex. Or if they are simple, then the need for words is due to the personal and emotional character of that in respect of which help or sympathy is desired.

§ 23 THE BASIS OF SPEECH

The ultimate basis of speech is the fact that individual thoughts and feelings are, as such, entirely inalienable. One man cannot think the thoughts of another, or behold an object with another's mental vision. Nor can anyone take his enjoyment of a sunset and transfer it directly to a companion's mind. It is the penalty of individuality that the inner life is solitary, that perceptions and feelings cannot actually be shared. Sympathy and understanding are indeed possible, but two minds cannot interpenetrate one another in any literal sense. From this follows the important consequence that a physical substitute has to be found whenever anything intellectual or emotional is to be imparted. Such physical substitutes are called **signs**, and are subject to the conditions (1) that they should have a pre-arranged 'meaning', or associated mental equivalence, and (2) that they should be handy objects of sense transferable at will. Any material thing which conforms to these two conditions will serve as a 'sign', and any system of signs is a kind of language. Examples are the manual signs employed by deaf-mutes and the somewhat similar gesture-language that has been observed among the native tribes of America and elsewhere.[1] Other languages are of a more artificial and improvised character; there is the 'language of flowers'; also 'money talks'. Samuel Butler quotes the snuff-box which Mrs. Bentley, wife of the famous Dr. Bentley of Trinity College, Cambridge, used to send to the college buttery whenever she wanted beer; as Samuel Butler demonstrates in his own inimitable way, the snuff-box was, for that particular purpose, very good language indeed.[2]

[1] See Ribot, *Idées générales*, pp. 47 foll., 59 foll.
[2] Samuel Butler's outlook on language and speech is so sound, that I reproduce the entire passage below, pp. 104–5, Additional Note C.

Before closing this section, brief mention must be made of the human attributes from which speech obtains its driving-force. These are the twin, but contrary, attributes of self-seeking and altruism.[1] The former impels us to enlist the brains and muscles of our fellows for our own advantage, while the latter, born of sympathy, causes us to study the interests of others—interests often well-served by information, persuasion, or even commands.

§ 24. **The superiority of spoken language to all other systems of signs.** It was inevitable that the system of signs which the human race would adopt in preference to all others for its communicative aims should be the sound-signs which we call 'words'. Since the signs had to be susceptible of production at will and without delay, it was likely that they would make use of the natural movements most nearly akin to reflex action. Such are facial expressions or grimaces, manual movements or gestures, and emotional cries together with such semi-volitional sounds as grunts and laughter. All these have survived as frequent accessories to speech, where their chief function is to indicate the nature and intensity of the speaker's feelings towards the thing spoken about and towards his audience. Facial expressions are so valuable for the display of emotion, that it would have been a pity had they been schooled to the more unimpassioned task of representing external phenomena, even if they could have developed the needful variety. Movements of the hands are too useful for practical purposes to have been specialized for the function of communication, apart from the objections that they need light to be seen by and claim a corresponding direction of the listener's eyes. Articulate sounds, on the other hand, have the advantage of giving employment to an organ

[1] This point is rightly stressed by Wegener, *Grundfragen*, p. 68.

which would otherwise be idle except when engaged in eating. They have the further advantages that they are susceptible of almost infinite variety, and that they reach the other person in spite of himself, since he cannot shut his ears as he can shut or turn away his eyes. Furthermore, they are equally effective in the light of day and in the darkness of night.[1]

§ 25. **Words not really objects of sense, but psychical entities.** Our next step is to observe that it is only inaccurately, though by a sort of necessary inaccuracy, that the name of 'words' is given to the articulate sounds which pass between speaker and listener. There is no more fundamental truth in the entire theory of speech. To use a metaphor, the sounds of speech are not aeroplanes invented for the purpose of carrying thoughts as their passengers between man and man. It must be repeated that psychical life is completely inalienable. The impossibility of transferring thought is absolute and insurmountable. Only by an inference from his own thought can the listener conclude that the speaker has been thinking of the same thing. What passes in speech between the two persons concerned is mere sound, bereft of all sense. Now as I have pointed out more than once (e.g. §§ 9, 15), 'words' are two-sided in their nature, one side being that of meaning or sense, and the other that of sound. It follows that the physical results of articulate speech, not possessing the side of meaning, cannot be actual words. But there are other important reasons why the same conclusion must be drawn. In the first place a word can be used and re-used on many different occasions; and in the second place the same word can be employed by all the different members

[1] For the whole of this section see Ribot, *Idées générales*, pp. 62-3; Ward, *Psychological Principles*, pp. 290-1.

of a linguistic community. It can be learnt by study or looked up in a dictionary. It is, in fact, something relatively permanent, widespread, and capable of being possessed in common by a multitude of individuals. All these considerations prove, beyond possibility of contradiction, that words transcend, and are altogether less evanescent entities than, the sounds which issue from a speaker's mouth and vanish into nothingness soon after they have reached the listener's ear. As words exist in the possession of every individual, they are psychical entities, comprising on the one hand an area of meaning, and on the other hand the image of a particular sound susceptible of being physically reproduced whenever wanted. We now see, therefore, that the description of words as having a side of meaning and a side of sound, though the simplest and most practical description at the stage when it was given, is slightly misleading, inasmuch as it implies that words are partly psychical and partly physical. In reality they are wholly psychical, matters of knowledge and learning, though on one side of their nature they point to a physical occurrence reproducible at will.

What then shall be said of the articulate sounds which are uttered and heard in speech? What is their relation to the 'words' which exist in the minds of all potential speakers and listeners? The articulate sounds appear to be physical, audible, copies of one aspect of their psychical originals. It is only the sound-image connected with words which can be reproduced in a physical copy. When a word is 'pronounced', its meaning stays with the speaker. All that the listener receives is the sound, which he then identifies as belonging to a word in *his* possession, this identification enabling him to pass immediately to the meaning associated with the sound.

In practice, to refer to the sounds heard in speech as 'words' is unavoidable. Indeed, it is even desirable; we cannot always refer to them as copies or reproductions of words. To do so would be worse than pedantic, it would often be wilfully misleading. Nothing is less desirable in speech—however little logicians may relish this assertion—than a misplaced accuracy. Accuracy of that description often serves only to lay the stress in the wrong place, and so to prevent the listener from seeing the 'thing-meant'.

§ 26. **The 'modus operandi' of a simple act of speech.** An act of speech, as conceived of in this book, is no mere set of words capable of being repeated on a number of separate occasions, but a particular, transient occurrence involving definite individuals and tied down to a special time and place. Hence the example which I shall conjure up to illustrate the principles involved in all speech must describe in detail a particular 'situation' (§ 16). A certain James Hawkins is sitting in his study in the afternoon of the 18th of April, 1931, together with Mary his wife. Both are reading and completely absorbed in their books. At a given moment James becomes aware of a continued beating upon the window-pane, which he identifies as the sound of rain, a conclusion verified a moment later by a glance towards the window. The perception of the rain reminds him that his wife and he have decided to walk over to Riverside for tea, should the weather hold. Another glance convinces James that this is no mere shower and that the idea of the walk must be abandoned, as Mary ought not to sit about with wet feet. Since she, however, shows no signs of having noticed the rain, her husband decides to call her attention to it, which he does with the simple ejaculation, *Rain!* Hearing that word, Mary looks up, sees the rain falling in torrents, realizes the effect that this is going to have on her afternoon, and replies, *What a bore!*

The act of speech here described comprises a series of events, the succession of which can be distinguished with some degree of clearness. There are five principal stages, in which the parts played by the two actors alternate with purely external, physical happenings, as follows: (1) downpour of rain; (2) speaker's reaction; (3) speech-sounds as a physical event; (4) listener's reaction, culminating in (5) verification of the rain by a glance at the window. The part of the proceedings which interests us begins with the perception of the rain by James Hawkins. That perception would have been impossible, of course, without previous experiences of rain, such as are summed up in the meaning of the word *rain*. The question as to whether thought does or does not involve language must, I suppose, amount to the following: Perception, or the recognition of something external for what it is, undoubtedly involves a revival or use of past experiences of similar things. But those experiences are associated in the mind with the sound of a particular word. Is it possible for perception to take place without some consciousness, however dim, of the associated word? This is clearly a question for the psychologist, and I shall not attempt to decide whether the word *rain* emerged in James's mind now or only later in the proceedings. At all events the perception has set in motion a whole train of thoughts, the recollection of the proposed walk, its undesirability in Mary's interest, and the need, therefore, to inform Mary of the probable change of plan. The entire situation is now clear to James, but many possibilities confront him as he makes up his mind to address Mary. He might point to the window and say, *Look!* or simply, *Mary!*; or else he might choose a more wordy

(J) 1. The rain falls

J 2. James perceives the rain

J 3. James says *Rain!*

(J) 4 = M 1. Mary pays attention

(J) 5 = M 2. Mary sees what is meant

M 3. Mary replies *What a bore!*

FIG. 2. The visible aspects of a typical act of speech.[h]

method of achieving the same result, as by the sentence *Look at the rain!* or *What a storm!* But our analysis is concerned only with the course actually taken by James, which is to indicate the central fact in the whole business, i.e. the rain itself. The word *rain* rises automatically to his lips as he goes on to name the falling water which he sees. Let us be certain that we understand what the process of naming the rain really is. It is not the choice of some arbitrary new sound to represent this particular new happening. On the contrary, James does not really name the new rain at all; *what he names is only his previous experiences of rain, as represented in his memory by the class-name 'rain'*.[1] That name is, in fact, the one which he has always used, and heard other persons use, for similar experiences in the past. Otherwise expressed, the presently perceived rain is recognized as a member of the class of things associated with the sound-image *rain*. It is this sound-image, therefore, which rises to James's lips.

But there within James's lips the sound-image might have stayed but for his decision to articulate it and to send it forth as a physical complex of air-waves. Now in practice the decision to speak invariably assumes the form of *an intention to affect the listener in a particular way*, and it is this intention which, as I shall later show, makes of every genuine act of speech a 'sentence', not merely the use of words or a word. It is true that the status of 'sen-

[1] The previous experiences may sometimes be restricted to a single occasion, as when some one is introduced by name, and the name is employed a few moments later. Moreover, as Mr. Gunn points out, the experiences need not be direct. I may speak of an earthquake without ever having experienced one, its nature being known to me by descriptions, i.e. through the experiences of others. Such cases do not affect my point, which is that the word-sign used did not, at the moment of its choice for utterance, yet include in its meaning the thing in course of being referred to.

tence' is not usually conceded to single nouns pronounced exclamatorily, but the view just expressed proclaims me an adherent of the opposite opinion. In the present instance James's intention is to convey information to Mary, to make her 'see' the rain and its implications. Grammarians call such a sentence a 'statement', a term which rather unfortunately conceals the speaker's evident desire to coax the listener's attention in a given direction. Allusion has just been made to a subsidiary device employed by James for the accomplishment of his particular purpose. He does not simply pronounce the word as though it were a matter of indifference, but utters it in a rather high-pitched voice, with *sforzando* attack, sinking at the finish to a slightly lower note. In writing we must suggest this difference of intonation by an exclamation-mark; *Rain!* says James, not simply *rain*. Differences of pitch and intensity are always used in actual speech to convey such differences of sentence-quality. If James, on hearing the sound at the window-pane, had not looked up and satisfied himself as to the cause, he might conceivably have uttered the word *Rain?* with the rising intonation which indicates a question. But in the case before us, James is not asking a question, but making an assertion. To render the interpretation of the utterance still clearer, yet another auxiliary to speech might have been invoked, either a nod of the head or a raising of the hand towards the window.

The passage from volition to action, and the method by which the muscles connected with the organs of speech were innervated, are psychological and physiological events beyond my competence. So far as I am concerned, therefore, James's role in the act of speech is now ended, and we may turn from him to the physical occurrence which he has created. Unable to transfer his thought as such, and unable, therefore, to adopt that means of attracting his companion's attention to the object of his thought, his articulated word-sign has brought about certain changes in Mary's environment which work upon her in a way similar to that in which the rain worked upon James. The principal change is, of course, the emergence for Mary of what, alike to herself and to James, appears as 'sound'. This nomenclature combines, in a fashion which strictly is inaccurate, the actual physical occurrence, the creation of a certain complex of wave-lengths in the air, with the auditory sensations of the persons present. For my purpose, all that has to be observed is that, from the listener's standpoint, what constitutes and renders effective the act of speech, is not any modification of the speaker's thoughts, but an external audible occurrence, reinforced by other external occurrences of a visible kind.

We now pass on to examine the part played by Mary Hawkins. By way of contrasting her role with that of her husband, I call her the listener, though without implying that she had been expecting any words to be addressed to her. On the contrary, she is so immersed in her book as to be totally oblivious of everything around her. All the more remarkable, therefore, is the alertness with which she lends ear to James's ejaculation. This readiness to attend is an important and almost invariable feature in the operation of speech, though I shall not allude to it again. It arises, partly from the general recognition of speech as a source of mutual advantage, partly from the habitual courtesy which social life has engendered. The auditory sensation caused by the sound-waves which James's utterance has set in motion is immediately identified by Mary as a familiar word. But

§ 26   AN ACT OF SPEECH   77

which word? The sound of *Rain!* is very ambiguous, embracing all the possibilities of *rain* and *rein* and *reign*. For the listener there are, at the moment of audition, no homophones. In speech, though not in language, words which sound alike are, in effect, a single word. But Mary does not doubt that *rain* has been meant. To the generality of Englishwomen rain is a more frequent topic than reins or a reign, and long before her thoughts could travel to those more remote components of her vocabulary, Mary's mind will have become satisfied that *rain* has been intended. The brevity of James's utterance, the incisiveness with which it has been spoken, and indeed the entire set of circumstances attending that curt exclamation upon that particular April afternoon, will already have convinced her (through previous experiences of the like) that he was referring to some obvious thing physically present in the immediate environment.[1] The word *rain* itself has potentialities of application which are very far from uniform; within its 'area of meaning' as known to Mary from her past experiences, are references not only to water-drops betokening a now occurring downpour, but also to a meteorological condition prevailing over an entire season (e.g. *There has been nothing but* RAIN *this August*) or even to any descent of small particles that can be compared with the natural phenomenon (e.g. *a* RAIN *of ashes*). Nevertheless, it is solely the first of these possibilities which occurs to Mary. Since the possibility nearest to hand suits the situation, she has no reason for looking further afield. A glance at the window confirms her interpretation, and also shows her that her husband has

[1] Mary may also have a dim consciousness, derived from the fact of a noun being used, that the thing-meant is to be viewed as a thing. (See below, pp. 144–5.)

rightly marked the state of the weather. And now crowd in upon her all the considerations which prompted James to speak, supplemented by feelings of her own not identical with any which have on this occasion been felt by him. James had shrewdly calculated the effect which his ejaculation would produce, and though, as I have just noted, the total 'thing-meant' is not exactly identical for Mary and himself, still the similarity is close enough to convince him that his purpose has been successfully fulfilled. The act of speech chosen for analysis has come full circle. Mary has 'seen' what James 'meant', and that thing-meant forthwith becomes the starting-point for a reply which takes shape in the words *What a bore!*

§ 27. **Once again the thing-meant.** What exactly is it that James has 'meant' and Mary has 'seen'? A complex 'state of things' (*Sachverhalt*), as I characterized it in § 8, consisting of the rain at the window, the thought of the walk, the disappointment at its abandonment, and a good deal else as well. Mary also sees that James has meant her to see all this. The act of speech itself can no more be excluded from the thing-meant than the persons participating in the act. But, to employ a simile already used, not all parts of this complex state of things are equally illuminated. James has willed it that a brilliant beam of light should fall upon that constituent part of the whole which was its actual point of departure, namely the visible downpour of rain. Orthodox grammarians would, indeed, asseverate that the rain was all that the exclamation meant, so much and no more having been said. The most they would concede is that James had meant what formally correct parlance expresses by *There is rain*.[1] So far as

[1] The old logical doctrine demands that every sentence should be analysable into subject and predicate.

PHYSICAL STIMULUS TO JAMES — the falling rain

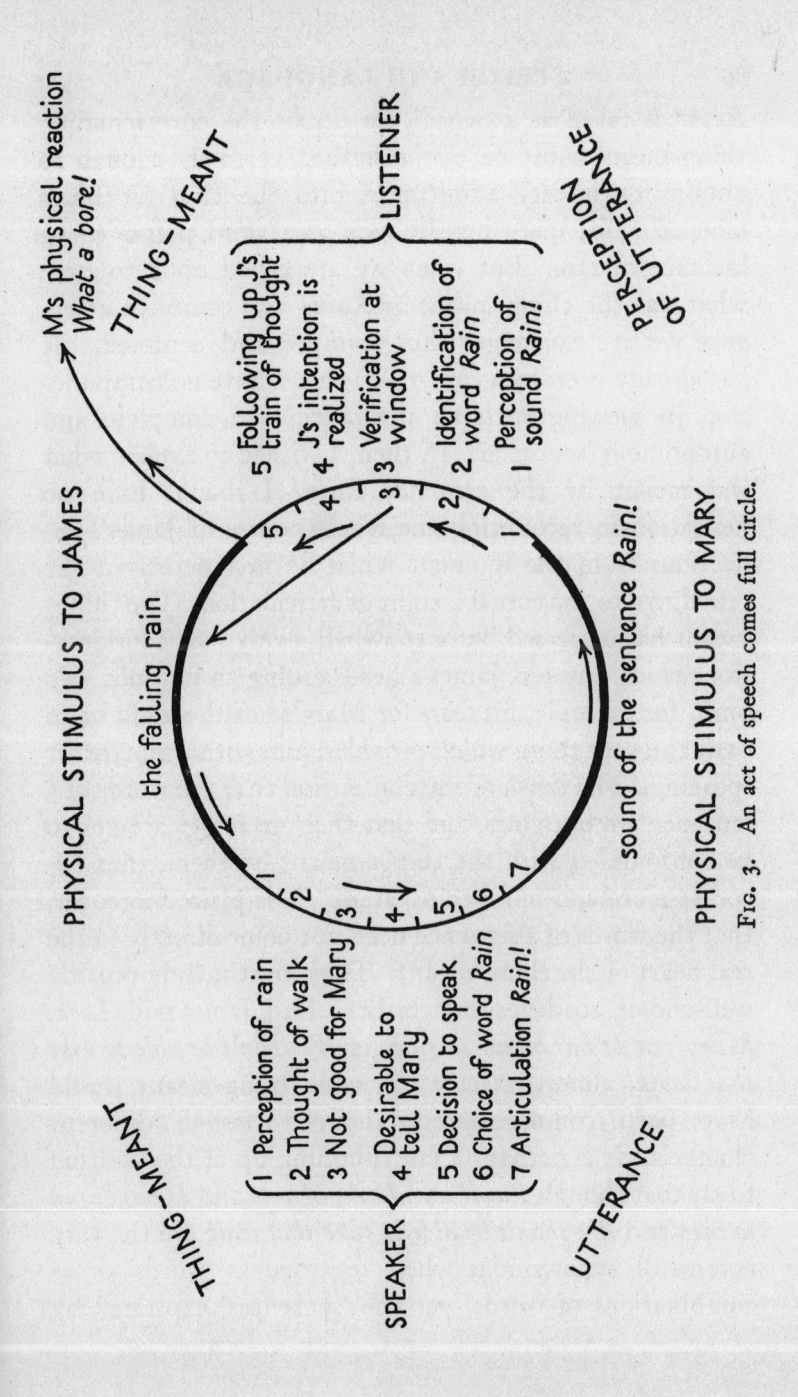

M's physical reaction *What a bore!*

THING-MEANT

LISTENER
5 Following up J's train of thought
4 J's intention is realized
3 Verification at window
2 Identification of word *Rain*
1 Perception of sound *Rain!*

PERCEPTION OF UTTERANCE

SPEAKER
1 Perception of rain
2 Thought of walk
3 Not good for Mary
4 Desirable to tell Mary
5 Decision to speak
6 Choice of word *Rain*
7 Articulation *Rain!*

THING-MEANT

UTTERANCE

PHYSICAL STIMULUS TO MARY — sound of the sentence *Rain!*

Fig. 3. An act of speech comes full circle.

Rain! is taken as a 'word', no doubt the corresponding thing-meant must be circumscribed narrowly enough to obtain for it easy admittance into the class of things labelled *rain*; more briefly, *rain* as a word points to an instance of rain. But when we are called upon to state what was the thing meant by *Rain!* as a complete utterance we are no longer thus cramped and confined. It has already been seen (pp. 74-5) that I have no compunction in viewing such an utterance as a complete and autonomous 'sentence'. If, then, I wished to explain what was meant by the sentence *Rain!* I should have no hesitation in recounting the whole course of James's reflections from the moment when he first perceived the rain down to the actual instant of articulation. The thing-meant has increased like a snowball, every new consideration which entered James's head adding to its bulk. To omit, for example, his fears for Mary's health would be to omit the very thing which provided him with a motive for speaking. The truth of my contention that the words of a sentence are but clues, and that their meanings are not to be confounded with the things meant by them, thus becomes more and more transparent. It is plain, moreover, that the words of a sentence need not point directly to the real heart of the thing-meant. They must merely provide well-chosen roads leading thither. Had James said, *Look, Mary!* or *It has begun to rain*, or *We shan't be able to take that walk*, almost exactly the same thing-meant would have been communicated, though through different channels. It is perhaps a fair summing up of the position to say that though *Rain!* and *Look, Mary!* and *It has begun to rain* and *We shan't be able to take that walk* are the very reverse of synonymous when regarded as 'words' or as combinations of words, yet the 'sentences' expressed by them in this situation are very nearly synonymous, indeed, are only not completely synonymous by reason of what may be described as different effects of lighting.

There is a further question with regard to the thing-meant which cannot be entirely evaded. Was the thing seen by Mary really the same thing that James had meant? In this question are involved deep metaphysical issues, upon which, for all their interest, we must resolutely turn our backs. My book has no other purpose than to investigate the nature of speech, and like all scientific inquiries, the plane upon which it moves is that of ordinary observation and common-sense assumptions. At the common-sense level the present question must be answered both affirmatively and negatively. Without the postulate that speaker and listener are able to direct their attention to the same thing, the very notion of speech is an absurdity, and any rational theory on the subject becomes impossible. But room must be left for such contingencies as contradiction and differences of feeling as between speaker and listener. In the instance before us, an element in James's thing-meant has been the expectation that Mary would be disappointed, whereas in fact she might answer, *I am quite glad, as I'm rather tired!* A less likely circumstance is that James, being short-sighted, has wrongly identified the cause of the sound heard by him, so that Mary can reply sharply, *Nonsense, it is not raining!* To that extent the thing-meant may not be identical for speaker and listener. It is indispensable for the success of the utterance that Mary should see the thing meant by James in its essential lines, but her own counterpart may reveal a somewhat changed and deepened perspective. On account of this possible divergence of views, as well as for other reasons, e.g. word-consciousness (§ 18), the entire act of speech, actors, words, and all, must be regarded as potential ingredients in the thing-meant, which thus runs the risk of being confused with the 'situation' (§ 16). At a word from Mary, James himself can be brought to see the thing-meant, as he would say, 'in quite a new light'.

The principles enunciated in the first chapter will enable us to draw a sharp distinction between 'situation' and 'thing-meant'. In so far as the thing-meant is a 'thing', there is no limit to the number of other things which subsequent thought may bring into connexion with it. Some of these super-added things are nearer, some more remote. All the nearer things, taken together, constitute the 'situation'. But within this, and strictly limited by the speaker's 'depth of intention' (§ 17), is what has been actually 'meant'. Inasmuch as it is 'meant', the thing-meant is only the volitionally illuminated part of the situation, namely that part of it which the speaker has intended to come to the listener's consciousness. Since every act of speech owes its existence to an exertion (however disguised by mechanization, § 14) of the speaker's will, it seems natural and right that the critic, if not the grammarian, should view the 'thing-meant' from the speaker's angle. But we must remember that it is by no means always the speaker's desire to divulge his private perceptions or emotions. He may deliberately wish to mislead, or may promise what he does not intend to perform. Or to take a subtler case, he may adopt a tone of certainty about what he knows to be doubtful. For all these reasons we dare not neglect the listener. The following will probably be found a good working definition: *The thing meant by any utterance is whatever the speaker has intended to be understood from it by the listener.*[1]

[1] A closely similar formulation was given in my article on *Word and*

§ 28. **The material and the standpoint of the theorist of speech.** Speaker and listener, uttered words and thing- or things-meant, have all come to light in the typical act of speech selected by me·for analysis. This act disclosed itself as a miniature drama, the action of which consisted in the interplay of those four factors. That they are involved in *some* examples of speech is thus conclusively demonstrated, but it would require a wide survey of other examples in order to justify generalization of the inference. For such an extended survey there is obviously no place in a book of this kind, and it must be left to the reader to discover, if he can, any instance of speech where the four factors are neither actually nor implicitly present. I shall deal in the next chapter (§ 36) with one or two cases which might seem dubious. Here I will mention only one. 'Do you really maintain', some one may object, 'that your four factors are present in that volume of Thackeray standing upon the shelf? And yet it undoubtedly contains written speech. I am ready to admit', he may continue, 'that the speaker is there, for I have named the author. But where is the listener, and where are the uttered words?' Now I shall have to acknowledge that speaker and listener are not present in the flesh, so that the thing-meant, here an imagination of the former, is also absent, and similarly no words are being uttered, only

Sentence, p. 360, though there I inexactly wrote 'meaning' for 'thing-meant'. Ogden and Richards (*Meaning of Meaning*, p. 315) criticize my view on the ground that ' "to be understood" is here a contraction. It stands for (*a*) to be referred to+(*b*) to be responded with+(*c*) to be felt towards referent+(*d*) to be felt towards speaker+(*e*) to be supposed that the speaker is referring to+(*f*) that the speaker is desiring, &c., &c.' I agree. But far from considering the vagueness of the phrase an objection, I think that is just its virtue. As I have shown, the thing-meant is always very complex, and the listener's powers of understanding must be equal to coping with all the various purposes embodied in the speaker's utterance.

visible written symbols for them being present. All this is true, and yet implicitly not one of my factors is missing. The speaker has already been conceded, and any bookseller might, if he would, indicate some 'listener' or other. The thing-meant is naught else than the story told, and the existence of this no one will deny. And lastly, what sort of symbols can those printed pages be, if they do not imply the utterances that they symbolize?

We may, therefore, regard the question of the four factors as settled, and proceed with good heart to inquire what further teaching our chosen act of speech can afford us. But a danger now arises lest we should be overwhelmed by the mass of information which closer analysis would impose. Accordingly, our next step must be to determine the exact problem which the theorist of speech sets before himself. A social act such as I have described calls for investigation from many different points of view. The psychologist might choose to consider it as a special type of behaviour, and might set himself to inquire what light such behaviour throws upon the workings of the mind. The physiologist will prefer to study the interaction of the organs of articulation, and the muscular movements involved. The task of the philologist differs from those of the psychologist and the physiologist, inasmuch as he is concerned only with the spoken words themselves, with the audible products of the act of speaking. Naturally he will take into account the three other factors, so far as they can help him to understand the special object of his efforts; but his researches will never wander far from the central region of words and sentences. Philology itself, however, comprises various branches or manners of approach. The phonetician seeks, among other things, to study the relations of the heard sounds to the exact place and mode of their articulation. The commentator deals only with written speech, with particular texts, interpreting the author's words and attempting to evaluate their aptness and aesthetic worth. The student of linguistic theory cannot, however, content himself with observing a given series or restricted total of linguistic acts. In search of general principles, he takes all possible utterances as his province, though he not only can, but also in my opinion must, use single and particular utterances as his points of departure. These utterances he treats solely as instruments of communication, as significant signs. His interest is, in fact, what has been variously called semasiology, significs, or semantics.[1] It is a wide field, and when rightly understood, embraces the entire domain of both grammar and lexicography. But whereas the grammarian and lexicographer devote themselves to detailed and specific facts, the linguistic theorist has no other aim than generalization. His task will include the right differentiation of all those strange entities which none whose business is with linguistics has ever been able quite to disavow. What is speech and what is language? What is a sentence and what is a word? What is a noun, a verb, subject, predicate, object, nominative, infinitive? Such are the questions which the inquirer into linguistic theory must try to answer. And his answers will fail to carry conviction and will be sterile, unless he can relate them to a comprehensive system or conspectus, this to be broadly conceived and presented in clear and unambiguous outline.

The standpoint of the linguistic theorist resembles that of the ordinary listener inasmuch as both are called upon to interpret. At all events the theorist stands nearer to

[1] Among English writers, the term 'semantics' seems to have carried the day.

the listener than he does to the speaker. By the time that the utterance comes upon the stage, the speaker has already made his exit. His perceptions, motives, and decisions are no longer of first-hand importance, for these, as we have seen, are inalienable. It is the utterance alone which is the immediate subject-matter of all philologists, and the theorist of speech will be concerned with the speaker only to the extent that his utterances are incomprehensible without him. But the theorist differs from the listener in his detachment and his unconcern for particular things-meant. He is a scientific observer, looking down on realities from a height. But though he be detached, let him beware of lacking sympathetic insight. There are some modern philologists who go much too far in the direction of denying the validity of feeling as a serious grammatical criterion. To them external form is everything, the felt quality nothing. I expressly reject this curious parallel to behaviourism in psychology. Everyone who is in the least sensitive to language knows the different feel of a noun, an adjective, and a verb. In linguistic matters feeling is of paramount importance.

§ 29. **How language enters into speech.** I now return to James and Mary Hawkins, but shall henceforth take into account a second possibility, namely that James might say *Look at the rain!* instead of simply *Rain!* These alternatives have nearly the same signification, but the longer of them testifies to a somewhat greater effort on James's part, whether out of courtesy to his wife or for some other reason. In either utterance we can distinguish between elements belonging to the present, and elements derived from the past. From the past James has taken, not only the words which he employs, but also the particular tone of voice in which he pronounces them; furthermore, in the case of *Look at the rain!* the order in which the words are arranged. The materials used by him are thus none of his making, though the choice of them out of the great multitude at his disposal must certainly be placed to his credit. But James's initiative itself is a momentary thing belonging exclusively to the present, and it has totally transformed the character of the word-signs selected for his particular purpose. Dead or slumbering these word-signs hitherto were, but by pronouncing them he has restored them to new life, imbuing them with fire and relevance. It is this double aspect worn by every utterance which has given to linguistics two of its most fundamental distinctions, that between speech and language, and that between the sentence and the word.

Speech has already been described, and I need only summarize the facts. It is a human activity which is called into being by an external stimulus subsequently forming the nucleus of the thing-meant. If the speaker considers the matter interesting enough to communicate to a listener, he uses word-signs for the purpose, articulating them and thus translating them into sound-waves, which the listener translates back into the word-signs of the code common to him and the speaker. 'Speech' is an abstract term, but can be used concretely and applied to the products of a speaker's articulations, as viewed from a standpoint similar to that of the listener (§ 28). The characteristics of speech in this sense are, firstly, that it is relevant to a particular occasion, listener, and thing-meant; and secondly, that it is due to the volition of a speaker, whose articulate utterance projects into reality the word-signs used, and endows them with a vitality absent from them at other times. It is clear that this description suits James's utterance *Rain!* or *Look at the* *rain!* extremely well. Now as a generic name for utterances like *Look at the rain!* grammarians use the term 'sentence', and I shall show that there is no valid reason for refusing the same name to many apparently less complete utterances, provided that they, like *Rain!* are felt to make satisfactory sense as they stand. Hence we arrive at a very important conclusion, namely that *the sentence is the unit of speech*.

Thus far we have not found it necessary to avail ourselves of the complementary notion of **Language**. But now language begins to be seen looming out mistily from behind every sentence, from behind every finished product of speech. Language is a collective term, and embraces in its compass all those items of knowledge which enable a speaker to make effective use of word-signs. But that knowledge is not of to-day or yesterday, for its main elements go back to early childhood. Our vocabulary is constantly being enriched, and the area of meaning belonging to specific words being widened. Words, as the most important constituents of language, may fairly be regarded as its units, though it must be borne in mind that the rules for combining words (syntactic rules, as they are called), and the specific types of intonation employed in pronouncing words, are constituents of language as well. We may now supplement our dictum concerning the 'sentence' with another concerning the 'word'. Together they run as follows: *The sentence is the unit of speech, and the word is the unit of language.*

Let us test these generalizations upon the alternative utterances to which James either did or might have given vent. Though at first sight the terms 'word' and 'sentence' seem, in the case of a single-word sentence like *Rain!* less names of separate and overlapping entities than names of distinct aspects of one and the same entity, yet many arguments prove this thesis to be wrong. The sentence *Rain!* is the private possession of James and Mary, whereas the word *rain* belongs to many millions beside them. *Rain!* being an example of speech, is uttered aloud, and has relevance both to a definite thing and to a definite listener; *rain*, as an item of language, has relevance to nothing except its own widely diffused area of meaning. And only one fragment of the area of meaning belonging to the word *rain* applies in the sentence *Rain!* It is, indeed, only by a sort of courtesy that the sentence *Rain!* can be said to 'contain' the word *rain*. The speaker of the sentence *Rain!* certainly 'utilizes' the word *rain*, and I have ventured to say that in utilizing it he also transforms it. But, strictly speaking, the word itself is not so easily altered, and the individual speaker, as we have seen, copies it rather than handles the original (§ 25).

The lack of identity as between word and sentence is much more clearly seen in the alternative form of James's utterance. For here *look* is not a sentence, and the same is still more obvious as regards *at* and *the*. It would be nearer the mark, as we have just seen, to call these 'copies' of words, rather than actual words, but we may waive the inaccuracy and say that the sentence *Look at the rain!* contains four words. Hence *look* and *at* and *the*, when pronounced, are at best parts of a sentence, and conversely, the sentence *Look at the rain!* is at best a combination of four words. To the ear of a foreigner ignorant of English the sentence presents no discontinuity, and might well appear as a unity. But Mary has no difficulty in detecting four different words therein, though doubtless unaware that she has done so. These words she has known in very different contexts and situations, and if she paused to reflect upon them, each would disclose its own individual feel and associations. No doubt alike in her experience and in that of James, the identical combination *Look at the rain!* had often occurred before, but it is not as a mechanized unit that he has produced or she received it. Structure is perceptibly present in this sentence, an unmistakable putting together. And so it generally is. Sentences are like *ad hoc* constructions run up for a particular ceremony, constructions which are pulled down and their materials dispersed as soon as their particular purpose has been served.

I have devised some diagrams which will help to display, in de Saussure's apt terminology, the 'diachronic' character of words, and the 'synchronic' character of sentences. In Fig. 4 the utterances *Rain!* and *Look at the rain!* are shown as sentences containing words. The volition of the speaker is indicated by arrows, and the sentences passing between him and the listener are enclosed in heavy black lines. Discontinuity is, of course, impossible in a sentence consisting of one word of a single syllable, but also is imperceptible where there are several words. For this reason no black dividing lines have been shown within the sentences. In conjunction with the arrows, the oblong shape of the sentences hints at their occurrence in present time. Strictly speaking, present time exists just as little as a point exists, and moreover in the four-word sentence a sequence and duration are definitely noticeable. But the time occupied by such a sentence is as nothing compared with the whole lives of James and Mary, so that the term 'present' must be allowed to stand. Entering into the sentences are the words employed, which have extensive areas of meaning here represented by dotted lines. Far back into the past they go, and only a tiny portion of the

§ 29 SPEECH AND LANGUAGE 91

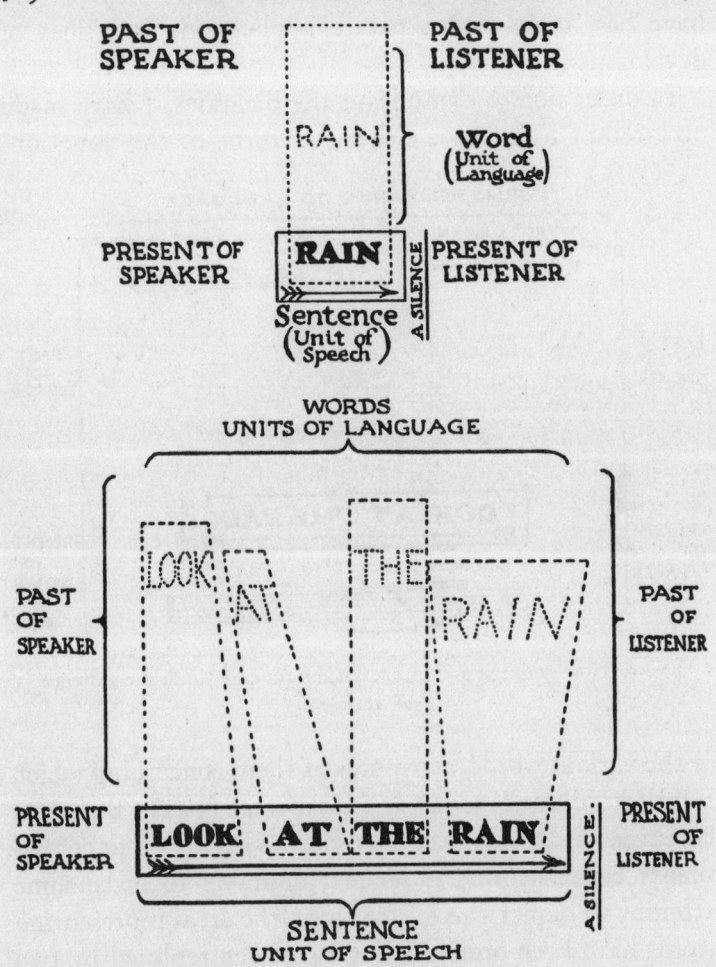

Fig. 4. How language enters into the sentences *Rain!* and *Look at the rain!*

areas touches and is concerned with the sentences. For the dotted areas are to be interpreted as planes converging upon the sentences, each at a somewhat different angle. This is intended to show that the four words of *Look at the rain!* have not always been associated as here, but have had their own separate applications and lines of development.

In order not to complicate the diagrams, I have made no attempt to indicate either the 'form' or the 'function'

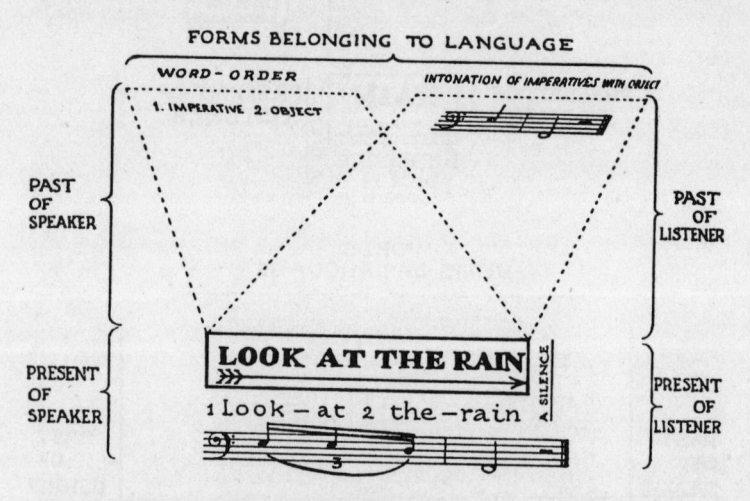

FIG. 5. How syntactic and intonational form enters into the sentence *Look at the rain!*

of the various words, attributes of them concerning which I shall have much to say at a later stage (§ 42). But since language has already been described as having other constituents beside words, it seemed desirable to make some attempt to depict these. In Fig. 5 the areas representing words have been omitted, but have been replaced by two areas representing **Syntactic** and **Intonational Form** respectively. On the left we see the rule that the verb precedes its object, congruently exemplified in the sentence *Look at the rain!* (To all intents and purposes *look-at* is a compound verb, so that no exception must be taken to construing this sentence as verb and object.) Both James and Mary are well acquainted with the rule, many examples of which have been encountered by them in the past, e.g. *Take a bite! Sell me a couple! Learn your lesson!* Hence Mary, through her linguistic knowledge, has no difficulty in concluding the kind of relation which has been meant between the action denoted by *look* and the thing denoted by *rain*. In precisely the same way the intonation given by James to the words *Look at the rain!* recalls a similar intonation given on many past occasions to commands consisting of an imperative and a noun. These enable Mary to recognize the present sentence as a command, though she does so automatically, and without referring it consciously to any type of previous experience. I will compare the part played in language by such forms and rules as these to the part played in astronomy by celestial movements. In astronomy the units are the stars and planets, just as words are the units of language. But the existence of such units in both sciences does not exclude the co-existence in them of other constituent facts of a more abstract and intangible kind.

§ 30. **The nature of the sentence.** We must retrace our steps a little and put to ourselves a question the answer to which has perhaps been assumed too lightheartedly. Are grammarians justified in postulating the separate existence of the two entities, or categories, which bear the names of 'word' and of 'sentence' respectively? It is true that these terms go back to the earliest period of Greek grammatical analysis, but a long tradition is in itself no adequate ground for their further retention. What if the distinction were based upon fallacious linguistic theory? What if there were solid reasons for banishing the names from our up-to-date linguistic terminology? Doubts such as these constantly make themselves heard, and in principle are not only legitimate, but salutary. It is right that we should be masters of the terms we use, not their slaves. And if there is nothing valid, or even useful, in the distinction of 'word' and 'sentence', by all means let us get rid of the one, or the other, or both.

Of recent times there has been a tendency to emphasize the reality of the sentence at the expense of the word. The phoneticians in particular have been struck by the audible continuity of sentences. These, especially when they are short, flow on without a break, and betray no indication of being composed of words. Since most speaking takes place unreflectingly, to assume the existence of components of speech which emerge only on reflection is to import extraneous elements into the utterance as heard. Hence, if words are not condemned out of hand as illusory, they are at least apt to be stigmatized as 'abstractions'. In point of fact, a word is no more and no less of an abstraction than the pound sterling. And who, especially in these days, would get any advantage out of calling the pound sterling an abstraction? The analogy is almost perfect, and deserves meditation. I shall return to this topic later (§ 38). But in the present part of my exposition, I am not really concerned with the word, but with the sentence. The reasons for regarding the sentence as an abstraction are little less serious than those for taking the same view about the word. As a general rule it is words that are catalogued in dictionaries, not sentences. There is no insurmountable difficulty, if we should really wish to do so, in regarding sentences as combinations of several words packed tightly together, with the result that some have become a little squeezed and unrecognizable in the process. Above all, against the existence of sentences one could cite the fact that they are only exceptionally remembered. As I wrote in the foregoing section, they are *ad hoc* constructions, run up for momentary use, and forgotten immediately after.

Nevertheless, the 'sentence' is a reality, and an irrefutable reality. And that it is so shall be known, not from any arguments or logical considerations, but from its 'feel' (p. 86). There is a sense of satisfaction arising from sentences which does not arise from any other samples of uttered speech. Suppose that James Hawkins had said *Look at the* . . . and no more, Mary his wife would have experienced a feeling of dissatisfaction, due to his having failed to complete the sentence. Suppose again that at some neighbour's party Mary chanced to overhear the words . . . *one of James Hawkins's friends* . . ., she would be left ill at ease and curious, unless she could ascertain, or sufficiently well divine, the remainder of the sentence. We thus see that the sense of satisfaction on the part of the listener corresponds to a quality of completeness in those utterances which we call sentences. But what is the secret of this completeness? Wherein does it consist? In the whole domain of linguistics there is no more debated problem. In his painstaking and instructive book on the sentence[1] John Ries prints no less than one hundred and forty definitions culled from different works. The divergences of these definitions would provide instructive reading for anyone who might imagine that this central problem of linguistics had been settled years ago.

The discussion of the sentence will occupy the whole of my fourth and fifth chapters, where many earlier explanations will be mentioned. Here I shall do no more than present the arguments in favour of my own view, which is, briefly, that the satisfactoriness perceived in any

[1] John Ries, *Was ist ein Satz?* (Part III of his *Beiträge zur Grundlegung der Syntax*), Prague, 1931, pp. 208-24.

sentence is due to the recognition of its perfect relevance and purposiveness. When Mary hears the words *Look at the* . . . she has no adequate idea what James is speaking about, or why he is speaking at all. When the words . . . *one of James Hawkins's friends* . . . catch her ear, she does not question the fact that a sentence has been spoken, but for her these words are no sentence, since she can make no sense out of them. More precisely, neither does she fully know the thing that was meant, nor can she discern the speaker's purpose in referring to it. No doubt she may form theories on the subject, and may reconstruct for herself a possible sentence in which these words played a part. But at most her reconstruction will be theoretical, and the chances are that it will be wrong. In fine, the spoken words . . . *one of James Hawkins's friends* . . . and *Look at the* . . . remain mere phrases, mere combinations of unintelligible words, until completed in such a way as to restore to them their original purposiveness and relevance.

Judged by this standard, both *Rain!* and *Look at the rain!* are very good sentences indeed. Mary knows both what James is referring to, and what she, Mary, is to do about it. Some grammarians have declared that a sentence is an utterance which 'has meaning', or 'makes sense'. But it is clear that these definitions are highly ambiguous and open, in this form, to serious objection. It cannot be denied that the utterances . . . *one of James Hawkins's friends* . . . and *Look at the* . . . mean (i.e. refer to) something in the context or situation in which they appear. But they fall short of being sentences because they do not succeed, without further additions, in supplying any intimation why the speaker should have uttered them. They fail to exhibit any communicative purpose on the speaker's part. They certainly have relevance to a thing-meant, but they cannot aspire to the title of sentences because they show no sign of relevance to the listener.

It is this combination of adequate relevance both to some definite thing-meant and to some definite audience or listener which alone can entitle an utterance to the rank of 'sentence'. And of the two qualifications it is the relevance to the listener which is the more essential. Thus ... *one of James Hawkins's friends* ... is a mere phrase, whereas *Look at the* ... must be described rather as an incomplete sentence (§ 55). This point of view is confirmed by comparing with one another the four classes of sentence usually distinguished by grammarians. In order to keep within the bounds of the concrete, some further possibilities must be added to the alternative utterances hitherto attributed to James Hawkins. In exactly the same circumstances it would have been natural for James to have exclaimed *Hark!* or *Hullo!* Or again his comment might have taken the form of a question, *Do you hear the rain?* Yet again, his implicit statement *Rain!* might have been given the more explicit form *It is raining*. Statements, exclamations, questions, and requests—these are the main types of sentence. In questions and requests the relevance to a listener is unmistakable, for an immediate responsive action is demanded. The listener's part is less obvious in statements and exclamations, but at least it is clear that the speaker is there drawing attention either to something objective or to a subjective emotion of his own. But to say that the speaker 'is drawing attention' to anything is to imply a purposive attitude towards a listener. An attentive and intelligent attitude on the part of the listener is the correlate to the speaker's purpose, and is the minimum requirement of speech.

I come back, therefore, to my dictum that the sentence

is the unit of speech. For a sentence to be uttered, the four factors of speech must be functioning harmoniously and adequately, and when they are so functioning there is no reason to withhold from the utterance the designation of 'sentence'. Thus James Hawkins's utterance *Rain!* is, in its own situation, just as good a sentence as *Look at the rain!* for its relevance both to Mary and to the rain on the window (with the attendant considerations) is evident and indisputable. Mary is perfectly satisfied by this brief utterance, and it is difficult to see why the grammarians should not be satisfied as well. Thus the door is opened for the admittance of countless short phrases and single words to the category of sentences, provided that they are spoken in such a way and in such a situation that their relevance to a listener is undeniable. At their own season and place, *Yes! No! Hi! Very well! Naturally! If you please! As you were! George! To your good health!* are all admirable sentences.

I have refrained from giving a formal definition, but schoolboys have to be taught, and provisionally I am inclined to recommend the following: *A sentence is a word or set of words revealing an intelligible purpose.* In this definition there is no reference to speaker, listener, or thing-meant, because I hold that, if the grammarian has done his duty, these will all have been mentioned long before the topic of the sentence is reached. One defect will probably be felt, namely the omission of any quantitative criterion. In the absence of this, my definition seems to suggest that *Mary! Do look! It is raining!* might be one sentence instead of three. I shall deal further with this objection in my fourth chapter (§ 55), and will here only add that those who prefer may extend my definition as follows: *A sentence is a word or set of words followed by a pause and revealing an intelligible purpose.*

§ 31. NATURE OF THE SENTENCE

Let us now consider for a moment how the sentence was defined by Dionysius Thrax in the first century before our era. This ancient grammarian, the father of grammatical analysis, probably wrote as follows: λόγος ἐστὶ λέξεων σύνθεσις διάνοιαν αὐτοτελῆ δηλοῦσα, 'A sentence is a combination of words displaying a self-sufficient meaning.'[1] Here αὐτοτελῆ is often rendered 'complete' (so already Priscian, ii. 45 *sententiam perfectam demonstrans*), and the entire phrase misinterpreted as 'expressing a complete thought'. But it is remarkable that Dionysius should have used an adjective compounded with τέλος 'purpose', and that the word διάνοια should cover the notion of 'intention', 'purpose' as well as that of 'meaning', 'signification'. Perhaps the Greek grammarian had a keener perception of the truth than the bulk of his modern successors.

§ 31. **The ambiguity of the word 'meaning'.** Those who define the sentence as a word or set of words revealing a complete meaning—and note that the Swedish term for sentence is *mening*—are etymologically nearer the mark than they themselves may be aware. For in its original sense, 'to mean' (Anglo-Saxon *mǣnan*, modern German *meinen*) signifies 'to purpose', at the outset an exclusively human action. To this day, German draws a distinction between *meinen* said of persons, e.g. *Er meint wohl etwas anderes*, and *bedeuten* said of things, e.g. *Dieser Satz bedeutet wohl etwas anderes*. In English the verb 'to mean' signifies either to intend an act (e.g. I MEAN *to go*) or to

---

[1] The existing text of Dionysius Thrax (ed. Uhlig, p. 22, 5) reads: λόγος δέ ἐστι πεζῆς λέξεως σύνθεσις διάνοιαν αὐτοτελῆ δηλοῦσα 'A sentence is a combination of prose diction displaying a self-sufficient meaning'. The version given above is that considered by Delbrück (*Vergleichende Syntax der indogermanischen Sprachen*, p. 2) to have been the probable original. It has been obtained by re-translating into Greek Priscian's *oratio est ordinatio dictionum congrua*, but omitting the word *congrua*.

intend a reference (e.g. *When I say a spade, I* MEAN *a spade*). But this originally simple and straightforward word has suffered irreparable harm from its secondary use with the names of things as subject, e.g. *But say, what* MEAN *those coloured streaks in heaven?* Our habit of transferring verbs from human to neuter subjects is not at all harmful in itself, and may indeed prove a real economy in certain cases. Thus to say *This knife* CUTS *very well* or *Your flat* WILL LET *without difficulty* makes it possible for us to concentrate our thoughts wholly upon the excellence of the knife or the flat, without reference to the person of its possessor. The same use is not uncommon when an object follows, as in *This* SHOWS *the folly of extravagance*, which is shorthand for *One* CAN SHOW *by this example the folly of extravagance*.

Now I believe that all the senses in which linguistic theory must employ the term 'meaning' conceal a similar abbreviation, and that the intending, purposing speaker must always be looked for in the background. Thus when we allude to the 'meaning' of a word, what is signified is the multitude of ways in which a speaker may, if he will, legitimately employ it. And by the term 'thing-meant', which I have invented for the convenience of my own theory, I wish to be understood whatever a particular speaker has intended on a particular occasion, both by way of reference to some objective thing, and by way of reference to the manner in which the listener should take his utterance.

The common practice of stating that a sign or symbol or symptom 'means' this, that, or the other, has led to an esoteric and, in my opinion, altogether baneful way of regarding 'meaning'. Signs, symbols, and symptoms are dead things, and as such can 'mean' nothing at all until human agents come to the rescue. Some element of purpose and intention enters, not only into the act of speaking, but also into the act of interpretation; hence the verb 'to mean' may be applied to significant things, even if they do not owe their significance to active intention. For instance, the symptoms[1] of a disease, which are but concurrent events the implications of which have been learnt by experience, can be said to 'mean' that the disease is present, but only because a doctor chooses to interpret them in that way. This employment of the verb gives it a new turn which we need not consider further. In language, at all events, the signs or symbols employed are all 'meant' in the sense of being actively intended by a speaker for reference to one thing or another.[2] Nor, as I have previously observed, does the fact that much speech has become almost automatic vitiate the truth that human will and endeavour lie at the root of all language and linguistic usage. The transference of the verb 'to mean' from human to inanimate subjects appears largely responsible for the confusion between 'meaning' and 'thing-meant'. Grammarians state that the objects of verbs

[1] Like other words, *symptom*, *sign*, and *symbol* are highly ambiguous, with overlapping areas of meaning. For semantic theory the following distinctions may be recommended: 'Symptoms' are indications of a non-psychical kind; hence the word excludes, not only intentional signs and symbols, but also significant cries and the like. 'Signs' and 'symbols' are, on the contrary, psychical, i.e. imposed by human beings or other living creatures, whether intentionally or unintentionally. Symbols are a subclass of signs in which some natural connexion exists between the sign and the thing signified, e.g. the cross is a symbol of Christianity. Among words only those which are onomatopoeic are symbols.

[2] The trend of my argument shows that I disagree with Ogden and Richards's verdict (*Meaning of Meaning*, p. 318) that '"Mean" as shorthand for "intend to refer to" is, in fact, one of the unluckiest symbolic devices possible'. In my opinion, human purposiveness lies behind every use of the verb 'to mean'. See further on this topic below, p. 147.

express relations of two different kinds. Either they designate something resulting from, or created by, the action named in the verb, as in *He built a house*; or else they denote some independent entity upon which the action is exerted or towards which it is directed, as in *He bought a house*; you do not create a house by buying it. These two kinds of object are sometimes called the 'effected' and the 'affected' object respectively. Now the verb 'to mean', so long as it was predicated solely of human beings, as a rule took an 'effected' object, e.g. *He meant mischief*. Only when it came to be used in the sense of 'to intend a reference to', as in *He meant me*, did it take an 'affected' object. In these cases there could be no risk of misunderstanding. But when it began to be said that words 'mean' this or that, not only was the possibility of the signification 'to purpose' eliminated, but also a doubt was cast upon the nature of the object appended to the verb. Perhaps the words could now be conceived of as constituting and creating the very substance of the things meant by them. Just as a house is a 'building', so perhaps the things meant by words might be a 'meaning'. Certainly some such fallacious conception appears to underlie the terms often employed to indicate the thing 'meant' by a sentence. Philosophers have felt no scruple in describing that thing as the 'content' (*Inhalt*) of the sentence.

§ 32. **Summary and conclusion.** The ultimate necessity for speech was shown to reside in the fact that thoughts and emotions are private to the individual, and not susceptible of communication in that purely psychical form. Hence if the desire should arise to acquaint a companion with something in which psychical elements have a place, use must perforce be made of signs, that is to say, physical substitutes the meaning of which both user and recipient know in advance. Articulate words were argued to be the most useful kind of signs, and evidence was adduced to show that these are nothing but copies of purely psychical counterparts. The elaborate account of a simple act of speech proved that word-signs could only represent classes of things similar to the thing now to be indicated, so that the discovery of the latter has to be left to the listener's active intelligence. The thing meant in any act of speech was defined as that which the speaker intends to be understood from it by the listener. The task of the theorist of speech was next investigated, and found to consist in the study of the various terminological entities necessary for the adequate description of speech and of the instruments employed therein. Behind individual utterances loomed out a whole body of previous knowledge called Language, which thus contrasted markedly with Speech, an activity taking place in the present. Words were seen to be the principal units of language, though, beside these, syntactic rules and specific types of intonation have to be named as less tangible elements. Words, as such, are not units of speech, for they lack the vivifying breath and the will-power of a speaker requisite to call speech into being. The units of speech are known as sentences, and their peculiarity was shown to be a manifest purposiveness, corresponding to the possession of a purpose by the speaker. The purposiveness diagnosed in the sentence was analysed partly as concern with some definite thing-meant, but principally as concern with the listener. Lastly, the word 'meaning' was found everywhere to involve the notion of human purpose.

By way of conclusion to this chapter let me stress the two points wherein the doctrine I expound differs from that usually expressed or implied by students of linguistics.

The section which dealt with the ultimate basis of speech (§ 23) is in effect a refutation of the assumption which has given to so many books the titles of *'Sprachpsychologie'* and the like. Hardly anywhere is the slightest hint found that the authors know how insufficient psychology is to cover the entire field of linguistics. In choosing such titles they ignore the very reason for which language and speech exist, namely the fact that speaker and listener do *not* possess a common psyche, wherefore communication between them has to take place through the medium of sound. And now for my second point. Philologists have been puzzled by the coexistence in linguistics of two units. Mineralogy deals only with minerals, botany only with plants, astronomy only with celestial phenomena, psychology only with minds. Why, then, should linguistics have as units both the 'word' and the 'sentence'? Passages could be quoted from the works of many scholars betraying uneasiness on this score, and revealing a tendency to deny either the one or the other. The mystery dissolves as soon as 'speech' and 'language' are sharply distinguished from one another, and when the sentence is seen to be the unit of the former, and the word the unit of the latter.

ADDITIONAL NOTE TO CHAPTER II

Note C (to p. 67). Extract from S. Butler, *Essays on Life, Art and Science*, pp. 201-4.

'Anything which can be made to hitch on invariably to a definite idea that can carry some distance—say an inch at the least, and which can be repeated at pleasure, can be pressed into the service of language. Mrs. Bentley, wife of the famous Dr. Bentley of Trinity College, Cambridge, used to send her snuff-box to the college buttery when she wanted beer, instead of a written order. If the snuff-box came the beer was sent, but if there was no snuff-box there was no beer. Wherein did the snuff-box differ more from a written order, than a written order differs from a spoken one? The snuff-box was for the time being language. It sounds strange to say that one might take a pinch of snuff out of a sentence, but if the servant had helped him or herself to a pinch while carrying it to the buttery this is what would have been done; for if a snuff-box can say "Send me a quart of beer" so efficiently that the beer is sent, it is impossible to say that it is not a *bonâ fide* sentence. As for the recipient of the message, the butler probably did not translate the snuff-box into articulate nouns and verbs; as soon as he saw it he just went down into the cellar and drew the beer, and if he thought at all, it was probably about something else. Yet he must have been thinking without words, or he would have drawn too much beer or too little, or have spilt it in the bringing it up, and we may be sure that he did none of these things.

'You will, of course, observe that if Mrs. Bentley had sent the snuff-box to the buttery of St. John's College instead of Trinity, it would not have been language, for there would have been no covenant between sayer and sayee as to what the symbol should represent, there would have been no previously established association of ideas in the mind of the butler of St. John's between beer and snuff-box; the connexion was artificial, arbitrary, and by no means one of those in respect of which an impromptu bargain might be proposed by the very symbol itself, and assented to without previous formality by the person to whom it was presented. More briefly, the butler of St. John's would not have been able to understand and read it aright. It would have been a dead letter to him—a snuff-box and not a letter; whereas to the butler of Trinity it was a letter and not a snuff-box. You will also note that it was only at the moment when he was looking at it and accepting it as a message that it flashed from snuff-box-hood into the light and life of living utterance. As soon as it had kindled the butler into sending a single quart of beer, its force was spent until Mrs. Bentley threw her soul into it again and charged it anew by wanting more beer, and sending it down accordingly.'

III
THE MUTUAL RELATIONS OF LANGUAGE AND SPEECH

§ 33. The antithesis of 'language' and 'speech'. The attentive reader will by this time have accustomed himself to think of speech as a form of drama needing a minimum of two actors, a scene or situation of its own, a plot or 'thing-meant', and as a last element the extemporized words. Such miniature dramas are going on wherever speech is practised, and it is little short of a miracle that the authors who deal with linguistic theory seem never to have thought of describing one of them. The plots are occasionally mentioned, and the words frequently so; here and there we hear of one of the actors, or both; and a few writers have insisted on the importance of the scene. But there has been a sort of conspiracy not to isolate or analyse in its entirety a single act of speech, instructive as such an analysis was nevertheless bound to be. Nor is it even easy to find in the indexes of the voluminous works on the philosophy or psychology of language any reference to 'speech' as the common name of the activity which unfolds itself in these linguistic dramas. If one is lucky enough to find any mention of speech at all, it is usually in the form, 'Speech, *see* Language', as if the two were identical. But no, I must correct myself. The commonest entry is 'Speech, parts of', whereas I shall be at pains to show that noun, adjective, and so on, are parts of language, and that the real parts of speech are subject and predicate. It is as though the critics were everlastingly discussing dramatic art without ever going to the theatre. One is tempted to conclude that philological science abhors the concrete no less than nature abhors a vacuum. It is of no avail for the writers here censured to answer that the act of speech is implied on their every page, for the business of science is not to imply, but to state; its task is to bring the embedded and entangled facts into the light of day, to separate them out, and to expose them to the public eye. Possibly my own account of an act of speech (§ 26) will, on closer examination, reveal crudities of which I am unaware. But no small part of my purpose will be served if later writers recognize the absolute necessity of examining single acts of speech in their total environment, and if the distinction between language and speech is never again suffered to fall into oblivion.

It is some relief to find that, though linguistic theorists have, as a rule, ignored the distinction between 'language' and 'speech', most civilized languages have not made this mistake.[1] In Latin we have *lingua* and *sermo*, in Greek γλῶσσα and λόγος, in French *langue* and *parole* (or *discours*), in German *Sprache* and *Rede*, in Dutch *taal* and *rede*, in Swedish *språk* and *tal*; so, too, in Arabic *lisān*, literally 'tongue' (= *lingua*), and *kalām*, 'speech', 'conversation', and ancient Egyptian sometimes uses *ro*, 'mouth', for our 'language', while our 'speech' is represented by *mūdet*, 'speaking'. In all these languages the equivalent of 'language' serves as a collective name for an organized system of knowable linguistic facts, and the equivalent of 'speech' is a *nomen actionis* for the activity of which the most evident symptoms are articulation and audibility. Comparing one language with another, there are, it is true, strange cross-currents: German *Sprache* and Swedish

---

[1] See de Saussure, *Cours de Linguistique générale*, p. 31. This scholar stands almost alone in making a clear distinction between speech and language, and in keeping it to the fore throughout his work.

språk are the same words as English 'speech', though the former couple are commonly employed in the sense of our 'language'; Swedish *tal* means 'speech', but Dutch *taal* means 'language'. The words for language, like Greek γλῶσσα, Latin *lingua*, French *langue*, English *tongue*, Arabic *lisān*, and Egyptian *ro*, 'mouth', connect it with one of the chief organs of articulation, perhaps seeking to stress the notions of continuity and permanence. French stands alone in possessing a word *langage* (from late Latin *linguaticum*, 'appertaining to the tongue') which, being neither a collective nor yet the name of an action, can serve as a wider and vaguer term embracing both 'language' (Fr. *langue*) and 'speech' (Fr. *parole*). Apart from this special case, the names for 'language' and 'speech' always come before us as etymologically unrelated pairs, eloquent testimony to the soundness of untutored instinct in its divination of real differences.

I have no desire to minimize the extent to which 'speech' and 'language' are intertwined and mutually dependent, and indeed the purpose of the present chapter is to elaborate that theme. To this intimate relation all languages bear witness, the meanings of the terms in question being everywhere extremely wide in area, with many overlapping applications. Thus in English one writer will prefer the phrase 'his native language', while another will prefer 'his native speech'. Beside the antithesis between 'language' and 'speech', there is another between 'speech' and 'writing', to which immediate attention will be given in § 34. It is in a rather different connexion that the term 'language' is most frequently employed, for many different systems of words and linguistic rules exist, to each of which this term can be applied. The collective word 'language' can thus be specialized with an adjectival epithet and used in the plural, like other collectives. Compare 'language and speech' with 'the people and democracy', 'the French language' with 'the French people', and 'the languages of the earth' with 'the peoples of the world'.

§ 34. **Secondary forms of speech.** So important for human life is the practical use of language that its employment could not for ever be confined to the articulate variety which we call 'speech'. An offshoot of pictorial art,[1] 'writing' at last came into existence as a means of translating audible speech into a visible but non-audible medium, whereby it was made relatively independent of time and space.[2] Writing is a genuine, though secondary, form of speech, so that linguistic theory, if sound, will apply alike to the spoken and to the written form. This is true, in particular, of the sentence; I can state, question, or command in writing no less than in speech. In this book but little notice will be taken of the differences between articulate and written speech, though these are greater than often supposed. The absence of a common physical situation for writer and reader makes it necessary for the former (the whilom 'speaker') to be more explicit than he would be in conversation. The topics themselves, and the knowledge that writing gives a certain durability to what in utterance is evanescent, counsel the selection of choicer expressions. The help afforded by intonation and gesture has gone, and is but clumsily replaced by

[1] For a recent comprehensive account see H. Jensen, *Geschichte der Schrift*, Hanover, 1925; for Ancient Egypt, A. H. Gardiner, 'The Nature and Development of the Egyptian Hieroglyphic Writing', in *Journal of Egyptian Archaeology*, vol. ii (1915), pp. 61 foll.

[2] See the luminous essay by H. Bradley, *Spoken and written English*, Oxford, 1919, where it is shown that spelt words are, and of necessity must be, far more ideographic than phonetic.

punctuation and italicizing. It must suffice to name these few differences.

Writing is not the only secondary form of speech. A derivative of writing is, for example, braille, in which the visible letters are converted into tactile signs for the use of the blind. Telegraphy and telephony have their special peculiarities, and telegraphy has even a style of its own. Gramophone records are now giving a permanence to articulate speech. May we anticipate, pleasurably or otherwise, a day in the near future when our correspondence by letter will be transacted by means of dictaphone records? The habits of reading and writing brought a welcome accession of silence into an unreasonably noisy world. There seems to be an unhappy likelihood that this boon will be ever increasingly diminished through the numerous mechanical devices for multiplying articulate speech.

§ 35. **Language as the product of speech.** We have seen (§ 29) how language enters into speech, but the complementary proposition that speech is the sole generator of language has still to be discussed. In a given act of speech, the thing-meant stands wholly outside the utterance, the words comprising which are, as I have repeatedly said, summaries of previous experience, and do not actually include the present experience. But at the very moment when any word is spoken or, to employ my own technical phraseology, is applied to some thing-meant, a fusion takes place and leaves a greater or less mark upon this particular item in the speaker's vocabulary. If the word be used in complete agreement with tradition, as when what is being called *green* is the grass, the effect is merely to confirm and strengthen a central feature in the accepted area of meaning. Wrong and repugnant applications of a word, even if intelligible from the situation or verbal context, have no influence upon its future, since they either meet with immediate correction or else are politely ignored. It is the slight departures from habitual usage which are the main sources of change in language. These departures rapidly find their imitators, the process being helped by the fact that 'every child, during the formative period of its speech habits, is more closely and intimately associated with children slightly older than itself than with adults, and is psychologically more receptive of influences from these children than from adults'.[1] Circumstances and shiftings of the environment play a large part, word-meanings which were restricted to a single trade or profession gradually passing into common currency, or again terms of wide general application being specialized to a narrower circle.[2] Most change is, no doubt, unconscious, but now and again conscious innovation gives the first impulse. A number of English words can be tracked down to authors who were, in all probability, their creators or adapters.[3] Much more often, however, the new coinage is anonymous. It must, of course, have been an individual wag who, struck by the peculiarly pungent fumes of Virginian cigarettes, first gave to them the name of *gaspers*. One thing, at all events, is clear. Every change in language, conscious or unconscious, great or small, whether of pronunciation or of meaning, has its

[1] J. M. Manly, 'From Generation to Generation' in *A Grammatical Miscellany offered to Otto Jespersen on his Seventieth Birthday*, Copenhagen, 1930, p. 289.
[2] Cf. the fascinating study by A. Meillet, 'Comment les mots changent de sens', reprinted in his book *Linguistique historique et linguistique générale*, Paris, 1921, pp. 230 foll.
[3] See the chapter on 'Makers of English Words' in L. Pearsall Smith, *The English Language*, London, 1912, pp. 109 foll.

origin in some single act of speech, hence passing, if it find favour with the multitude, from mouth to mouth, until at last it becomes common property.

Potent as are the factors making for change, those making for uniformity and stability are still more potent. It is the interest of the community to eliminate individual differences, which could, indeed, only render mutual comprehension more difficult. Such differences are to a large extent automatically effaced, because every speaker is himself equally often a listener, and hence forms his vocabulary as much from the applications made by others as from those for which he is personally responsible. Parents, nurses, teachers are all only too ready to correct or deride unorthodox applications of meaning or defects of pronunciation. The child gains his knowledge of the sound and meaning of any word by innumerable different applications, e.g. *Look, here's Daddy! Kiss Daddy, Funny Daddy, Don't bother Daddy, Daddy's tired, No, that's not Daddy, that's Uncle Tom*, and then, from the lips of the little girl next door, referring to a spruce male with raven locks so different from our own bald-headed parent, *That is my Daddy, Have you a Daddy?* But I will labour the point no further. There is no need for lengthier insistence on the universally recognized truth that language is, and can only be, the outcome of countless single examples of speech.[1]

§ 36. **Is all use of language of the type already described?** It is difficult to believe that any one acquainted with the literature of linguistic theory will fail to find a large measure of truth in my complaint concerning the general neglect of the aspect of linguistics called 'speech'. At the same time a suspicion may perhaps haunt

[1] See H. Paul, *Prinzipien*, pp. 18 foll.

his mind that I, on my part, have exaggerated the importance of this aspect. He will doubtless agree that writing is a form of speech, and so include the 'writer' within the technical meaning of the term 'speaker' as here employed, and similarly the 'reader' within the meaning of the term 'listener'. But he may still feel that there are some uses of language in which the whole paraphernalia of speaker, listener, situation, and so forth can legitimately be dispensed with, as in such simple generalizations as *Two and two make four*, or in the formulation of scientific truths like the following random example: *A liquid at rest takes the shape of the lowest part of the vessel containing it, and has a horizontal surface*. Such statements are couched in a form which makes them relatively independent of any particular situation, and certainly the truth or falsehood of their import holds good without reference to any particular speaker or listener. It might seem, therefore, that there are some samples of speech which elude the kind of analysis demanded by ordinary conversational utterances. What if such exclamations as *Rain!* proved untypical of the use of language when viewed from a broader and more comprehensive standpoint? Is it not possible, after all, that sentences like *Two and two make four* may simply 'contain' their meaning, and that here, in the most highly developed employment of words, we have the pure linguistic article purged of all such contaminating circumstances as speaker, listener, and the rest, and showing the true metal liberated from the dross of its native ore?

Suppositions of this kind are nothing but illusions due to neglect of that selective attention which I have described in §15. Deeper thought will show that no use of language whatsoever is emancipated from the shackles of interpretation, that interpretation demands an interpreter who is the 'listener' of linguistic theory, and that unless the words had once been put together by some rational 'speaker' there would be nothing to interpret. To say that *Two and two make four* holds good in *any* situation is not to say that this statement holds good *without* any situation, nor indeed is the former assertion true. Put two drops of water in a test-tube, and add two more; so far as immediate observation goes, the result is one. Put two male rabbits in a hutch with two female rabbits—but it is unnecessary to insist. The fact of the matter is that, on hearing or reading the words *Two and two make four* the listener or reader at once attunes his mind to the 'Situation of Mathematical Verities', as we might call it. He has heard the statement many times before, and has no difficulty whatsoever in understanding *and* as *added to* and *make* as *yield the number*.

It may be objected, however, that *Two and two make four*, being a cliché, is by no means a suitable touchstone for ascertaining the truth about speech. The scientific formula quoted above will perhaps serve better. Here it is undeniable that the words contain their own unequivocal meaning in the sense that it is difficult or impossible to attach to them any *rational* interpretation other than that intended by the writer. But how do the words come by their 'meaning', as untechnical parlance has it? Obviously only through a complex process of rapid deductions by any reader capable of understanding the words. In the lack of constructive intelligence nothing could be made of them. What, apart from such interpretative intelligence, is a sequence of words? Nothing but a sum of highly complex areas of meaning indicated by a string of sounds or written symbols. At the very outset the word *a* presents an almost unlimited field of possibilities. By the time that *a liquid at rest* has been read the educated reader has already conjectured the trend of the sentence as a scientific formulation. Through 'selective attention', and without being aware that he is doing so, he will have taken *a* in the sense of 'any', and treated *liquid* and *rest* as substantives, not as adjective and verb respectively. In short, he will have chosen out of each word-meaning whatever was requisite for the ascertainment of the thing-meant, just as the writer has chosen each word in order to illumine some part of the total thing meant by him. This account of the matter is not vitiated by the facts that the interpretative deductions are instantaneous, and that expression, by dint of long practice, is mechanized. The linguistic analysis of such a scientific formula must proceed on exactly the same lines as that of our type-sentence *Rain!* only the details will be more complex. The mind of the speaker or writer is set on the 'Situation of Scientific Verities' at the start; so probably is that of the listener or reader. The proposition to be expressed is perceived by the speaker with greater or less clarity before the words are fitted to it. These follow one another like a series of consecutive notes on a piano, each opening up a vista of possibilities, each simultaneously limited by what has preceded. The word-clues pass to the listener or reader as a sequence of audible or visible signs bereft, as such, of all meaning. By him they are identified with those mental possesssions of his called words, and his intelligence makes busy with the search after whatever can have been meant by these clues. It is, perhaps, not always a very apt mode of description, when the more intellectual things-meant are in question, to say that the listener finds these in the situation, as happened in the case of the utterance *Rain!* Sometimes, as when the speaker recounts a dream, the listener has, in order to fulfil the act of understanding, himself to reconstruct the thing-meant in his imagination. Still the fact remains that from the outset the thing-meant has always been a potential common object for both speaker and listener. To conclude, I see no possibility anywhere for any use of language essentially different from the sample discussed in § 26.

§ 37. **The undifferentiated word-sentence of prehuman times.** Since, then, failing some negative instance still to be adduced, all use of language involves the various factors of speech enumerated in Chapter I, we are free to continue our study of the mutual relations of speech and language without the fear of thereby deviating too widely from the main channel of linguistic theory. By way of a beginning, let us return for a moment to the highly problematic question of the speech of animals. Zoologists whom I have asked are strongly of opinion that animals do converse with one another by means of sound-signs, though I have found them unwilling to make any very definite pronouncements as to the degree or scope of these linguistic attainments. For the purpose of contrasting it with human language, I propose to assume that all animal language is of the type exemplified by the warning-cry of the chamois or the nest-call of the pigeon. It will be further assumed that such cries only occur uncombined, that in fact there is among animals no such joining together of words to form sentences as is universal in human speech. This position may or may not be zoologically correct, but in either case it is instructive, if merely as a dialectic exercise, to consider what results would ensue as regards the relations of animal language and animal speech. The utterance would, on these assumptions, be of a kind best described as the undifferentiated word-sentence.[1] Undifferentiated word-sentences of the type I am supposing are represented in fully developed human speech by the class of words called interjections, like *Yes! No! Alas! Fie!* which do not readily and completely combine with other words in order to form a sentence. For though one can say *Yes, I am going out!* or *Fie, you should know better!* the words *Yes!* and *Fie!* here are little sentences in their own right, and what follows is merely corroborative explanation. I imagine that a very similar character should be attributed to the warning-cry or the nest-call.

A fairly large vocabulary of different cries might be in the possession of a given species of animal, and the sum of these would constitute the language of that species. In such circumstances it would be almost nugatory to contrast speech with language as a separate aspect of animal linguistics, since speech would betray no construction or arrangement, but would simply be the close reproduction of the sound heard in all previous utterance of the same

---

[1] The view that language originated in utterances where word and sentence were not yet differentiated from one another is now accepted by most authorities; see, for example, O. Jespersen, *Language*, pp. 428 foll.; G. A. de Laguna, *Speech*, pp. 259 foll.; J. Ries, *Was ist ein Satz?*, p. 41. We must beware of mis-statements to the effect that the sentence is prior to the word; for an example, surprising in so great a scholar, see K. Brugmann, *Die Syntax des einfachen Satzes im Indogermanischen*, Berlin-Leipzig, 1925, p. 1: 'In der Tat geschieht alles Sprechen in Sätzen, und nicht zu bezweifeln ist auch, dass, was zuerst als sprachliche Äusserung aufkam, Ausruf, Wunsch, Befehl, Frage, oder Aussage, nicht "Wort", sondern "Satz" gewesen ist, oder, genauer und vorsichtiger gesagt, dass sich im Bewusstsein der Sprechenden der Begriff "Satz" eher hat einstellen können als der Begriff "Wort".' The last part of this quotation is, indeed, a classical example of what William James called 'the psychologist's fallacy', the fallacy defined by J. Ward (*Psychological Principles*, p. 19) as 'a confusion between the standpoint of a given experience and the standpoint of its exposition'.

cry. In fact, the unit of animal speech would be identical with the unit of animal language, except in so far as the former would require muscular effort and translation into sound.

The same warning-cry and nest-call being constantly repeated, each in its own appropriate situation, these word-sentences would, like human words, acquire areas of meaning exhibiting (1) a certain attributive quality peculiar to each cry, and (2) an adaptability enabling it to be applied, without sense of strain, to any of a large number of different situations all exhibiting that quality. But such meanings would have an exceedingly wide range of application, and would in consequence wear an appearance of extreme vagueness. As regards reference to things, the warning-cry, for example, could point equally well to the exciting stimulus, to the utterer, or (if it had any element of purpose) to the comrades addressed. Thus included in its area of meaning would be the applications indicated in translation by 'it-dangerous' or 'it-frightening', 'I-afraid' or 'I-helpless', 'you-beware' or 'you-attack'. Similarly, if any intention as regards the listener were involved, it might often remain uncertain whether statement, exclamation, or command was meant. All three might be combined, without bias on the part of the utterer in any single direction. At other times, however, a louder or more emotionally modulated pronunciation, accompanied by significant demonstrative movements, might be deliberately adopted with a view to specifying more closely the particular thing-meant. Thus on one occasion the warning-cry might be made to mean 'there is a dangerous animal in the neighbourhood', at another 'gird yourselves for battle'. Widely diffused meaning does not necessarily exclude more precise things-meant, and indeed it can be taken as an axiom of linguistic theory that the variety of possible things which the speaker may intend is always far greater than the variety of the expressional means contained in his vocabulary.[1]

In such a condition of affairs, linguistic change would in no way be improbable. As regards the sound of the cries, the young generation might fail accurately to reproduce the traditional notes. Differences of pitch, cadence, or tempo might lead to the evolution of new varieties of cry. On the side of meaning, external changes might effect new developments. The disappearance of some dangerous bird of prey, or the first experience of the crack of the rifle, might modify the area of meaning of the warning cry by this novel exclusion or inclusion. And lastly, specialization of a particular pronunciation to suit some particular class of thing-meant would result in enrichment of the vocabulary.

§ 38. **The word as a linguistic entity distinct from the sentence.** Between the animal utterance and human speech there is a difference so vital as almost to eclipse the essential homogeneity of the two activities. For whereas the animal cry appears to be an indissoluble unity, the majority of the sentences spoken by mankind can be broken up at will into the smaller linguistic units called words. In detail, it is true, there are plenty of difficulties in connexion with this breaking up of sentences into words, since the spoken sentence flows on without audible discontinuity and its divisions are, therefore, not directly observable. Nevertheless, the existence of the word is not in doubt, since obviously examples like *but*, *wrangle*, *boy* cannot be regarded in any other way. I have already

---

[1] For Locke's classical treatment of this topic see Additional Note D at the end of this chapter, p. 176.

remarked upon the futility of calling the word an 'abstraction' (p. 94). If all that is meant is that the word is a psychical rather than an audible entity, then I agree (see above, § 25). But more is often intended than this, one scholar actually telling us that words are nothing but the result of scientific analysis.[1] Any dictionary can testify to the contrary, for I need hardly say that the words have not been manufactured for the sake of the dictionary, but rather the dictionary compiled for the purpose of registering the words. There is, however, just one element of truth in the view here criticized. The unreflecting user of language makes no difference between homophones, at least so long as they are written alike.[2] It is only the historian of language who is interested to find separate words in (e.g.) the resinous *gum* and that *gum* in which the teeth are embedded, the *helm* of a ship and the *helm* which protects the head, the *capers* cut by a mountebank and the *capers* used in the sauce. But for everyone, the word *boy*

[1] J. Ries, *Was ist ein Satz?*, p. 60: 'Laute, Worte und Wortgruppen sind künstliche Einheiten der Grammatik, gewissermassen Abstraktionen; der Satz ist eine natürliche Einheit und eine sprachliche Wirklichkeit; jene sind nur die durch eine zu wissenschaftlichen Zwecken erfolgte Zerlegung gewonnenen Bestandteile der Sprache, die aus ihrem natürlichen Zusammenhang herausgelöst sind und für sich allein kein wirkliches Leben haben.' See too Wellander, *Bedeutungswandel*, Part I, p. 15: 'In der Wirklichkeit existieren nur Wortindividuen. Das Wort, von dem man in dem Wörterbuch oder in der Grammatik spricht, ist eine Abstraktion aus vielen Wortindividuen, die zu verschiedenen Zeiten gesprochen und gehört worden sind.' No one denies, of course, that words originate in speech and have obtained their characters of sound and meaning from that source. I repeat, to call 'words' in the lexicographic sense 'abstractions' is to convey an utterly false impression. They exist as necessarily presupposed mediums of linguistic exchange, and differ from sixpences and halfpennies only in being psychical, rather than physical, coinage.

[2] See R. Bridges, *On English Homophones*, being Tract No. 11 of the Society for Pure English, Oxford, 1919.

is different from the word *wrangle*, the word *but* from the word *moreover*.

As a matter of fact, the spoken word can usually be obtained by asking a speaker to repeat quite slowly some sentence that he has uttered; be he parson or be he peasant, he will in all probability separate off the words in exactly the same way as a grammarian. Since, however, the influence of education might always be suspected in any such test, and since this predominance of the word, undoubted in the classical and modern European tongues, might not necessarily hold good in more remote linguistic fields, it is interesting to quote the testimony of an expert in American Indian languages who is exceptionally well qualified to offer an opinion. 'Linguistic experience,' writes Professor Sapir,[1] 'both as expressed in standardized, written form and as tested in daily usage, indicates overwhelmingly that there is not, as a rule, the slightest difficulty in bringing the word to consciousness as a psychological reality. No more convincing test could be desired than this, that the naïve Indian, quite unaccustomed to the concept of the written word, has nevertheless no serious difficulty in dictating a text to a linguistic student word by word; he tends, of course, to run his words together as in actual speech, but if he is called to a halt and is made to understand what is desired, he can readily isolate the words as such, repeating them as units. He regularly refuses, on the other hand, to isolate the radical or grammatical element, on the ground that it "makes no sense".' I myself am able to add a tittle of evidence from a different source. Egyptian hieroglyphic writing is in the main phonetic, but a large number of ideographic or directly pictorial signs occur signifying the actual thing or kind of

[1] E. Sapir, *Language*, London, 1921, p. 34.

thing meant. Among such pictorial signs are those known as 'determinatives', which stand at the end of phonetically written words to indicate their meaning, whether general or specific. Most, though not all, phonetically written words have determinatives, which effect, therefore, the practical result of dividing up sentences into their component words. For example, in the sentence ⌂△⌂ ⌂⌂⌂⌂⌂ *pr·k r pt, mȝ·k nṯr im*, 'thou goest-up to heaven, and seest the god there', the words *pr* △, 'go up', *pt* ⌂, 'heaven', *mȝ* ⌂, 'see', and *nṯr* ⌂, 'god', all end in determinatives, whence the division of the sentence into words is seen to correspond precisely to that which every European philologist would demand. A broad survey of hieroglyphic texts shows that Egyptian feeling in this matter coincided almost exactly with our own. The only exceptions are some grammatical endings, about which the scribes seem to have felt a doubt whether they should take them as part of the word or whether they should not; for sometimes these endings follow the determinative, while sometimes they precede.

§ 39. **The emergence of words in the many-word sentence.** Throughout the preceding argumentation there has run, as a kind of *Leitmotiv*, the thought that the essential function of words is to serve as clues. But that is practically equivalent to saying that every sentence containing more than a single word is fundamentally a succession of little one-word sentences or predicates. As each of these falls upon the listener's ear it exhorts him to seek in the situation something corresponding to the class indicated by the word.[1] On this showing, a sentence such as *He likes pudding* would ultimately signify 'Look out for a him! Look out for a liking! Look out for something

[1] Wegener, *Grundfragen*, p. 100.

being-a-pudding!' Well as this view agrees with the hypothesis that all human speech has developed out of the undifferentiated word-sentence, yet it clearly fails to do justice to the statement as a whole, which is felt as a unity composed of definitely related parts, and not as a series of disjointed predicates. The problem now before us is, accordingly, to find some explanation of the fact that the many-word sentence is felt as a single predication or as the presentation to the listener's mind of a single composite thing, the several parts of which are seen as of this or that particular character and as standing in particular relations to one another. The solution of this problem is a most formidable undertaking, but the general lines of a satisfactory theory are traced in many passages of Wegener's epoch-making treatise. His book is a mine of wisdom whence philologists could draw inspiration for many valuable investigations. But probably owing to the circumstances of an over-busy professional life, the brilliant suggestions which he makes are presented in somewhat disconnected form, and I do not wish it to be assumed that he would have subscribed to all points of the argument which, having once again expressed my indebtedness, I shall now proceed to unfold.

Towards the end of § 37 I sought to show that the animal cry, in spite of its extremely vague and diffused meaning, might in particular situations refer to a fairly definite and narrowly circumscribed thing-meant. Herein lay the possibility for the development of single-word sentences the meaning of which approximated to that of our own words. The evolution of communicative purpose would lead to the multiplication of significant signs, for conscious effort would be directed towards making oneself understood, and in all but the simplest conditions a single sign would no longer suffice. It is remarkable how little attention to the broader semantic aspect has been paid by students interested in the origin of language. Their speculations have turned almost wholly upon how this particular notion came by that particular sound. Hence the famous hypotheses nicknamed 'the bow-wow theory' and 'the pooh-pooh theory' respectively. With that topic I shall not deal at all, the more so since English readers possess a sober and sensible discussion in Jespersen's recent book on Language.[1] My immediate concern is with the emergence of the 'word' as an entity distinct from the 'sentence'. Here Wegener's theory of exposition by successive correctives is evidently of the highest importance.[2] No details can be seen distinctly, but the general trend of the process may be surmised from the stages to be observed in the linguistic development of children. Between the ages of eight to thirteen months the little son of the Serbian scholar Pavlovitch could talk only in isolated word-sentences. At this stage *pàpā* signified 'I am going for a walk', 'One is going for a walk', 'I want to go for a walk', 'Go for a walk', and 'Papa is going for a walk' indiscriminately.[3] When the child heard his father's footsteps on the stairs he would cry *tata*, but the same cry, accompanied by a demonstrative gesture, served to express the request 'Papa, give me this or that'.[4] Clearly, this kind of speech, if the listener were no more highly developed than the child-speaker, could meet with suc-

[1] O. Jespersen, *Language*, pp. 412 foll.
[2] This thought occurs in various connexions in Wegener's *Grundfragen*, e.g. in the discussion on the importance of the situation, pp. 19 foll.; again in dealing with apposition and relative clauses, pp. 34 foll.; best of all in his summary of conclusions, p. 181.
[3] M. Pavlovitch, *Le langage enfantin*, Paris, 1920, p. 143.
[4] Op. cit., p. 145.

cessful response only in the most favourable circumstances. From the fourteenth month onwards, combinations of two sound-signs begin; *tato-vōde* was now used for 'Papa, give me water', and *tato-cecela* for 'Papa, give me sugar'. The additions *vōde* and *cecela* here serve as corrections to the indefiniteness of *tata* alone, and would effectively indicate the child's desire even if the things in question were absent from the room. The least intelligent of listeners, drawing rapid deductions from the clues successively given, and combining them with a deduction drawn from the physical situation, could not have failed to conclude that the child wanted a glass of water or a lump of sugar.

But the transition from utterances consisting of one member to utterances consisting of two or more would bring about a remarkable transformation both of the whole and of its parts. An essential feature of Wegener's theory is the stress it lays upon the psychical effects of mechanization. The listener would soon no longer be aware that he was drawing separate deductions from successive clues, but viewing the utterance as a whole, would seize its signification in a flash. The entire utterance would now appear as effecting a single purpose, and would thus be felt as a single sentence, not as two. And simultaneously the component parts, if their separate existence became the subject of reflection, would be viewed as the names of things, the things meant by them relating themselves to one another in the listener's mind as the situation showed that they were related in fact.

When a transformation such as this has taken place, so closely interlinked have the words and the things meant by them become, that the words themselves seem to be related.[1] Thus in the sentence *Fetch me my hat*, the words

[1] See below, § 44.

my hat are said to be the object of the verb *fetch*, whereas in truth it is only the thing meant by *hat* which is the object of the action denoted by the imperative *fetch*. But now, when this stage has been reached, the speaker is able to communicate things much more remote than the things perceptible in the immediate 'Situation of Visible Presence' (*die Situation der Anschauung*). The worlds of imagination and memory are henceforth potential common objects for individuals in association with one another. The less easily accessible the things spoken about, the more clues or explanations that must be offered. But once the method of the many-word sentence has been found there is no assignable limit to the intellectual wealth which, by the help of speech, human beings may share with one another.

The custom of uttering two-word or three-word sentences having been firmly established, the variety of combinations into which each sound-sign could enter would greatly increase its individuality and definiteness. Pavlovitch expressly states that what was destined later to appear as a vocative meaning 'Daddy!' was at first mixed up with various verbal notions. It is evident that with each new combination the common element of meaning 'daddy' would receive reinforcement, while the variable associated verbal notions would sink into the background. But those notions would not disappear without leaving a trace; rather would they appear as qualifications of the common nucleus, lending it character and definiteness. Daddy would now become familiar as someone constantly present, who went out for walks, who brought sugar or water when asked, and so forth. Thus word-signs would be more and more clearly revealed as means of reference to 'things', and the things meant by words—not necessarily what we know as things, but also actions, qualities, relations, the forerunners of verbs, adjectives, and prepositions—would gain in significance with every new application. The area of a word's meanings becomes very complex by reason of its many applications. And just on account of that complexity, words acquire the individuality and feeling-tone which adheres to persons. Take, for example, the word *respectability*. We come to think we know as much about 'respectability' as we know about any of our friends or enemies, and according to our temperaments we like or dislike that thing.

The foregoing paragraphs need be read neither as a theory of origins, nor yet as an incursion into child psychology. If they contain anything of interest in either direction, it is because the general conditions of speech remain the same at all times and all places. Wegener's standpoint, like my own, is dominated by the notion of the importance of the 'situation'. In simple situations a single-word sentence, or else an utterance in which word and sentence have not yet been differentiated, would suffice for the fulfilment of the speaker's purpose, and in such circumstances a single sound-sign is still often employed. But to indicate anything more remote, i.e. in a situation of time or place different from the present, or anything more complex, the many-word sentence is a necessity. A listener's comprehension is based primarily upon the situation in which he finds himself; this provides the foundation for all his deductions. If now the speaker wishes to refer to something not immediately deducible from the present situation, he must employ one or more 'clues' or sound-signs to supplement the latter. When more than one sound-sign is used, a divorce between word and sentence occurs. The separate sound-signs are not sentences, because singly they do not accomplish the speaker's purpose.

The utterance as a whole is not a word, because it contains a reference, not to one thing, but to several. We can see, moreover, how the sentence becomes the unit of speech and the word the unit of language. A combination of sound-signs is obviously of less general utility than a single sound-sign, since the situations in which it can be effectively employed are less numerous than the situations in which the component sound-signs can be used. Hence the combination of sound-signs, as such, perishes from the memory, while the single sound-sign is retained as a permanent means of reference to some thing. In this capacity it is a 'word'.

§ 40. **The many-word sentence as a whole.** Viewed from a certain angle, all the words of a sentence are on a par. Each consists of a larger or smaller complex of articulate sound, each is a class-name embracing a wider or narrower area of meaning, and each, when employed in speech, has a particular thing-meant corresponding to it. And if again we consider the different things meant by the various words of any sentence, we shall note that they seem to stand at a certain dead level of superficiality. Take once more the example *Pussy is beautiful* as spoken in reference to some definite living cat. So far as this sentence is concerned, Pussy is not that complete, interesting, and versatile creature we know so well, but is merely herself in the aspect of being beautiful. I do not know how more aptly to describe what is meant by the words of any sentence than by saying that they have no profundity, no dimension of depth. Pussy is not beautiful all through, but only in the way that cats are said to be beautiful, namely externally; neither her character nor her inside are included in the predication. Again, beauty is undoubtedly involved in the sentence, but not all that wondrous attribute which manifests itself in landscapes, in music, in women, but only the beauty of fur, of whiskers, and of gambollings. It is by virtue of this superficiality of speech that we can say in two consecutive sentences, *Alice is growing quite a big girl* and *Alice's parents live in a dreadfully small house*. The smallness of the smallest human abode would be a bigness if predicated of a girl. In fact, as used in speech, word-meanings are applied in an entirely one-sided way. Speech seems to skate but lightly over the surface of things.[1]

Arguing along these lines, we might conceive of the many-word sentence as a mere sequence of clues having each the same importance and functional power, comparable, let us say, to the even ticking of a watch, where every second resembles every other with a dead monotony. It suffices, however, to enounce this possible thesis in order to realize its falsity. The various words of any sentence differ enormously among themselves in point of importance, as well as in other respects. In a very real sense the whole of Pussy does enter into my statement *Pussy is beautiful*, and what is more, there is something about the word *Pussy* which makes us feel it. And again, will any one seriously affirm that, in the sentence *Sutton is almost a mile from here*, the words *almost* and *is* are as important and significant as the word *mile*? The lilt and rhythm of speech, and the way in which speakers scurry over some words and dwell with emphasis upon others, give the lie to any assertion of equality among spoken words. And the like is true when one sentence is compared with another. There are differences both in importance and in quality, and the principal problem before us is to investigate in detail wherein these differences consist.

[1] Examine in this connexion the examples quoted by Paul, *Prinzipien*, § 56.

§ 41. **Word-form.** As regards the relative importance of the words in a sentence, some differ, then, from others simply through the whim or the need of the speaker. He knows what things he desires to emphasize and what things are only contributory to his purpose, and he uses the resources of word-order, modulations of the voice, speed of utterance, and so forth, to mark these differences. But apart from such occasional and momentary differences between words there are others which are constitutional, and which are connected with distinctions in **word-form**.[1] As here to be understood, *word-form is the name of a special kind of meaning which attaches to words over and above their radical meaning.* This additional meaning is of various kinds, but its characteristic feature is that it is always subsidiary to the meaning of the root or stem. Word-form may be simple, as in the cases of *in*, *lo*, and *gently*, where it amounts to no more than the feeling associated with these words that they are a preposition, an interjection, and an attributive adverb respectively. Or else word-form may be intensely complex, as in *puerorum*, *vidissem*, *plurimae*. The first of these conveys, in addition to the root-meaning 'boy', notions of (1) being the name of something presented as a thing, (2) referring to several boys, not to one boy only, and (3) the fact that the boys stand to something else in one or other of a number of cognate relations of which possessorship and authorship are two. In grammatical terms, *puerorum* is the genitive plural of the noun *puer*. In saying that the form-meaning of a word is always subsidiary, I do not imply that it is ever lacking in importance. All I wish to state is that

[1] An extremely interesting and valuable account of word-form is given by Sapir, *Language*, chs. ii, iv–v, but this scholar unfortunately draws no clear distinction between 'speech' and 'language'.

such importance as the form has is dependent on the root-meaning. It would be useless to know that *puerorum* is a plural unless it were simultaneously known what it is the plural of. In view of its subsidiary nature, word-form may be compared to the overtone of a musical note.

In understanding 'word-form' as the name of a kind of meaning I am deliberately opposing the view of certain grammarians that external differences of inflexion are the really fundamental feature of 'word-form', and that where such external differences are absent a word is without form.[1] But true enough it is that differences of **inner word-form**, as I shall call the semantic aspect, are often accompanied by **outer word-form**, and that the term 'word-form' owes its origin to the latter. In order to be sure that I have made myself clear, let me say that in my terminology the sounded or written word *puerorum*, with its inflexion in *-orum*, constitutes the outer word-form of *puerorum*, while the three subsidiary notions specified above constitute its inner word-form. When I speak of word-form without qualification, I shall refer primarily to whatever subsidiary meaning a word may possess, and only secondarily to the external marks, if any, whereby this subsidiary meaning is shown. Thus both the Latin *omittunt* and its English equivalent *omit* have the word-

[1] The standpoint of Jespersen, expressed in the following quotation, may be regarded as on the whole sound, at least as a practical counsel: 'While we should be careful to keep out of the grammar of any language such distinctions or categories as are found in other languages, but are not formally expressed in the language in question, we should be no less averse to deny in a particular case the existence of distinctions elsewhere made in the same language, because they happen there to have no outward sign,' *Philosophy*, p. 51. But this formulation does not cover the distinction in form between, e.g., the Latin preposition *in* and the Latin conjunction *an*. Ultimately, felt inner word-form is decisive, if only we can make certain of its presence.

form of verbs, since both are felt to present the action of omitting as an action, not as a thing. But of the two, only the Latin word has outer word-form, namely the ending *-unt* which marks it as present indicative active, 3rd person plural.

The term **word-form** (together with the related collective term **morphology**, from the Greek μορφή 'form') arose in connexion with the outer forms or inflexions seen in the ancient classical languages. In the non-linguistic sense 'form' properly means 'shape', and refers to physically visible appearances. Both 'form' and 'shape' are attributes belonging to single objects, and these single objects can have only one form at a time. A vase, for example, has only one form, though a lump of putty of a particular form may be squeezed into a number of forms. By a natural extension, the word 'form' came to be used of constituent characters other than those which were visible, as in *musical form, the democratic form of government*. Now though 'form' ostensibly refers to the character of a single thing, in practice the word is employed only when the thing in question is one of a class of similar objects; thus *a crystal hexagonal in form* or *of hexagonal form* is so called because a class of hexagonal objects has been segregated by experience; we talk of *the democratic form of government* because among governments several have been compared with one another and recognized as democracies. Applying these notions of 'form' to linguistics, we must suppose that first of all the term was applied to identical inflexions such as *rosam, casam, dominam; cantas, amas, rogas*. It should be carefully noted that at no period have merely visibly identical or rhyming endings been deemed sufficient to constitute a class of word-forms. *Incipite* and *limite* are not of the same form, nor in English are *rill, fill,* *still, ill.* Form in the grammatical sense doubtless applied from the outset only to those resemblances among words which combined identity of inflexion with identity of the kind of subsidiary meaning above described. *Rosam, casam,* and *dominam* were said to have the form of the accusative case, or more shortly, to be accusative forms, because they could all be used in one or other of the ways in which accusatives are used, namely as direct objects of verbs, after certain prepositions, and the like. This being so, there could be no objection to extending the term 'form' to other groups of words which were externally different in appearance but semantically identical; thus not only *rosam* and *casam* are accusative in form, but so too are *dominum, ignem,* and *mare.* Once this stage had been reached, little difficulty could be felt in extending 'form' still further to words from which inflexions had disappeared, or in which they had never been present. Thus it can be said that the singular and the plural forms of the word *sheep* are identical, or again that *boy* is singular in form. It must not be forgotten that the concept of grammatical form arose among grammarians of the classical languages. Calling *oves* a plural and *puer* a singular form, they would naturally do the same to the modern translations of these Latin words, without troubling themselves with the nicer theoretic questions which are our concern in this book.

Since common practice countenances the use of the term 'form' in certain cases where there are no outer marks to show it, that term is certainly permissible as a description of the felt character enabling us to assign words to this or that word-class. Accordingly I shall not hesitate to say that *give* is a verb in form, *table* a noun, and *upon* a preposition. Expressing this view as a generalization,

I maintain that the so-called 'parts of speech' are distinctions of word-form. Much more disputable is the legitimacy of employing the term where, when a word is quoted out of context, its 'form' can be neither felt nor heard. This topic is reserved for my second volume, where it will become a vital issue in connexion with the controversy whether English distinguishes several cases in the noun, or only two, or none. To anticipate my conclusion, I must confess myself unable to agree that in *He gave the boy a book* the word *boy* should be called a dative case or form, though it seems to me quite correct to say that *the boy* here 'functions as a dative'.

I now come to a fact of high grammatical importance. *The form of a word, like its meaning, is a fact of language, not of speech.* Word-form belongs to a word permanently, and is no merely temporary qualification which becomes attached to it in the course of speaking. This is obvious in some of the examples already quoted, such as *lo*, *vidissem*, *puerorum*. As these words stand, linguistic tokens to be hoarded or put into circulation at their possessor's pleasure, they have each a particular form-meaning as well as a radical meaning. The first is felt as an exclamation, the second presents sight as an action which at some past moment was both contingent and prospective, with the speaker as its performer, and the third—*puerorum*—possesses the additional notions already described. But in other cases, such as the Latin *pueris* or the English *like*, the word-form presents itself in the guise of alternatives: *pueris* is either dative or ablative plural, *like* may be an adjective or an adverb or a noun or (with a different radical meaning) a verb. This ambiguity of certain word-forms does not, however, vitiate the statement that word-form belongs to language, not to speech. Wundt, quoting

§ 41 WORD-FORM 135

the very word *like* which I have just used as an example, takes up the curious position of asserting that, while 'outer form', i.e. inflexions and so forth, belongs to language, 'inner form' belongs to speech. Of course he does not express his standpoint in this way, since the distinction between language and speech is not in his purview. The following is a translation of what he actually says: 'Nevertheless there can be no doubt that such a word (as *like* or the German *gebe* or *Gabe*) has on each occasion the meaning of a definite word-form, that of a noun, a verb, an adverb, &c., and that under suitable conditions the meaning of a definite case, tense, or number may adhere to it. Yet it acquires that meaning only through the relation to other words into which it enters in the course of speech. This conceptual definiteness which is lent to the word through its position in the sentence we may call "inner word-form".'[1] But how exactly this conjuring trick of lending conceptual definiteness to a word is performed,

[1] *Die Sprache*, vol. ii, p. 2: 'Nichtsdestoweniger kann es keinem Zweifel unterliegen, dass ein solches Wort jedesmal die Bedeutung einer ganz bestimmten Wortform, eines Nomens, Verbums, Adverbs usw., hat, und dass ihm unter den geeigneten Bedingungen eine bestimmte Kasus-, Tempus-, Numerusbedeutung usw. zukommt. Doch es gewinnt dieselbe erst durch das Verhältnis, in das es im Zusammenhang der Rede zu andern Wörtern tritt. Diese dem Wort durch seine Stellung im Satze verliehene begriffliche Bestimmtheit können wir hiernach die *innere* Wortform nennen.' In fairness to Wundt let it be admitted, however, that in the sentence preceding my quotation he appears to have noticed that the application of *like* is restricted to a limited number of possibilities (pp. 1–2): 'Vollends ein Wort wie das englische *like* (gleich, Gleiches) kann Adverb, Adjektiv, Substantiv oder (in der Bedeutung 'gern haben') Verbum sein, ohne dass der Wortform diese verschiedene begriffliche Stellung anzusehen wäre.' Mis-statements analogous to that of Wundt are not rare. For example, see J. Vendryès, *Le langage*, Paris, 1921, p. 111: 'C'est seulement lorsqu'on dit *l'aurore est belle* ou *l'abîme est profond* que les mots *aurore* ou *abîme* ont un genre'; but possibly this was not intended to be taken quite literally.

Wundt does not explain. The fact of the matter is that he has not really wrestled with the problem as to how language works in its practical application as speech, nor was this indeed possible for him without adopting the sociological standpoint. To those who do so the form of words such as *like* presents no more difficulty than does their radical meaning. We saw in the first chapter that the meaning of a word is a complex area of often quite heterogeneous potential applications. When a speaker says *horse* he leaves it to the listener to infer from the context whether a live race-horse, a gymnasium horse, or a towel-horse is meant. In just the same way the speaker who utters the word *like* leaves it to the listener to infer from the context in what way the word is to be taken, whether as an adjective or an adverb or a noun or a verb. Indeed, the speaker has no choice in the matter, for the word occurs to his mind complete with all its various possibilities of application, among which he cannot pick and choose. This is true as much of radical meaning as of word-form. But both the speaker who selects the word and the listener who has to interpret it are guided by their knowledge of the kinds of word-form which it has displayed in their past experiences of its use, and it is only to one or other among these kinds of word-form that the word itself can actually point.[1] For example, a speaker cannot without some sense of strain use *like* as an interjection or the listener interpret the word as such, since the interjectional use of *like* is not prescribed by language. I do not deny, of course, that speakers sometimes make innovations in employing words, but that is quite another story.[2] As a rule, words are used

---

[1] For a practical demonstration as to how the form applicable to a given context is elicited see below, pp. 144–5.

[2] We shall see later (§ 44 foll., and particularly § 47, first paragraph) that

as language has decreed that they shall be used, and this applies alike to radical meaning and to the additional sort of meaning designated by the term word-form.

On several previous occasions I have voiced my conviction that the practice of philologists has generally been sound even where their theory may be at fault. This thesis is well illustrated in the present connexion. What happens to word-form in a dictionary? Turning up *like* in the *Concise Oxford Dictionary*, I find the following entries:

like[1], a. (often governing noun like trans. part.; *more*, *most*, rarely or poet. *-er*, *-est*), prep., adv. (archaic), conj. (vulg.), & n. Similar, resembling something . . .

like[2], v.t. & i., & n. Be pleasing to (archaic or facet.; . . .); find agreeable, congenial, or satisfactory . . .

Now a dictionary is a catalogue or synopsis of the wealth of words which any linguistic community possesses, appending to each word itemized some account of its range of applications. The entries quoted above show that some of the leading authorities in English philology have been in no practical doubt whatsoever as to the status of word-form. For them it is a fact of language, not a chance adhesion which may come about in the course of speech. Otherwise the word-forms would not have been given in this dictionary, the purpose of which was to state what is vouchsafed or dictated by the English language, and which fulfilled that purpose, first by naming the word-form, and then by describing the area of meaning. The reasons for distinguishing between homophones such as the two different words *like* will be discussed in my second volume.

'incongruent function', as I shall call it, is always accompanied by a feeling of difference between form and function.

We are now in a position to give a definition of word-form which will suit the requirements of our present quest. In doing so I shall disregard the outer aspect altogether, and look at word-form solely in its inner or semantic aspect. As so seen, *word-form is a kind of meaning permanently attached to words over and above the meaning of the stem, intimating the formal character in which a listener may expect any future speaker to intend the thing-meant to be taken.*¹ It is highly important to realize that all linguistic form arouses an expectation of use. The reason is that language is only a name for established habits of speech, built up out of innumerable repeated acts of the same type. A habit, once formed, excites in any observer the expectation that its owner will act in the same way on all new occasions. That expectation may not be fulfilled, and then a position arises which will be discussed in the next few sections.

I have attempted to show that language is the outcome of single acts of speech (§ 35), and it is now necessary to illustrate this truth in connexion with word-form. For this purpose, however, I shall deal only with the so-called 'parts of speech', which are really different kinds of words, or more precisely, words differing permanently from one another as regards their inner word-form. At rock-bottom there can be no doubt that the distinction between nouns and verbs, to take an example, is based upon differences in things-meant, in the things talked about. There is a sound reason grounded in the very constitution of the universe why we should prefer the mode of speech *Did you hear that horse neighing?* to *Did you hear that neigh horsing?* though we can easily both speak of the *neigh* of a horse, the *bray* of a donkey, the *roar* of a lion, and the *moo* of a cow, and also form verbs from the names of animals, as to *monkey with*, to *ferret out*, to *pig it*. The fact is that horses are insistent things, always requiring that we should speak of them as being so and so, as having been treated in such and such a way, or as things in relation to which other things stand thus and thus. Grammatically stated, *horses* are always obtruding themselves either as subjects of predication, as objects of verbs, or as cases after prepositions. *Neighing*, on the other hand, seldom comes before us except as emanating from some horse which was its cause. Because the horse is constantly presenting itself to us in live form we predicate *neigh* of the horse, rather than the horse of neigh. But something of which we are constantly predicating something else is not only a thing, but is also felt to be substantival, i.e. to possess the substance of a thing. We see that horses are big and spirited and steaming and thirsty, we can ride them, pat them, or spur them on. Objects of sense, and among them living creatures most of all, are things naturally predestined to be viewed as things. The names of the objects of sense are the natural nouns.

But since, according to my creed, everything which a word can be employed to designate is a thing, there is obviously no reason why it should not also, in suitable circumstances, be viewed *as* a thing. When such a view becomes a fixed habit, the word is felt as a noun, and whether the view does or does not become habitual depends upon the vagaries of human interest and convenience. The emergence of abstracts—attributes considered as things—is a comparatively recent development in linguistic history; I refer to definitely independent substantives, like *beauty*, *poverty*, *goodness*, as distinct from *nomina actionis* or infinitives, which are of very ancient date. But even such insignificant words as prepositions and conjunctions may gain currency as nouns or verbs, e.g. *But me no buts, the ins and outs of the matter, pros and cons.* Around these purely intellectual substantival creations, however, there clings a hollowness absent from the natural substantives described in the last paragraph.

Natural fitness, therefore, and human caprice are the two sources to which nouns trace their origin. The same is true, *mutatis mutandis*, of the other parts of speech. Slowly the form of words is built up, by one act of speech after another, until it becomes sufficiently characteristic of them to merit mention in the dictionary.

In the above account of word-form, little attention has been paid to its outer aspect, since in speech inner word-form alone is of decisive importance. Language itself seems particularly careless of uniformity in outer word-form, as witness pairs of words with identical inner word-form like the following: *amat, monet; pulchra, fortis; lisez, dîtes; geschrieben, beendet; came, walked.* Nevertheless, outer word-form is of high importance for linguistic theory as the means which the habit of speech has invented for exhibiting inner word-form. But the details of outer word-form are only of historical interest; moreover, it is only from history that their eccentricities obtain an explanation. The principal sources of outer word-form are, firstly the fusion of two words to become one, e.g. French *du* from *de illo* (through *de illum*); *finirai* from *finire habeo*; German *schmerzvoll* from *schmerz* and *voll*; English *lovely* from *love* and an old Teutonic noun *likom 'appearance'; and secondly, analogy or a conforming of one word to another based on the fact that other pairs of word-forms from the same stems are identical in appearance. Analogy has as motive simply the desire for uniformity. Its operation is seen, for example, when a French child says *vous* *disez* in place of *vous dîtes*, assimilating it to *vous lisez* on the strength of the identical endings in *je dis, je lis; nous disons, nous lisons; dire, lire*. Beside the two sources of outer word-form mentioned above, some others of less importance have been suggested.[1] To these, however, I shall pay no attention. In linguistic theory outer word-form is a datum with which we start and, beyond a general statement how it came about, no further details as to its historic evolution are required.

§ 42. **Word-form and word-function as correlated linguistic facts.** We have seen that word-form is a fact of language; the corresponding fact in single acts of speech is **word-function**. Etymologically, 'function' is only a rather grand synonym of 'performance', but it is often used in a peculiar way to designate the capacity in which something acts in subservience to a certain aim. Thus a nail driven into the wall can function as, or have the function of, a peg to hang one's hat on. Two conditions govern this use of the word: firstly, that some particular type of service should be named to indicate the capacity in which the functioner acts; and secondly, that the aim or purpose subserved should be that of a human employer. These notions reappear in the linguistic use of the term, where it has reference to the results achieved in the course of a particular act of speech. In such an act the speaker's aim is to draw attention to something, and the words are, as it were, his functionaries whose office it is to present the thing-meant as possessing some particular formal character. However, grammarians seldom avail themselves

---

[1] For fusion of independent elements and analogy as the two main sources of outer word-form see the essay entitled 'L'évolution des formes grammaticales' in Meillet, *Linguistique*, pp. 130 foll. But see further Jespersen, *Language*, ch. xix, and particularly its § 13 on 'secretion'.

of the term 'function' in reference to the general duties of a word in the fulfilment of its inherent 'form' or capacity. The term comes into play only when details of the work done have to be described, or when the word is found doing work which is not, properly considered, its own. For example, in the phrase *the boy king* the word *boy* is a noun, but functions as an adjective; or again, the rhetorical question *Have I ever done you an injury?* is a sentence having the form of a question, but functioning or serving as a denial. Such conflicts between form and function will concern us greatly in the sequel. For the moment I will leave on one side **incongruent function**, as I shall call it, and will concentrate my attention upon the more usual cases where function is **congruent**, i.e. where form and function agree.

But a preliminary difficulty must be faced before we can proceed successfully with the discussion of word-function. I regret the necessity, because it compels us to take a view of the things meant by speech somewhat different from that of the ordinary man, whereas my endeavours have been directed towards confining linguistic theory to the plane of common sense. It was seen in § 8 that speech deals with things of the most heterogeneous kinds; material objects, abstractions, figments of the imagination—all these indifferently are grist to the speaker's mill. The reason, which hitherto needed but passing mention, is that in reality the things spoken about are not external phenomena, but the reflections of these, immediate or mediate, mirrored in the speaker's mind. If I ask for a piece of cake, the thing I refer to is primarily the piece of cake as perceived by me, and only secondarily the piece of cake itself. So long as we were dealing with the thing-meant apart from linguistic form, it would have been foolish to complicate matters by emphasizing this point. The ordinary man believes he can speak about a piece of cake directly, and it was better not to disturb him in his illusion. But at the present stage he must be disillusioned, as I shall show by reverting to James and Mary Hawkins and to the words which passed, or might have passed, between them. Outside the house in which they are is the rain, and no way in which James may refer to it will alter its nature by a hair's-breadth. But the form in which the rain may be presented to Mary's mind differs according to James's caprice. If he says *Look how it rains!* the rain is presented as an action, as full of movement and activity. If, on the other hand, he says *Look at the rain!* then he presents the rain as a thing, i.e. as though it were a fixed object with a vague similarity in this respect to a table or chair. Hence we have to conclude that the things referred to in speech are always mentally conditioned, and that the conditioning of them is subject to the speaker's will. I hope that no reader will imagine me to be maintaining that we cannot really speak of external things at all. An illustration already employed in connexion with the general meaning of the word 'form' will here stand us in good stead. Putty, it was said (p. 132), can be moulded into different forms. Human agency can effect this change for its own purposes, but the putty remains the same all the time. So, too, it is with the things spoken about. When spoken about, they have already assumed a particular form in the speaker's mind, and he presents them in that form to the listener. But the listener, though he has received the thing as a mental reflection, can subsequently deal with it according as the possibilities connected with it permit. I ask my wife for a piece of cake. My wife receives the piece of cake from me as a mental reflection, and hands it back to me as a reality.

Word-function is the work which a spoken word has to perform in order to present the thing meant by the speaker in the formal character in which he must be supposed to have intended the listener to see it. In order to ascertain the function of a spoken word in a given situation, the forms of all the other words in the sentence have to be taken into account. Paying careful attention to these and to the situation as a whole, the critic will usually be able to judge the way in which the speaker intended the thing named by the word to be taken. In the sentence *Look at the rain!* the three words *look*, *at*, and *the* together indicate with high probability the formal character that the thing named by rain was meant to assume in the listener's mind. *Look* alone is insufficient to bring about this result, since, though one looks at 'things', yet the alternative possibility *Look how it rains!* shows that the real object of the looking may be presented in the character of an action, not in that of a thing. However, the word *at* awakens the expectation that a noun, i.e. the name of a thing presented as a thing (pp. 9–10), will follow, and still more is this true of *the*. Those expectations are involved in the forms of the words *at* and *the* as preposition and definite article respectively. The word *rain* itself is ambiguous in the expectation which it arouses, but at least it tells us that the thing meant by the speaker ought to be taken *either* as an action *or* as a thing. The best dictionaries distinguish two different words *rain*, the one a noun, and the other a verb.[1] In the present context the listener has not the slightest ground for suspecting that *rain* is being used in

[1] In point of fact *O.E.D.* always uses the term 'substantive' in place of 'noun'. I have adopted the latter in deference to the recommendation of the Joint Committee on Grammatical Terminology (see their *Report*, London, 1917, p. 18), though I believe 'substantive' to be free from objection, if properly defined.

incongruent function. The preceding words point to something presented as a thing, and the word *rain* itself offers that conclusion as of equal possibility with the presentation of the rain as an action. Consequently, the grammarian will pronounce the verdict: 'Here the noun *rain* is being used.' This is the usual manner in which congruent function is announced. Unless there are strong reasons for the contrary view, it is always assumed that words are functioning in accordance with their form. James, if consulted upon the point, would undoubtedly admit that he meant the noun *rain*, not the verb *rain*.

We have just seen that when function is congruent, it often suffices to mention the form of the word which is used. But the use of the term 'function' becomes desirable when the specific work done by the word in a particular sentence has to be emphasized. Thus in *There are several persons here of the name of Miller*, the noun *miller* is said to 'function' as a proper name. I shall proceed to show that the term 'function' often provides the most scientific way of describing the subdivisions habitually made by grammarians in order to define the scope of a particular word-form. For example, among other kinds of present tense, grammarians of English distinguish the Habitual Present, e.g. *He* TAKES *sugar in his tea*, and the Historical Present, e.g. *Now on each side the leaders* | GIVE *signal for the charge;* | *And on each side the footmen* | *Strode on with lance and targe*. To illustrate the implications of such subdivisions I shall take two particular applications of the Latin genitive as my illustrations. It appears that the original function of the genitive case was to express authorship rather than ownership, but the matter is uncertain and of no importance for the question here to be investigated. Whatever the original meaning of the form, it is clear that this was extended gradually and doubtless unwittingly so as at last to cover a large number of uses or functions, the connexion of which with the starting-point is often barely perceptible. Thus the grammarians distinguish a Genitive of Respect, a Genitive of Price, and so forth. In *amor hominum in te*, 'the love of men for thee', *hominum* is said to be a Subjective Genitive, because the thing meant by it bears to the thing meant by *amor* the same relation as exists between the subject and the finite verb in a sentence like *Homines amant Balbum*. In *amor patriae*, 'love of country', on the other hand, *patriae* is called an Objective Genitive, because the relation involved is that subsisting, e.g. between *Balbum* and *amant* in the sentence just quoted. Now to say that *hominum* is a Subjective Genitive in the first case, and *patriae* an Objective Genitive in the second, suggests that Latin morphology has here two separate forms in precisely the same way that it has two in the genitive *aulae* and the dative *aulae*. But this is not true. Apart from the fact that at an earlier moment Latin distinguished the genitive *aulāī* from the dative *aulai* (with *-ai* as a diphthong), in countless other words (e.g. *mentis*, *menti*) there is a difference in outer form between genitive and dative.[1] Any Roman who had any grammatical consciousness at all would doubtless have felt the genitive *aulae* and the dative *aulae* as two separate forms, the outward coincidence of which was purely accidental. In all probability he would have had no such feeling about *hominum* and *patriae* in the above examples. Even if well aware of the semantic differences between them, he would have declared merely that the genitive was present in both cases. The uneducated Roman would almost certainly have spoken the two words without a

[1] See Jespersen, *Philosophy*, p. 177.

§ 42 CONGRUENT WORD-FUNCTION 147

suspicion that different relations were described. But scientifically it is highly undesirable to make the terms we use rest upon speculations as to the feelings of a remote people of foreign race. This can be avoided by recourse to the term 'function', behind which always lies the verdict of a skilled interpreter. The proper way of describing *hominum* and *patriae* is to say that the first functions or serves as a Subjective Genitive, and the second as an Objective Genitive.[1]

Exception may perhaps be taken to the course just recommended on the ground that my own definition deprives the term 'word-function' of the detached scientific quality which I am seeking to attribute to it. It is true that in the definition I refer to 'the formal character in which' the speaker 'must be supposed to have intended the listener to see' the thing-meant. But I maintain, not only that to assume intention in the speaker is essential for linguistic theory, but also that at the moment of utterance the speaker may not be aware of what he intends. On the common-sense plane intention is always presupposed by the listener, and a speaker can usually be brought by questioning to state 'what he really meant'. I do not dispute that speech is often nearly automatic. Habit provides short-cuts to many results which, despite all apparent absence of feeling, we really desire, and linguistic form

[1] Another method which may, however, sometimes serve better is to use the phrase 'refer to' and to describe, not the word-function, but the factual character of the thing-meant. For example, the Egyptians seem to have distinguished in their verb-forms only the two 'aspects' (*Aktionsarten*) of (1) repetition or continuity, (2) simple action. It is therefore doubtful whether they ever rose to a conception of 'tense' at all. For this reason I have been careful, in my *Egyptian Grammar*, not to state (e.g.) that the Imperfective tense has past, present, or future 'meaning', but to say merely that it may be employed 'in reference to past, present, or future actions'.

is simply inherited habit. We shall see that when educated persons talk consciously, their word-consciousness frequently consists in applying certain grammatical rules without awareness of the deeper-lying factual relations which these grammatical rules imply (§ 44). If the right words have been chosen, those factual relations can be revealed to consciousness by a careful analysis of 'what was really meant', the surrounding words and the situation forming the basis of the deduction. Accordingly, the function of words is, after all, something objective and scientifically ascertainable.

§ 43. **The application of words.** The diagrams on p. 151 (Fig. 6) are designed to illustrate the application of three words discussed in the last section, namely *rain* in *Look at the rain! patriae* in *amor patriae*, and *boy* in *the boy king*. Both stem-meaning and word-form are taken into account, but since the sole object has been to elucidate the very difficult topic of word-form and word-function, only one possibility in the application of word-meaning has been envisaged, namely the case when this is acceptably and correctly applied. The application and function of the words are represented by dotted lines connecting the large areas of meaning and form on the left with the things-meant on the right. I must explain that the terms 'application' and 'function' have roughly the same signification, inasmuch as both designate the work done by words in pointing to things-meant. But since 'form and function' is a familiar antithesis, it seemed desirable to restrict the linguistic term 'function' to the work accomplished in the way of attributing grammatically formal character. The meaning (stem-meaning) of the words is represented by lines of medium thickness, and seeing that their form (*ffff*) is constant and adheres to them in every conceivable

§ 43   WORD-FUNCTION ILLUSTRATED   149

application, the thinner lines representing word-form follow the meaning wherever it goes. If the rectangles were completed, we should have the words as they exist in language, as yet unapplied but possessing form (*f*) as well as meaning (*m*), i.e. possibilities of varied application (*abcde*). When a word is applied in speech, one particular tract of its area of meaning becomes protruded, as it were, to characterize the thing-meant; the latter is represented as an area enclosed by thick lines. The word-meaning and word-form must be conceived of as casting jets of light upon the thing as intended by the speaker, revealing its true characters as so intended or meant. These characters are twofold, meaning-character (C) and formal character (Fc). Corresponding to them in the protruded part of the word are the specific meaning of the word as applied (χ), and the specific capacity in which the word functions (*F*) as attributor of form. Note that in examples of correct and wholly congruent application the pairs χ : C and *F* : Fc correspond exactly, but we must beware of equating χ with C, or *F* with Fc, for χ and *F* are characters of the words, whereas C and Fc are characters of the things.

To turn now to the separate diagrams. In the topmost the word *rain* (*m*) in its character of designating-visible-rain (χ, see p. 77) applies admirably to the rain (T); the rain (T) is suited to the word which describes it (*m*) in its character of being-visible-rain (C). Correspondingly, the word functions congruently in the capacity of a noun (*F* = *f*), inasmuch as it presents the thing-meant in its true character of being-thought-of-as-a-thing (Fc).

In the middle diagram, we again have correct and congruent application, but the congruence of function is of a special type represented by γ. In *patriae* the capacity (*F*) in which the word functions is that of a genitive, but just

Fig. 6. Diagram to illustrate the application or functioning of the words: (1) *rain* in *Look at the rain!* (2) *patriae* in *amor patriae*, (3) *boy* in *the boy king*.

Thick lines indicate the thing-meant or characters of it.
Medium lines indicate word-meaning (stem-meaning).
Thin lines indicate word-form (formal word-meaning).
Dotted lines indicate the functioning or application of a word.
Roman letters denote the thing-meant or characters of it.
Greek letters denote the characters (capacities) in which a word is applied or functions.
Italic letters denote the meaning (stem-meaning or formal meaning) of a word.

T = the thing-meant.
C = the character of the thing-meant as expressed by the stem-meaning.
Fc = the formal character of the thing-meant.
m = the area of meaning belonging to a word.
$abcde$ = the field of possible applications belonging to a word.
$ffff$ = the area of word-form.
χ = the specific stem-meaning in a given application.
F = a specific form as the capacity in which the word is functioning.
γ = the same, more closely specified.
S = the Syntactic Form, position between article and noun, see p. 160.
F' = the capacity in which the Syntactic Form is functioning.

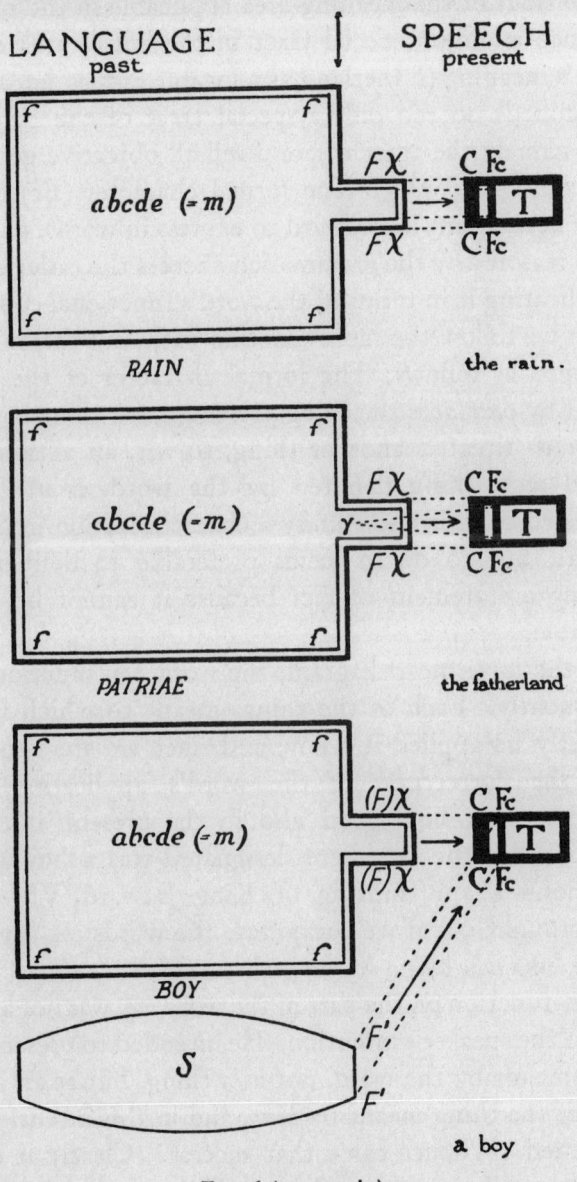

FIG. 6 (see opposite)

as the tract of the meaning-area applicable in the present instance is only a special tract in the entire area of the word's meaning (fatherland as a lovable entity, i.e. almost personified), so too only a special tract of the genitive-area, namely the tract where dwell all objective genitives (γ), comes into play. The formal character (Fc) of the thing here meant is awkward to express in words, and this is the reason why the grammarian chooses the easier course of indicating it in terms of the word's functional capacity. But if we follow the more exacting path, our formulation will read as follows: The formal character of the thing meant by *patriae* is the being presented as a thing towards which is directed another thing, to wit, an action presented as a thing denoted by the word *amor*. I am distressed to inflict so clumsy a characterization upon my readers, but to do so seems preferable to deliberately evading a statement of fact because it cannot be made palatable.

In the lowermost diagram, the word *boy* functions incongruently. Each of the things-meant to which it can correctly be applied is a boy, and since we are assuming here the correctness of the word's application, this assertion must hold good also in the present instance. And indeed, the king here designated was a boy at his accession—I am thinking of King Edward VI—as is well brought out if we paraphrase the words *the boy king* by *the king who was a boy when he ascended the throne*. But a noun-function on the part of the word *boy* was not a vital part of the speaker's intention. He intended to present the thing meant by the word, not as a thing, but as an attribute of the thing meant by *king*, and in this intention he succeeded. Whence came that success? Clearly it came from somewhere, and so I have depicted the attribute-character (Fc) of the thing meant by *boy* as proceeding from a linguistic form (S) outside the area of the word *boy*. The capacity (F') in which the said form acts or functions is that of conferring on the thing meant by a given word the value of an attribute, and I shall return to it again in § 45.

To make the lowermost diagram complete, some device ought to have been discovered for showing a faint stream of light proceeding from F, the functional capacity of the word *boy*, towards the thing meant by the word. For although the speaker did not primarily intend the thing-meant to be regarded as a thing, yet he is unable to prevent the word chosen by him from exerting some of its innate power. The word has been correctly applied, and if we look at the thing meant by it, we note that in a secondary way the thing is indeed presented as a thing. This we have already seen. That Edward VI was a boy when he came to the throne is admitted, and at all events the speaker did not intend the fact to be disguised. In choosing the noun *boy* he may even have meant to imply this fact; but if so, he meant it less than he meant the attributive function of the word. Hence the grammarian will rightly sum up the position by saying: The noun *boy* here functions as an attributive adjective.

§ 44. **Form and function become grammatical.** The starting-point for my discussion of word-form and word-function was the inquiry whether or no all words are on an equal footing, whether they resemble one another in intrinsic value and functional power (§ 40). The result has been to show that, apart from all considerations of outer word-form, words do differ greatly among themselves by reason of certain varying over-meanings known as 'inner word-form'. But inner word-form was found to consist in qualities of words permanently attaching to them, which were simply prophecies of certain characters in the things meant by the words, whenever the latter should be correctly or congruently used. The differences between words might thus seem, at first sight, to be differences merely in the things meant by them. There is some element of truth in this proposition, and it is one so often overlooked that to lay excessive emphasis upon it would do more good than harm. Few practical grammarians realize that the formal characters belonging to words are ultimately and fundamentally formal characters belonging to the things meant by them. The diagrams explained in the last section have, it is hoped, helped to reveal this truth. To add a new example, *aedificare* is called a transitive verb, and is said to 'take after it' an object in the accusative case. Behind this purely grammatical statement lie the facts that *aedificare* means 'to build', and that the physical act of building brings into existence an effected thing, a wall for instance, such as demands a noun in the accusative case for its expression. In *Balbus murum aedificavit*, 'Balbus built a wall', the true cause of the relation between *aedificavit* and *murum* is that the thing meant by *aedificavit*, i.e. Balbus's past act of building, effected or brought about the thing meant by *murum*, i.e. a wall. Similarly, in *amor patriae* the relation between the two words depends on the factual love of some person or of people in general for the real thing known as his or their fatherland. Every relation between words rests genetically upon a relation of non-verbal fact.[1] The historian of grammar attempts to unearth and prove these relations between the things meant by words, though he may be unable to give a correct

[1] Wegener and Kalepky seem to stand alone among grammarians in emphasizing this.

theoretical account of his practice. Thus when he explains that, in Latin *fruor* with the ablative, the case is really instrumental, his explanation implies that historically *fruor* meant something like 'I enjoy myself' and that (e.g.) in *fruor vita* the ablative *vita* referred to life in its aspect of being the instrument or means of my enjoyment.

But to insist unduly upon the semantic character of all grammatical forms and constructions is to ignore the equally important fact that, through the gradual mechanization of speech, through the establishment of those fixed habits which we call language, the words themselves and the relations of these with one another have undergone a profound change. This can be proved by various arguments, still without recourse to the criterion of outer form. In the first place, the inner form of words makes itself felt, sometimes with unpleasant insistence, in uses of them which are incongruent or wrong. If we hear someone say *Mary and John's down with the 'flu*, the slurred over and abbreviated *is* jars upon us for all its unobtrusiveness, even though the thing-meant is quite unmistakable. Again, in *the boy king* the word *boy* is not felt to be on the same footing as *good* in *the good king*. There is a sense of *boy* having been somehow diverted from its true use, and that true use gives a peculiar flavour to the combination. It is perfectly well understood that *boy* is here used as an attribute, not as a thing presented as a thing, but the word has a character of its own which can no longer be taken from it. From *the boy king* arises a certain feeling of two persons being identified with one another, not merely of one person being provided with an attribute. We must conclude that the development of language has made the word *boy* differ from such a word as *good*. They belong to different classes, and are tenacious of their rank in every circumstance and situation.

The same point may also be demonstrated by the fact that some words have inner word-form which no longer bears any relation to the things designated by them. The peculiar linguistic phenomenon of gender is here particularly instructive. It is not to be imagined that the Romans really thought of every flower as masculine, but Latin *flos* is masculine. Opinions differ as to how grammatical gender originated, but no one doubts that, at some distant moment in the dim past, it arose in some dual (or triple) classification of the things meant by words.[1] In historic times, however, the inner word-form known as gender is dead or half-dead as a semantic reality; only half-dead, perhaps, because humans and animals of female sex are still named by feminine words, and males by masculine words, so that these exceptional cases still reveal a felt correspondence between observed character in the things and grammatical form in the words. The example quoted is the more interesting because the French derivative *fleur* (from *florem*) is feminine, and this change of gender is due, not to any change of conception with regard to the sex of flowers, but to analogic assimilation of the word to other words ending in *-eur*; in French these words are feminines (e.g. *chaleur*, *douleur*), except such of them as are names of agents (e.g. *joueur* from Latin **jocatorem*).

Word-form thus becomes a fact mainly of grammatical import. Words have grammatical status, and this now determines their relations to other words to some extent independently of the things to which they refer. In a combination like *cette belle fleur*, the separate words may

[1] For an excellent discussion of grammatical gender, with bibliographical indications, see Vendryès, *Le langage*, pp. 108 foll.

be analysed to mean 'this (female person)+beautiful (female person)+flower (as a female person)'. But no Frenchman, in saying *cette belle fleur*, goes through the mental process here indicated. Whenever his speech is not purely automatic and unconscious, he strives to use his words congruently, i.e. in the forms dictated by language on the one hand, and by the context on the other. But the congruence which is now his goal is a congruence of grammar, no longer one of meaning. Instead of making *cette* and *belle* agree with his conception of the thing of which an attribute is thereby denoted, he makes them agree with the word *fleur*, with the separately expressed name of that same thing. Concord, together with its subtler variety 'sequence of tenses', takes place directly as between word and word, without reference to the factual character which the two words signify in common.

Thus, in developed speech, one word fixes the form of another, and schoolmasters teach their pupils, not to fit word-forms to the things spoken about, but to talk grammatically and idiomatically. The reasons for given modes of parlance are historic rather than semantic. For English 'by him' the Roman said *ab eo*, but the Greek ὑπ' αὐτοῦ; nor is there any reason except established idiom why the former should have used the ablative, and the latter the genitive. Grammar tells us simply that *a, ab* 'takes' the ablative and ὑπό the genitive.[1] Objection is sometimes raised against the grammatical phraseology that one word

[1] The old Indo-European ablative has not survived in Greek, and is there absorbed by the genitive. In Latin the agent of a passively conceived action seems to have been thought of originally as its 'source', so that the ablative, which conveyed a notion of coming from a distance, was the obviously suitable case. But the Roman of the Augustan era will have associated no such conception with *ab eo*; to him this will have seemed merely the natural and right way of indicating the agent.

'governs' another, or that the second is 'dependent upon' the first. Nevertheless these terms are exact and unimpeachable presentations of the truth. The practice of grammarians here scores yet another victory over defective grammatical theory.

In *Balbus murum aedificavit* it is, therefore, quite legitimate to say that *murum* functions as object of *aedificavit*. Every Roman knew, as a matter of practice, that *aedificare* took the accusative and automatically followed that rule. Nevertheless, the sense is sometimes chosen as a guide rather than grammatical precedent, as is proved by instances of conflict between the two. From such conflict arises the linguistic phenomenon which grammarians call 'construction according to the sense' (*constructio ad sensum*, κατὰ σύνεσιν), a term which testifies eloquently to the predominance in educated prejudice of grammar over meaning. A Latin example is *omnis aetas currere obvii* 'every age ran to meet them', where *obvii* is congruent in sense, but grammatically incongruent as failing to agree with *aetas* in number and gender; cf. in Greek ὦ φίλε τέκνον. Similar anomalies are frequent in English, e.g. *None of them* WRITE *well; The lowing herd* WIND *slowly o'er the lea; Your committee* ARE *of opinion*.

§ 45. **Syntactic and intonational form and function.** In connexion with the genitive *patriae* and the accusative *murum* it was impossible to avoid discussing the relation of each to another word in their respective contexts, whence it is evident that word-form and syntax cannot always be kept apart. **Syntax** (Greek σύνταξις 'a putting together in order') may be defined as *the study of the forms both of the sentence itself and of all free word-combinations which enter into it*.[1] By an act of grace one-word sentences are

[1] See J. Ries, *Was ist Syntax?* Ries has the merit of having realized

§ 45   SYNTACTIC FORM   159

included under the head of syntax, though etymologically the term does not sanction their admittance. Much that is syntactic would have to be included in a descriptive work on morphology (word-form), but the same material would require to be reviewed again in a treatise on syntax. There, however, the angle of vision would be changed, each word being regarded as a member of a combination, not as an individual. Such combinations of words would be seen to have **syntactic form**, which like all linguistic form is a fact of language, built up out of countless syntactic functionings of words in single acts of speech. Like word-form, syntactic form is a kind of meaning heard as an overtone above the stem-meanings and wordform-meanings imparted by the component words. Thus from *the good king* a listener unconsciously concludes that *good* designates an attribute of the person referred to by *king*. This particular syntactic form has as its outer manifestation the word-order (1) article (or demonstrative)+(2) adjective (or word serving as such)+(3) noun, and in the example quoted the syntactic combination functions with perfect congruence, since *good* denotes goodness as an attribute of the king in question—naturally I am assuming some particular situation in which the words are uttered. Here again we find 'form' and 'function' as complementary terms, the one belonging to language and the other to speech. I will not dwell on syntactic form at length, since it was illustrated diagrammatically in connexion with *Look at the rain!* (p. 92, with Fig. 5), and since many

that the combinations of words called 'phrases' or 'clauses' are no mere component parts of the sentence, but substitutes for words deserving study for their own sakes. Hence the equation of syntax and *Satzlehre* is fallacious. In my definition the word *free* is added to exclude purely mechanized phrases, which are already, to all intents and purposes, actual words.

other examples will be discussed in the second half of this book.

Yet another type of linguistic form and function received illustration in the diagram just alluded to. **Intonational form** is the name given to those differences of tone, pitch, stress, &c., with which combinations of words having a certain syntactic over-meaning are habitually spoken. Statements, questions, commands, and so forth have all their specific intonational forms, and it is a strange fact—to receive further comment in the next chapter—that intonational form always functions congruently. *C'est le ton qui fait la musique*, we can appropriately quote, leaving further discussion to a later stage (§ 54).

The two new varieties of linguistic form and function gain an added interest for us, when we note that they throw considerable light on incongruent function. The word-order (1) definite article, (2) attribute-word, (3) noun is, indeed, the source from which the thing denoted by *boy* in *the boy king* obtained its attributive power, and this is the particular syntactic form which is depicted in cylindrical shape (*S*) in the lowermost diagram of Fig. 6 (p. 151). We saw above that *the good king* is another congruent example of the same form. A second incongruent instance would be *the then king*, for the word *then* is, as an adverb, not naturally entitled to serve as attribute to a noun. Nevertheless, when placed between the article and a noun, it has attributive force conferred upon it in the same way as *boy* in *the boy king*.

On this single type of incongruent function I shall venture to base two important inferences, which others must test for themselves. The first is that, where incongruent function arises in speech, it is more often than not due to the conflict of two linguistic forms. In *the boy king* word-form commands the word *boy* to function in one way, and syntactic form commands it to function in another. I come now to my second inference. Which of the two mandates is to be obeyed? I believe that syntax always secures the victory. Word-form goes on feebly asserting its rights, but syntax proclaims its triumph in no uncertain voice. Such at all events is the result in *the boy king*. But further, I believe that intonation has a similar priority everywhere over syntax. This position will be demonstrated later so far as sentence-function is concerned (pp. 204–5), so that here it is advisable to adduce a different type as evidence. Let us suppose two schoolgirls to be debating their preferences in English history. One of them says, *Í prefer the* BÓY *king*, stressing both *I* and *boy*. In this sentence *boy* ceases to be the simple epithet that the syntactic form intended it to be, and by virtue of its intonational emphasis secures for the combination in which it occurs the status of logical predicate, the highest dignity which speech has to bestow. The sentence may be paraphrased *The king whom I prefer is the* BOY *king*, a form in which the logical predicate is displayed as also part of the grammatical predicate (see below, § 69). Observe, in conclusion, that the stressing of BOY does not cease to make it an attribute of *king*, though this syntactically functional character of the word is somewhat obscured, much in the same manner as its noun-quality sank into relative obscurity when syntax claimed it for an attribute. For interpretational purposes intonation, syntax, and word-form thus seem to exert influence in this hierarchical order.

§ 46. **Final remarks on incongruent word-function.** It may be thought that, in devoting so much space to incongruent word-function, I am insisting unduly on what, after all, is a comparatively rare and exceptional linguistic phenomenon. My answer is that nowhere else can the interaction of speech and language be better exhibited. Here language is seen dictating, and speech ever so mildly rebelling. And if the cause itself be good, very possibly the rebellious utterance may win through, and gain recognition as a fact of language.

Incongruent word-function is not necessarily an individual twisting of word-form, though it may be such. When a friend once wittily described my lawn-tennis as *Doherty strokes with Gardiner results*, he was using my surname incongruently, though not altogether incorrectly; and he was using it in a manner not heard by me before or since. This is an example of purely individual incongruence. The use of *boy* in *the boy king* is, on the other hand, quite common. In the limited sense of 'being a boy', the word *boy* can be employed freely in the capacity of an adjective, cf. *boy friend*, *boy actor*, *boy lover*, *boy cousin*. One particular case of this use, namely *boy-scout*, has recently become so mechanized that it must be regarded as a compound word, not a combination of two. In the other sense 'pertaining to boys', the attributive function is considerably rarer, but *boy-kind* and *boy-nature* have been quoted. In all these employments, however, a certain recalcitrance on the part of the word can be felt, and the *Oxford English Dictionary* is, accordingly, fully justified in refusing to it the rank of adjective beside that of noun. The position is there accurately characterized by the statement that in combinations '*boy* often approaches the force of an adjective'. For the senses 'pertaining to boys' and 'boy-like', 'puerile', there is a derivative adjective *boyish*, e.g. *boyish pastimes*, *boyish vanities*. Contrast now with *boy* as an attribute the adjective *silver*. The same dictionary rightly classifies this word as both noun and adjective. In the latter capacity its range is very wide; compare the various types of application in a *silver needle*, *silver mines*, *silver standard*, *silver chloride*, *his silver beard*, *silver laughter*. Nevertheless, there appears to be no doubt that *silver* originally was only a noun, and that, in becoming an adjective as well, it passed through various degrees of incongruent function.

These examples suffice to illustrate the way in which all new linguistic form comes about. Single acts of speech gradually push some old form in a new direction, and a function once completely incongruent at last becomes wholly congruent. In the case of word-form, analogy may then move the word with the altered form to assume some of the outer characteristics of its new colleagues. Jespersen writes: 'The Latin adjective *ridiculus* according to Bréal is evolved from a neuter substantive *ridiculum* "objet de risée" formed in the same way as *curriculum*, *cubiculum*, *vehiculum*. When applied to persons it took masculine and feminine endings. . . .' Jespersen continues, '. . . and it is this formal trait which made it into an adjective; but at the same time its signification became slightly more general and eliminated the element of "thing".'[1] Surely this is putting the cart before the horse. The reason why the old noun *ridiculum* ultimately took on the masculine and feminine endings is that its originally incongruent function as an attribute of persons had become congruent. *Ridiculum* had in meaning acquired the status of an adjective, and for that reason was declined as such. Inner word-form is always the cause of outer, not vice versa.

There is, however, another kind of incongruent function which can never lead to new form, and for which the

[1] Jespersen, *Philosophy*, p. 76.

future holds in store nothing but extinction. This is found in the employment of words that have been, or are in course of being, superseded by others of different outer form. Thus *mine* as an epithet has given place to *my*, though retained in poetry before vowels, e.g. *mine eyes*. But *mine* sometimes occurs incongruently in conversation as a playful substitute for *my*, which it can then hardly fail to suggest to the listener's mind; so in *mine host, mine enemy*. Analogous in the field of stem-meaning are the occasional applications of words in obsolescent senses. An elderly person might easily speak of a quill as *that pen*, and though this employment is etymologically far more correct than the current usage, it would doubtless sound strange in the ears of a boy for whom a *pen* is a fountain-pen; he would expect to hear the quill referred to as *that quill*. We must realize, therefore, that incongruence may be felt in employments which are perishing, no less than in those which are of recent birth. Incongruence is the mark of transition. In both varieties a feeling of strain is perceptible, and there is some impression of an alternative possibility. But in the one case the incongruence is due to innovation, in the other to archaism.

In conclusion, let it be noted that, subject to the view of linguistic intention defined above, p. 147, incongruent function is seldom quite motiveless. It is a correct but unusual mode of parlance, and is frequently chosen because there is no suitable alternative. In *the boy king*, the adjective *boyish* obviously would not fit. But often some stylistic motive operates in addition. Thus in *God made the country, man made the town*, the word *man* is preferable to *men* for two reasons. Firstly, it hints better than the plural would have done that the creation of towns is the outcome of man's perverted nature; the singular acts almost as though it personified the idea or concept of human nature. Secondly, the choice of the singular displays two individuals face to face with one another, the one acting wisely, the other foolishly. The antithesis is dramatically impressive.

§ 47. **Metaphor.**[1] I now turn to a linguistic phenomenon which plays, in the domain of word-meaning, much the same part as incongruent word-function in the domain of word-form. Metaphor, from the Greek μεταφορά 'a transference', signifies, in its technical use, any diversion of words from their literal or central meanings. The chief point wherein metaphor resembles incongruent word-function is the sense of a blending, of a mixture, which arises from it; not a disharmony, however, since the feeling excited is that of enrichment rather than the contrary. The one ingredient of the mixture is derived from speech and from the thing-meant; the other from language and from established semantic usage. Metaphor and incongruent word-function can be described by a common formula: speech obsessed by language. There are, moreover, other points of resemblance having a deep interest. Each of these two linguistic phenomena starts as an isolated occurrence in a single act of speech. Sometimes it takes place almost unconsciously, as the mode of parlance most naturally suited to the occasion; sometimes very deliberately, with specific rhetorical intention. Each is subject to many degrees, proportional to the popularity acquired by a particular metaphor or an incongruent word-function. The new meaning introduced by speech

---

[1] For 'metaphor' see Paul, *Prinzipien*, §§ 68–9; Wundt, *Sprache*, vol. ii, pp. 554 foll.; [H. W. and G. Fowler], *The King's English*, Oxford, 1906, pp. 200 foll.; the same and A. Clutton-Brock, *Metaphor*, being Tract No. XI of the Society for Pure English, Oxford, 1924.

gradually gains the upper hand over the old meaning imposed by language. If at last the old meaning ceases to be felt when the word is used, incongruent word-function becomes congruent, and metaphor dies. A new word-form or a new word-meaning has become established. Speech has become language.

A distinction has been rightly drawn between natural or spontaneous metaphor and metaphor as a carefully planned artistic device. But in practice the distinction is difficult to maintain, since the early stages of the former are always hidden. The principle involved is best illustrated by reference to a very common type. Here something which is more remote, less concrete, less vivid, is referred to in terms of something similar which is more familiar, less abstract, more pictorial.[1] Natural metaphor often comes before us only at so advanced a stage, that the presence of imagery demands philological scrutiny for its recognition. We are scarcely aware of the image in speaking of the *arm* of a chair, the *foot* of a table, the *mouth* of a river, the *neck* of a bottle, or the *veins* in a piece of marble. Metaphor is moribund when we say that prices *sink* or *rise*, that a voice is *high* or *low*, that someone's character is *hard* or *coarse*. So, too, in descriptions of mental happenings: to *feel* tired, to *grasp* a thought, to *imagine* a situation, to *direct* one's attention.

---

[1] Not all metaphor is of this type, however. Sometimes the thing compared is no less concrete and vivid than the comparison, e.g. the frequent metaphors by which the Egyptians, for adulatory reasons, compared the Pharaoh with a lion, a bull, and so forth. Sometimes the metaphor may even be more abstract than that to which it is applied, e.g. in Siegfried Sassoon's poem describing the impressions left by an evening in the company of archaeologists; he refers to the moon, '*But, as her whitening way aloft she took, I thought she had a* PRE-DYNASTIC *look.*' Metaphor of this kind is rare, and dictated by very individual and unusual aims.

§ 47 METAPHOR

For my present purpose, the illustration of the relations between speech and language, deliberate metaphor is far more instructive. The most full-blooded form of the tendency underlying this is seen in parable or allegory. Here the prophet or teacher has a message to deliver, but conceives the best way to the hearts of his audience to be through the description of some homely incident embodying the lesson to be taught or the truth to be inculcated. The method is analogous to the personification of abstract notions. The same process is exemplified in similes, where the less pictorial fact is first explicitly named, and then brought home to the listener by means of a highly coloured parallel introduced by some word marking the comparison as such. Many elaborate instances are found in Homer, e.g. *They two in front of the high gate were standing like high-crested oaks on a mountain, which abide the wind and the rain through all days, firm in their long roots that reach deep into the earth.* It has sometimes been said that metaphor (i.e. the metaphor of individual speech) is a shortened simile; for instance, *Rebellion blazed forth* might be taken as a shorter version of *Rebellion spread abroad, even as when a fire blazes forth.* If this explanation is offered in illustration of the psychological principle involved, no fault can be found with it. If, on the other hand, it is offered as a statement of historical origin, it is certainly false. Metaphor, as we have seen, is so natural a phenomenon, that it frequently takes place unbeknown to its employer. It would be little wonder, accordingly, if the effectiveness of this natural device became consciously recognized and if it were adopted as a deliberate means of enhancing the interest of a sentence. But one more approximation to metaphor must be mentioned before we turn to the genuine article itself. It is a misnomer to apply the term metaphor to the mixed mode of diction of which the Bible contains so many magnificent specimens: *And there shall come forth a shoot out of the stock of Jesse . . .; and he shall smite the earth with the rod of his mouth, and with the breath of his lips shall he slay the wicked.* Here the allegory and the prophecy allegorized are so closely interwoven that no separation is possible; a number of images are combined in so rich a texture, that we are unable to discern which is the comparison and which the thing compared. True metaphor, at least in the lexicographical sense, begins only where the thing-meant can be distinctly recognized as such, though presented figuratively by a pictorial word conjuring up some other scene.

If the account I have to give of metaphor marks any advance upon previous accounts, it will be because I display it as a phenomenon of language belonging midway between a word as used figuratively by an individual speaker and a word of stereotyped meaning from which imagery once present has completely vanished. The two extremes are separated by any number of intermediate stages. To witness the birth of metaphor we must turn to poetry. So well-trodden are the paths of literature that even among the poets entirely new figurative uses are not easy to find. An instance recently quoted from Thomas Hardy[1] is *In the waves they bore their* GIMLETS *of light*, said of lamps on a sea-wall; this use of the word *gimlet* appears to be quite unprecedented, nor is it likely to be repeated. The following examples from well-known poems are far less individual: *The frolick Wind that* BREATHES *the Spring; While the Cock with lively din,* SCATTERS *the* REAR *of Darkness*

---

[1] An interesting collection of unique words or uses of words in Thomas Hardy's poems is given by G. G. Loane in *The Times Literary Supplement* for 21st January, 1932.

THIN; *Ever let the Fancy* ROAM, *Pleasure never is at* HOME; *Her mirth the world required, She* BATHED *it in smiles of glee.* Even if we confine the term 'metaphor' to figurative uses adopted by language, doubtless these will already come under that head. In commonplace writing, more hackneyed metaphors are often employed to give colour to drab surroundings: *Contentment is the* FOUNT *of all happiness;* STEALTHILY *the shadow of the house* CREPT ACROSS *the wall; My thoughts* HOLD MORTAL STRIFE. If *source* were substituted for *fount*, and *are in conflict* for *hold mortal strife*, we should have metaphor well within sight of death. At this stage, however, the addition of some other word elaborating the image may still resuscitate it: *Contentment is the* SOURCE *whence all happiness* FLOWS. Three-quarters dead metaphor, as H. W. Fowler has called it, can be brought to life again, but disastrously, by a mixture of images; he quotes a particularly crass example in *All the evidence must first be* SIFTED *with acid tests*. Apart from the final qualification, the *sifting* of evidence would barely be felt as metaphorical. Stone-dead metaphor, to borrow a phrase from the same writer, is exemplified in English *ponder, depend, explain, examine, test*, whence the Latin images of *weighing, hanging, straightening out, swarming*, and *bearing witness* have departed beyond recall. The disappearance from a word of more concrete collateral possibilities of application may be the cause of a metaphor's death; the metaphor in *towel-horse* is kept alive by the application of *horse* to Derby winners. But imagery can nearly perish in a word if its secondary and metaphorical use be much more frequent than its literal sense; the slang employment of *awful* and *dreadful* for what is bad or unpleasant is scarcely felt as metaphorical, though the literal applications, 'awe-inspiring', 'fraught with dread', are not quite extinct. The name 'dead metaphor', though illuminating as a means of realizing the phases through which many words pass, is not to be taken too seriously. A dead metaphor is a live word, but one which is a metaphor no longer.

§ 48. **Correct and faulty speech.** The perspective must now be widened so as to afford a glimpse of faulty speech. The very mention of such a possibility implies a standard of language which individual utterance may neglect or fail to reach. First, therefore, we must ask what a language is and by whose authority rules of grammar and right usages of words are formulated and imposed. The questions are more easily put than answered, although a rough approximation is found in the statement that, just as a speaker stands behind every isolated product of speech, so, too, the linguistic community stands behind any language as a whole. On looking closer, all kinds of difficulties confront us. There are local dialects, and there are social classes, each with its own set of linguistic habits, often directly contradicting one another. And yet the belief in a definite standard is universal and ineradicable; this is English and that not English. Little more than a generation ago, the attitude of philologists to language was purely normative; grammar had to teach rules of correct speaking, and the dictionaries declared, not only what words meant, but also what they ought to mean. The pendulum has swung far, perhaps too far, in the opposite direction. Linguistic treatises have become, for the most part, simply descriptive of usage, past or present. A French philologist has even had the happy idea of compiling a *Grammaire des fautes*, to show in what directions the French language is veering.[1] The foregoing sections

[1] H. Frei, *La grammaire des fautes*, Paris, 1929.

will have indicated the position which, in my conception, the theorist of language ought to adopt in regard to his subject-matter. It is a necessary assumption that the broad principles of linguistic theory are the same in all places and at all times. The theorist of language will, therefore, take his own linguistic habits and feelings as a basis. These, for him, are the 'language' of which he seeks the theory. But within his own language he will find much that is doubtful and indistinct. He may not be certain of the meaning of a specific word, and may not have made up his mind as to the validity of a particular rule. What is the exact significance of *sardonic*? Should *whose* be employed in the sense of *of which*? These examples are typical of the doubts which assail everyone interested in his mother-tongue.

If the theorist of language eliminates all such questionable elements in his own linguistic outlook, there will remain a large nucleus of words and rules about which he has no hesitation whatsoever. Concerning these he cannot fail to think normatively, but his approval and condemnation will have many degrees. In a given context one word may be more appropriate than another, though the second is not absolutely wrong. In the individual linguistic consciousness the dualism of speech and language is always postulated, and the claims of each are settled by strong and often dogmatic feeling. No grammar or dictionary, therefore, is adequate to the facts unless it recognizes and records the degrees which lie between unquestionably correct and unquestionably faulty speech. The normative standpoint must be combined with the purely descriptive, corresponding to the truth that at any given moment the language of any particular individual is not only in being, but also in course of becoming. Thus even in his own field of dispassionate scientific recording, the philologist is not entitled to overlook what I venture to call linguistic ethics. A few words require to be added in defence of the purists and their propaganda, now often unjustly reviled in the name of Science. If, as I have pointed out, there is an ethical element in all linguistic feeling, surely it is only natural and right that those who value their own language should seek to influence others in the directions which seem aesthetically or logically preferable. In writing 'logically' I touch upon a point which demands some emphasis. Scientific grammarians and purists of English will be ready to join hands in admitting an inherent, almost objective, ugliness in logical discrepancies. *These sort of things* is heard even from the lips of highly educated people, despite the existence of a simple alternative in *things of this sort*. Here obviously the purist should be encouraged to speak. But I will venture to suggest that even the ablest defenders of pure English occasionally spoil their cause by defective theory. The term 'split infinitive' is a case in point. Whatever the grammars may assert, *to dig* is not an infinitive, but only an infinitival phrase.[k] No doubt the union of the component words is closer than in free combinations of preposition and gerund, e.g. *in digging*. But if an intervening adverb be permissible in the latter case, it is at least defensible in the former. Moreover, the prevalence of the 'split infinitive' shows that *to*+infinitive is not felt as a unit.[1] Another example can be quoted by me the more conscientiously because here my feeling is in conflict with my opinion. My prejudice in favour of *different from* has increased with

[1] I have no fault to find with the conclusions of the witty article on the Split Infinitive in H. W. Fowler's *Modern English Usage*, except that he omits to point out the *petitio principii* involved in the term.

years. But I believe it to be wrong-headed. If the commonly favoured *different to* has brought about a disharmony with Latin, it has brought about a harmony in English itself; *similar to, different to* form a good pair! Is there any reason in common sense or good feeling why a live language should for ever hang upon the coat-tails of a dead one?

Mistakes in speech arise either from failure to envisage the thing-meant or else from incapacity to find the right word. Cases of total failure in one direction or the other are probably very rare; no one tries to name a cathedral and says *electrically*. Most errors are due to confusion or laziness. The short-sighted man who points at a cow and says *Look at that horse!* has in all likelihood had correct perceptions of colour and movement, but will have jumped to an over-hasty conclusion. Often the speaker will not take the trouble to identify an object about which he desires to speak; laziness in respect both of thing-meant and of word gives rise to utterances like *Pass that thingummy!* Slovenliness of this kind has doubtless been a potent factor in the history of language. But linguistic theory is barely concerned with situations where the speaker has failed to envisage the thing-meant. It is, on the other hand, deeply interested in incapacity to find the right word, for this state of affairs illustrates the fundamental antithesis between language and speech. Such incapacity is of many kinds. Malapropism is a familiar variety; I recall a gamekeeper who said *Them there birds is gone over th'ill, and the* CONSOLATION *is we shan't get 'em to-day*. Individual mistakes of this type are very frequent, and presuppose a common element of sound in the words confused. Especially conducive to error are words which resemble one another alike in sound and in sense; the interchange of *efficient* and *effective* or of *perspicuity* and *perspicacity* suggest themselves as examples. Grammatical forms may be similarly confused; *will* and *shall*, German *mir* and *mich*. But it serves no good purpose to illustrate the various possibilities of incorrect speech. I will merely note that much change in language has its root in individual errors. Popular etymology is an obvious type, and it is only one among many.

Finally, mention must be made of a fallacy which for a time enjoyed an unwarranted vogue—the fallacy of the *mot juste*. Some eminent authors have been pleased to toy with the illusion that there is only one correct way of saying a thing, and conversely, that each word has only one correct application. To hold such a view is to affirm the rights of language, but to deny those of speech. Individuality in speaker or writer is seemingly forbidden, and it is difficult to imagine, on this presupposition, how new thoughts could come to expression or old ones take on a new aspect. One of the most precious characteristics of language is its elasticity, which permits speech to stretch a word or construction to suit the momentary fancy or need. The true position is summed up by Walter Raleigh[1] with great profundity: 'The business of letters, howsoever simple it may seem to those who think truth-telling a gift of nature, is in reality twofold, to find words for a meaning, and to find a meaning for words. Now it is the words which refuse to yield, and now the meaning, so that he who attempts to wed them is at the same time altering his words to suit his meaning, and modifying and shaping his meaning to satisfy the requirements of his words.' Without the notion of a give and take between speech and language, linguistic theory is an impossibility.

[1] *Style*, London, 1898, p. 63.

§ 49. **Conclusion.** Instead of summarizing the argument of this lengthy chapter, I will bring it to a close with two similes which may help to keep in remembrance the principal results attained. Words do not all resemble one another. They may be likened to the stones in a builder's yard, of different materials and of different shapes. They have been hewn into diverse shapes for special purposes, some meant for this position in the building and some for that. In themselves they carry a presumption of their future use, but at the last moment the builder may change his mind, and use a particular stone in a way for which it was not intended. In skilled hands, a stone so employed may perhaps be even more effective than another originally destined for the same place.

Language and speech are admittedly closely akin, but to ignore the distinction between them is to ignore the ever-balancing principles of conservatism and reform which are the mainspring of development in linguistic, as in other matters. Language is the mother of all speech, educating it and by past example setting the standard it is expected to follow. But the youngster is vigorous and experimental, and will often go its own way. Wise is the mother who tempers discipline with good grace in yielding, for she in time will pass away and her offspring become the parent in turn. In the interest of the family fortunes, rules of conduct must always be open to revision, though it is inevitable that the transitional stages should reveal some trace of friction.

ADDITIONAL NOTE TO CHAPTER III

Note D, on my statement (p. 119) that *'the variety of possible things which the speaker may intend is always far greater than the variety of the expressional means contained in his vocabulary'*.

See Locke, *An Essay concerning Human Understanding*, Book III, chap. iii, sect. 2–4:

'2. *For every particular thing to have a name is impossible.*—First. It is impossible that every particular thing should have a distinct peculiar name. For the signification and use of words depending on that connexion which the mind makes between its ideas and the sounds it uses as signs of them, it is necessary, in the application of names to things, that the mind should have distinct ideas of the things, and retain also the particular name that belongs to every one, with its peculiar appropriation to that idea. But it is beyond the power of human capacity to frame and retain distinct ideas of all the particular things we meet with: every bird and beast men saw, every tree and plant that affected the senses, could not find a place in the most capacious understanding. If it be looked on as an instance of a prodigious memory, that some generals have been able to call every soldier in their army by his proper name, we may easily find a reason why men have never attempted to give names to each sheep in their flock, or crow that flies over their heads; much less to call every leaf of plants or grain of sand that came in their way by a peculiar name.

'3. *And useless.*—Secondly. If it were possible, it would yet be useless, because it would not serve to the chief end of language. Men would in vain heap up names of particular things, that would not serve them to communicate their thoughts. Men learn names, and use them in talk with others, only that they may be understood: which is then only done when, by use or consent, the sound I make by the organs of speech excites, in another man's mind who hears it, the idea I apply it to in mine when I speak it. This cannot be done by names applied to particular things, whereof I alone having the ideas in my mind, the names of them could not be significant or intelligible to another who was not acquainted with all those very particular things which had fallen under my notice.

'4. Thirdly. But yet granting this also feasible (which I think is not), yet a distinct name for every particular thing would not be of any great use for the improvement of knowledge: which, though founded in particular things, enlarges itself by general views; to which things reduced into sorts under general names, are properly subservient. These, with the names belonging to them, come within some compass, and do not multiply every moment beyond what either the mind can contain, or use requires. And therefore in these, men have for the most part stopped: but yet not so as to hinder themselves from distinguishing particular things by appropriated names, where convenience demands it. And therefore in their own species, which they have most to do with, and wherein they have often occasion to mention particular persons, they make use of proper names; and there distinct individuals have distinct denominations.'

PART II
THEORY OF THE SENTENCE

IV
THE SENTENCE AND ITS FORM

§ 50. **Function as the criterion of the sentence.** After the necessary excursion into the mutual relations of language and speech I return to the consideration of the sentence. This, as we saw in Chapter II, is the unit of speech, by which must be understood that sentences come into existence only through purposeful acts of human beings seeking, for different reasons of their own, to draw the attention of their fellow-men to various matters of interest. In my preliminary account the sentence was viewed from a dramatic standpoint, with speaker and listener as the actors, and a given situation as the scene. But at the same time it was pointed out (§ 28) that the philologist as such is concerned only with the products of speech, and that the intentions, motives, and other psychical occurrences in the speaker, as well as the attitude of the listener, are proper objects of philological analysis only in so far as the spoken (or written) sentence is inexplicable without them. It is, therefore, with the concrete sentence itself, a meaningful compound of articulated words, sounds, and gesture, that I shall henceforth deal. And the standpoint to be adopted, as I have previously noted (§ 28), is that of an observer in a position similar to that of the listener (or reader), but outside the actual situation of speech.

Regarded from this angle, the characteristic feature of the sentence, as opposed to mere unintelligible words, is its purposiveness, the satisfying sense which arises from it that the speaker has purposed or intended something (§ 30). Let us suppose that the words *reasonably that*, or *strength by lifting* catch my ear. To me they are no sentences, since I can imagine no reason why these words, taken in isolation, should ever have been spoken. A place in the domain of the sentence can be conceded to them only when it is realized that they formed part of the larger utterances *He spoke so reasonably that everyone was convinced* and *Show your strength by lifting this weight*. And even then they are but parts of sentences, the title of 'sentence' being reserved for those single words or combinations of words which, *taken as complete in themselves*, give satisfaction by shadowing forth the intelligible purpose of a speaker. It is only when, in a given situation, a word or words betray such a purpose, seem fired or galvanized by some reasonable communicative intent, that the dignity of sentence-rank can be conferred upon them. Such is the revolutionary view which has been steadily gaining ground of late. Psychologists like Bühler, as well as philologists like Wegener and Kretschmer,[1] are agreed that the sentence is a purposive structure, though opinions differ as to the way in which this, its essential nature, is to be interpreted or defined.

This view of the sentence is widely at variance with that practically universal half a century ago and still lingering on in many a school primer. According to the traditional view, which was a direct borrowing from formal logic, the sentence is simply a combination of words that can be analysed into subject and predicate; sentences like *Romulus built a wall* or *Paris is a beautiful city* were classified as such for no other reason. Thus, whereas modern theory makes purpose or intention the criterion, the old view regarded the sentence merely as a matter of outer form. For the grammarian this error had unpleasant consequences,

[1] See Additional Note E at the end of this chapter, below, p. 237.

though they did not exist for the logician. In teaching to parse, the schoolmaster found himself obliged to draw a distinction between 'main sentences' ('principal sentences') and 'subordinate sentences', though he could not fail to perceive that 'subordinate sentences', so called because they possessed a subject and predicate of their own, were in fact only parts of sentences. It was noted that these 'subordinate sentences' functioned as though they were single nouns, adjectives, or adverbs; they were, indeed, nothing but word-equivalents of a special outer form. To have smaller sentences serving as integral parts of larger sentences was naturally felt to be inconvenient, and English grammarians got over the difficulty by substituting the term 'clause' for 'sentence' whenever, within the body of a single sentence, it proved necessary to distinguish between the *main clause* and certain component *subordinate clauses* having a subject and predicate of their own.[1] Unfortunately, German grammarians have not yet realized the practical necessity of inventing a term similar to the English 'clause', so that *Hauptsatz* and *Nebensatz* still persist beside *Satz*, the name given to the whole of which they are merely parts.[2] In France a distinction is sometimes made between *phrase* (='sentence') and its component parts—the *proposition principale* and one or more *propositions subordonnées*; however, it cannot be denied that the name *proposition* in the sense of 'clause' is not particularly happy.

The recognition that a 'clause' is not the same thing as

---

[1] See *On the Terminology of Grammar, being the Report of the Joint Committee on Grammatical Terminology*, revised 1911, 5th impression, London, 1917, p. 14, Recommendation VIII, n. 2.

[2] The need for new terms in German is clearly recognized (e.g.) by Kalepky, *Neuaufbau*, pp. 16–17.

a 'sentence' ought to have led to the conclusion that the sentence cannot be merely a matter of outer form, but only a few theoreticians have taken this further step. In the present section I shall follow up this question of sentence-form, and shall show that the fallacy inherent in the old view was due to the failure to distinguish between language and speech, and can be laid bare as soon as that distinction is firmly grasped and utilized. The constant necessity of combining words for declarative or stating purposes would lead naturally to a particular outer form being adopted, and the outer form which has, in fact, everywhere been adopted may be represented by the formula 'subject + predicate'; I use this formula without reference to word-order, for some languages (e.g. Egyptian) normally place the subject after the predicate, if the latter is a verb. Thus there is such a thing as 'sentence-form', and like all other linguistic forms, it is a fact of language, not a fact of speech. To take an example, *he is well* has sentence-form; on its 'inner' side that of a statement, but evidenced outwardly by the presence of subject and predicate. If the words be considered apart from any context, they appear to state that some person referred to is in good health. More fully, they seem to embody the purpose of a speaker to convey the information that some one is in good health. They are clearly not a sentence by virtue of the outer sentence-form (subject 'he' + predicate 'is well'), but only become a sentence when, in a given situation of speech, they actually *do* embody the said desire or purpose. It is function, not form, which makes a set of words into a sentence. And this is proved by the fact that the same form of words can be used, with some slight degree of incongruence, in another way. For instance, in *I hope he is well* the words *he is well* are merely a noun clause pointing to the object of my hope, or as the grammarian says, serving as object of the verb *hope*; here *he is well* is not a sentence at all. Why? Because, though as a fact of language *he is well* seems destined to embody a speaker's declarative purpose, though indeed it is a statement in form, both outer and inner, yet in function, i.e. as a fact of speech, it embodies no such purpose, but serves simply as a noun bereft of any purpose of its own apart from that of the entire sentence *I hope he is well*.[1] Thus the distinction between language and speech, or what amounts to the same thing, the distinction between 'form' and 'function', proves to lie at the root of the distinction between 'sentence' and 'clause'.

§ 51. **General and special sentence-quality. The four kinds of sentence.** Let us take a few complete utterances: *I thought you were dining at home this evening. Has any one telephoned? Hush! How stupid! You have only to ask. It is a fine afternoon.* Every one has heard such utterances at one time or another, and when spoken they deserved the title of sentences because they both were, and were recognized to be, adequate expressions of a communicative purpose on the part of the speaker. As I have argued in § 30 (p. 97), the minimum qualification which makes a set of words pass muster as a sentence is that it is felt to be making a claim upon the attention of a listener in respect of the thing indicated by the words. The possession of this qualification might fitly be described as **general sentence-quality**. But it is not enough for a listener to be aware that the speaker has entertained the

---

[1] Ries discusses almost the same example (*I hope you are well*) in *Was ist Syntax?*, p. 33, together with its German equivalent, and rightly maintains, as against Kern, that *you are well* is a 'Nebensatz'. But he has not recognized the real reason. Nevertheless, his discussion is of interest from several points of view.

general purpose of communication; as a rule he wishes to know further details with regard to that purpose, so as to shape his receptive attitude accordingly. And equally from the speaker's point of view it is desirable that his listener should know precisely what aim or intention he had in mind. In fact, it is not enough for an utterance to have recognizable function as a sentence, as the vehicle of the general purpose to make a communication; it must somehow reveal or hint at the special purpose entertained by the speaker. We shall have to study later the different ways in which **special sentence-quality**, as it may be called, is indicated. For the moment we are concerned only with the fact that sentences are used for many different purposes, and with the inquiry as to which of these are of grammatical interest. In sum, we want to know what different kinds of sentence ought to be distinguished.

On a broad survey there might seem hardly any limit to the variety of purposes with which a sentence can be uttered. Sometimes a speaker makes an affirmation with intent to persuade, protest, or even deceive; sometimes he may give a description for his own amusement or for that of his audience; or again, he may speak merely for the sake of speaking. His sentences may be aspirations, prayers, promises, threats, judicial verdicts, sarcasms, witticisms, sneers, teasings, exhortations, complaints, flatteries, and much else. But although it would be interesting to know, if life were long enough, the various forms which these different types of sentence might assume in different languages, still neither the enumeration of them nor yet their further investigation is an urgent task for the theorist of speech. He would find the same form of words (e.g. *I shall certainly do so*) serving at different times under half a dozen or more different heads. The classification of sentences along the lines mentioned above is possibly the business of the student of Rhetoric or '*Stylistique*', to use a term that has become very fashionable on the Continent, but it is not the business of the grammarian. The grammarian and the theorist of speech are concerned only with the general principles governing the use of words. They have little to do with lexicographical matters, with the choice of words employed. They want to know the different kinds of sentence only from a formal point of view. Now if my argumentation be sound, every act of speech is the purposeful performance of a 'speaker' employing 'words' in order to draw the attention of a 'listener' to some 'thing'. Is it not clear, then, that our classification must turn on the greater or less degree of prominence accorded to some one of the three factors other than the words ? All speech assumes the presence of 'words', and in a sense the words are equally important whatever the kind of sentence. But the prominence of the speaker, the things spoken about, and the listener may vary greatly. Evidently we must make this variation the basis for our classification.

Few would dispute my contention that practical grammarians have, as a rule, accomplished their task with instinctive common sense and soundness of judgement, and that grammatical analysis has usually gone astray only when misled by erroneous theoretic considerations. Is it not good testimony to the validity of my own linguistic theory that the classification of sentences now almost unanimously accepted can be shown to follow the lines indicated in the last paragraph ? The *Report of the Joint Committee on Grammatical Terminology*[1] recommended

[1] Recommendation X, p. 15. (For full title of this pamphlet see above, p. 183, n. 1.)

that sentences should be divided into the following four classes: (*a*) *statements*, (*b*) *questions*, (*c*) *desires*, which are explained to include commands, requests, entreaties, and wishes, and (*d*), as a less important group, *exclamations*. A like division is found in the writings of many grammarians and theoreticians outside England. For instance, Sheffield[1] distinguishes between exclamative, imperative, assertive, and interrogative sentences, Bühler[2] between *Kundgabesätze* ('proclamatory sentences'), *Auslösungssätze* ('evocative sentences'), and *Darstellungssätze* ('descriptive' or 'depictive sentences'). The substitution advocated by Bühler of three for four classes has the approval of Kretschmer,[3] but only because he has realized that the two equally important groups of 'questions' and 'desires' belong together as subdivisions of the larger class called by him *Aufforderungssätze* or 'demands'. His trio presents simpler names than those proposed by Bühler, namely, (*a*) *Gefühlssätze* ('sentences of feeling'), (*b*) *Aufforderungssätze* ('demands'), and (*c*) *Aussagesätze* ('statements'). This appears to me a singularly neat arrangement, and fits in particularly well with my linguistic theory inasmuch as 'sentences of feeling' are those in which the part played by the speaker looms largest, 'demands' those in which successful achievement of the speaker's purpose depends upon an action to be performed by the listener, while 'statements' are more objective, lay no stress on speaker or listener, but concentrate their energies upon drawing attention to the thing or things spoken about. Still, as Kretschmer is well aware, we cannot refuse to distinguish

[1] *Grammar and Thinking*, New York, 1912, pp. 178 foll. This writer seems at times to approach my purposive view of the sentence without stating it definitely or clearly.   [2] *Theorien des Satzes*, pp. 16 foll.
[3] *Sprache*, pp. 61 foll., in Gercke and Norden, *Einleitung in die Altertumswissenschaft*, vol. i, part 6, Leipzig, 1923.

questions, i.e. those demands which call for information, from those other demands which call for an action, or it may be merely for some passive attitude that can be regarded as an action, e.g. *Stay!*, the more so since questions possess sentence-form of their own closely akin to that of statements. Thus, while retaining the triple division advocated by Bühler and Kretschmer, we must divide 'demands' into the two subclasses of (1) 'questions' and (2) 'requests'. I prefer the name 'requests' to the designation 'desires' favoured by the Committee on Grammatical Terminology, firstly because their term is somewhat colourless, and secondly because the common element *quest-* (from Latin *quaero*, 'demand') marks the kinship between the two subclasses. But the distinction between these is just as important as that between 'exclamations' (= *Gefühlssätze*) and 'statements' (= *Aussagesätze*), so that in practice we return to the quadruple classification recommended by the English Committee. This may be presented in diagrammatic form as follows:

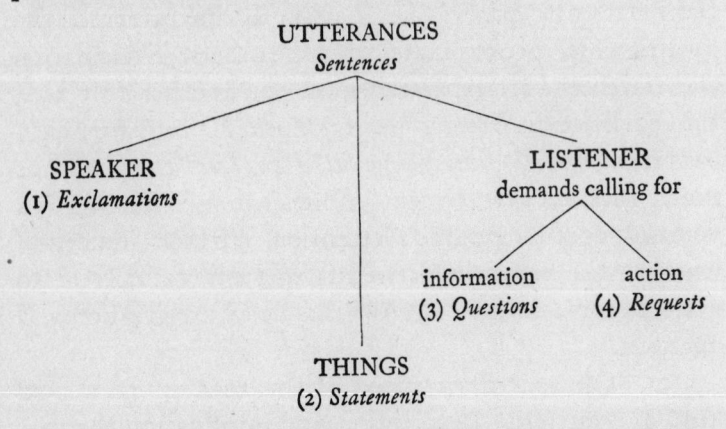

```
                        UTTERANCES
                         Sentences

      SPEAKER                         LISTENER
   (1) Exclamations              demands calling for

                              information        action
                            (3) Questions    (4) Requests
                        THINGS
                     (2) Statements
```

It is no contradiction of my analysis, but an argument strongly in its favour, that the four classes tend to merge into one another. For it is my contention that in all speech whatsoever, except in a few border-line cases like involuntary ejaculations (§ 21), all four factors of speaker, listener, words, and things are invariably interacting, so that any type of sentence cannot fail to possess, at least in rudimentary form, also the characteristics of the other types. A statement, for instance, is an exclamation to the extent that it never fails to voice the speaker's real or pretended sentiments, and a demand to the extent that it looks forward, with greater or less eagerness, to the listener's reaction, verbal or otherwise. I shall later deal with the four classes of sentence in some detail, and for the present will merely give examples to exhibit, on the one hand their real difference, and on the other hand their close relationship. A typical example of 'exclamations' is *Alas!*, of 'statements' *It is a rainy day*, of 'questions' *Have you seen my spectacles?* and of 'requests' *Give me another helping, please!* The following sentences, however, illustrate my point that the fourfold classification is only a classification *a potiori*, i.e. having as its principle the quality which predominates over the others. Exclamation and statement are separated from one another only by a thin partition in *How well he sings!* and *He sings very well.* Sentences like *You are going out, I suppose!* are almost as much question as statement. An exclamation like *Hi!* is a demand upon some one's attention, without indicating whether the person addressed is to reply verbally or to perform some action. *Really?* is at once exclamation and question.

§ 52. The specific purpose of the speaker as a new kind of overtone. Description and implication the two methods of speech. If we now take an arbitrary selection of sentences, e.g. *Did you give that poor beggar anything?*

I gave him a shilling. How kind of you! Give him a shilling yourself! we shall note that one and all convey some specific intention on the part of the speaker, but that this intention is never directly named. Of the sentences quoted, the first is a question, the second a statement, the third an exclamation, and the fourth a request; but they contain no explicit acknowledgement that they are of these several qualities. For example, *Did you give that poor beggar anything?* is a question, but does not state that it is a question. Nor is this observation contradicted when the same sentences are prefaced by further words describing their quality;[1] for *I ask you, did you give that poor beggar anything?* is at least primarily two sentences, of which the first does not tell us that it states, nor the latter that it asks a question. And again, if we transform the second half of this pair of sentences into an indirect question, viz. *I want to know whether you gave that poor beggar anything,* we now have a statement about a wish concerning a question, but no statement that this statement is a statement. It is true that such additions do indicate descriptively the manner in which the speaker has intended his sentence; but with them comes a new importation of sentence-quality, the nature of which is not declared. Thus the attempt to assert the quality of a sentence within that sentence itself does but involve us in an infinite regress.

Now in connexion with word-form (§ 41) we learnt that individual words may possess, in addition to the direct reference to things given by their stem-meaning, a sort of subsidiary meaning which is best compared to the overtone of a musical note. Thus the word *boy*, a noun, carries with it a feeling that the thing signified by it is substantival, is

[1] For these see below, p. 226.

to be taken as a thing. In just the same way, sentence-quality may be compared to a kind of overtone or harmonic spread over the whole of the sentence taken as a unity, and not necessarily or permanently attaching to the constituent words. Or to employ a different image, the purpose inherent in a sentence is like a thread running through a chain of beads, a means of binding them together and yet no part of them.

But is sentence-quality really as distinct from the direct signification of the words of a sentence as the above account seeks to make out, and if so, what is the explanation? It must be acknowledged that in many sentences the speaker's purpose is so entangled with the thing denoted by the words that the two cannot but appear as continuous and inextricable. For example, in *Please, pass the jam!* the thing-meant loses its very core and heart if the notion of a request on the part of the speaker be amputated from it. Equally so with the question *Have you seen my cousin?* and perhaps even more with exclamations like *Bother!* or like the salutation *Good morning!* But there are other sentences—and they are extremely frequent—where the sentence-quality is felt as lying, so to speak, in an utterly different dimension from the actual drift of the sentence. Thus in *He must have known that his speculations were bound to end badly* we receive the impression of a speaker asserting something with warmth and energy, but this something, the knowledge possessed by a person perhaps many thousands of miles away, lies in a totally different situation from the assertion of that knowledge. The term 'situation' which I have just employed will, on reflection, be found to provide the key to the linguistic mystery which we are seeking to run to earth. **Sentence-quality,** *that character of a sentence which reveals the speaker's*

§ 52   SENTENCE-QUALITY   193

specific purpose, is indeed nothing more than the linguistic indication of the particular relations of the four factors of speech constituting *the present situation* of the utterance, as the listener must deduce those relations to have been intended by the speaker. The matter referred to may be worlds apart from the speaker who is referring to it, worlds apart also from the listener to whom the speaker addresses himself, but a dim consciousness of those present factors arises out of the sentence, however remote the topic may be. In maintaining that sentence-quality is always perceived out of a present situation of speech underlying the sentence I must explain that I do not mean an absolute present, but rather the kind of present which may be mentally imaged as a bridge connecting the speaker with his listener. Thus when I am studying Virgil the present situation of his verses is that which somehow links the poet, as he was when he lived and wrote, with me his twentieth-century reader.

A picture will perhaps explain my conception of sentence-quality more comprehensibly than words can do. In this picture (Fig. 7) I have attempted to illustrate the thing meant by *He must have known that his speculations were bound to end badly*. In the situation which I have in mind a man is talking with his wife about a nephew of hers in Australia. The parties are aware that a discussion between them is in progress, so that the picture necessarily displays both husband and wife with some degree of distinctness. There is no great consciousness of the words spoken, and they are but barely discerned issuing from the speaker's lips. The thing spoken about, on the other hand, is indicated a good deal more boldly than the situation of speech (A), and it is in an entirely different region (B) far removed from that situation. We see the nephew in

Australia contemplating an imaginary scene of closed shops, these divided from him by a certain lapse of time, even as he himself is separated from his aunt and uncle both temporally and spatially; see Situation c in the figure.

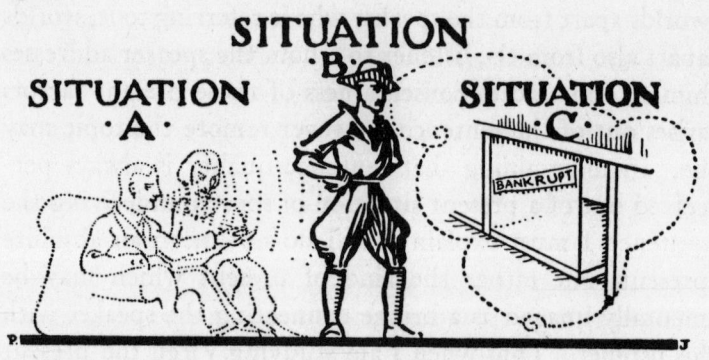

FIG. 7. To illustrate the sentence *He must have known that his speculations were bound to end badly*

To return now to the starting-point of this section, we saw that the specific quality of a sentence cannot be directly affirmed by the constituent words, but emerges from it as a sort of overtone. It is evident that the outer form of the sentence is at least in some degree responsible for the overtone which sounds in the listener's ears, and much of the remainder of this chapter will be devoted to investigating the various devices which language has called to its aid in the constitution of this outer sentence-form. But a number of preliminaries will have to be settled before starting on that lengthy undertaking, and to these it may be a useful prelude to indicate my opinion in a controversy which has recently arisen between two writers on the theory of the sentence, both of whom accept the view that this is a 'purposive structure' (*Zweckgebilde*).

Bühler maintains that the nature of the sentence cannot rest upon 'depiction' or 'delineation' (*Darstellung*) alone, although the part which that activity plays in speech is overwhelmingly important. Dempe takes the opposite view.[1] It is hardly possible for an Englishman to participate in a controversy conducted on exactly these lines, since for him neither 'depiction' nor 'delineation' is a term suitable in reference to speech, and to render *Darstellung* by 'description' (in German *Beschreibung*) seems hardly justifiable. Consequently, the only course open to him is to change the issue, so as to make it debatable within the framework of English idiom. Here I shall follow up the problem with an eye more to my own linguistic theory than to the way in which it has been set by the two German scholars. In my first two chapters I showed that the essential method of speech consisted in presenting to the listener successive word-signs each possessing a definite area of meaning. Employing these clues, the listener reconstructs the thing-meant by an effort of his intelligence, using the situation as an additional source of inference. The method thus summarized corresponds closely to the idea suggested by the term **description**, with which my own feeling, at all events, associates notions both of deliberate effort and of gradual approximation. But in the third chapter a new method employed by speech began to appear on the horizon. Words and sentences not only have immediate reference, resulting from intentionally directed meaning, but they also have 'form', a method of conveying knowledge by a sort of overtone, less well characterized by the term 'description' than by the term **implication**. Speech achieves its ends partly by describing, partly by

[1] The argument forms the main subject of Dempe's book, *Was ist Sprache?* where the references to Bühler's various articles will be found.

implying. The former method is the more direct and the more intentional; it instructs the listener as regards the kind of thing he has to attend to. 'Implication' is more subtle, and works less consciously. For example, the form of an interrogative sentence intimates that the speaker has intended a question, and if the situation warrants it, the listener draws that very conclusion without being aware that he has done so. Previous experience of similar form mediates the conclusion, and the listener reacts to it without directly attending to the fact, much as we react involuntarily to a person's looks or general bearing. The speaker himself 'implies' without clear knowledge of what he is doing.[1] At all events, the element of intellectual effort is far less marked in 'implication' than in 'description'. Apart from these two, so far as I can see, speech employs no other method.

§ 53. **Sentence-quality, sentence-function, and sentence-form.** In the preceding argument use has been made of the three technical terms which serve as heading to the present section, and it is high time that we should examine their precise signification. All three are attributes of uttered words, and describe what they are, what they do, and what they appear likely to do respectively. In order to elucidate these attributes and to explain their relations to one another, it might have been profitable to give a diagram similar to that in which I attempted to exhibit the application of words (Fig. 6, p. 151); but since it would have been difficult to escape depicting the speaker and listener, as well as the utterance and the thing meant

---

[1] 'Implication' appears to me the last clear analogy left in speech to the animal's automatic cry of pain. But in such psychological questions I am out of my depth. Dempe's distinction between the spontaneous cry *Ow!* and the interjectional *Ow!* of language is here of interest; see the discussion in *Was ist Sprache?* p. 59; also below, § 75.

thereby, I have shrunk from the complexity involved, and shall attempt to make myself comprehensible without a diagram. The attributes of the sentence being, however, completely parallel to those of the word, I would request the reader to keep in view the Figure afore-mentioned. With the help of this, it ought not to be difficult to gain a clear conception of the distinctions in question.

All speech has as its task to call attention to something wearing an aspect chosen and intended by the speaker, and these three attributes of an utterance which refer to it as a sentence are all connected with the attitude intended by the speaker to be adopted by the listener towards the thing designated by the words. Since this attitude to be adopted by the listener lies outside the sentence itself, it corresponds to what in Fig. 6 is represented as the formal character (Fc) of the thing-meant. For example, in the sentence *Come!* the attitude which the speaker means the listener to adopt is the factual performance of the action designated by the word *come*. But the best way of describing this attitude is in terms of the manner of utterance employed by the speaker in order to bring it about; the speaker is said to request, question, state, or exclaim. Correspondingly, the utterance itself is called a request, question, statement, or exclamation, and these descriptions constitute its **special sentence-quality** (§ 51). It will now be apparent why I defined special sentence-quality as 'that character of a sentence which reveals the speaker's specific purpose'. Here the word 'reveals' assumes that the listener has been successful in detecting the special sentence-quality of the sentence; if the listener has detected that quality, the speaker's purpose is *ipso facto* revealed to him. Clearly special sentence-quality corresponds, in the domain of the sentence, to what I called 'functional capacity' in connexion with the word (F in Fig. 6). **Sentence-function** now comes into view. This is *the work which a given sentence does in the capacity indicated by its special sentence-quality*. A given sentence functions as a statement, as a request, as a question, or as an exclamation. Had a diagram been made for the sentence as it was for the word, the sentence-function would have been indicated by dotted lines (see Fig. 6) connecting the spoken words with the thing they designate, and then, after running through it, connecting this again with the listener.

Now the speaker may have had the best of intentions, but the listener may nevertheless fail to understand what was meant. In that event the sentence does not function, and its special quality has been in vain. The act of speech desiderates an intelligent act of understanding as its counterpart, and this, however much mechanized, is always a deduction from both the words and the situation. Wegener[1] employs a very simple example to illustrate his contention that sentence-quality is always ascertained by a deduction on the part of the listener. A child is heard exclaiming *Butterbrot!* in a whimpering manner. But since bread and butter are not normally a cause of sorrow, and since the child's tone of voice recalls the tone of other exclamations uttered when something was wanted, we conclude that he desires some bread and butter. The sentence expressed by the word *Butterbrot!* has, accordingly, the special sentence-quality (§ 51) of an exclamatory request. Even without the whimpering tone the same conclusion might have been reached, if indicated by the entire situation. I will elaborate Wegener's argument by a further example. Suppose the child had given utterance

[1] *Grundfragen*, pp. 16, 68, 70.

to the name of a dog instead of exclaiming *Butterbrot!* our conclusion would have been different; we might now infer that the dog had snapped at or otherwise annoyed the child. In this case the sentence would be an exclamatory statement. Thus the total situation, including the nature of the thing referred to by the words, must always be taken into account in determining sentence-quality, and the listener's interpretation is always a matter of reasoning. But through constant practice in speaking and listening to speech, the drawing of the right inference has become as nearly automatic as possible, and the listener is seldom aware that he has been engaged in any such logical process.

On occasion an intelligent listener might be able to deduce the special quality of a sentence without the guidance of **sentence-form**. But it is doubtful if such cases actually occur. Even in a whispered exclamation like *Thieves!* the brevity is significant and the startled manner would suggest an exclamatory statement. Be this as it may, sentence-form is indisputably the main device by which speakers ensure the right acceptance of their utterances. All sentence-form has developed out of single utterances in the same way as word-form, to which it is parallel in almost all respects. Once constituted, it arouses the expectation that future utterances of similar form will have the same sentence-quality. As in 'word-form', the element 'form' in the compound 'sentence-form' must be taken as referring primarily to meaning, for we cannot do otherwise than regard special sentence-quality as a kind of meaning. It is proved by *boy* (a noun), *great* (an adjective), *give* (present indicative of a verb) that single words may possess 'form' without any outer mark to show it (§ 41). This is hardly possible with sentences except in so far as single uninflected words like *alas* and *fie* have inherent sentence-form. Such exceptional instances at least reinforce my point that 'form', whether of single words or of whole sentences, has reference primarily to meaning and only secondarily to outer appearance. Outer sentence-form differs from outer word-form in being usually disembodied. Concrete illustration will best explain my thought. The sentence *Did you go to church yesterday?* exemplifies a familiar type of question-form, of which *Have you been to Rome?* and *Am I ever going to see you again?* provide other instances. But we do not carry about in our minds a stock-example of this outer form of question, as is proved by the hesitation which might be experienced in choosing one. So far as it depends upon words at all, outer sentence-form exists in the mind as a certain aptitude for putting the right words together in the right way so as to yield the appearance appropriate, as the case may be, to a statement, an exclamation, a request, or a question. For the purposes of grammatical teaching, we can exteriorize this aptitude or knowledge in two different ways: either by using a formula, as when we say that French questions for corroboration usually take the form verb+pronominal subject with or without further addition; or else by choosing illustrative examples such as *Vient-il? Iras-tu? Jacques est-il malade?*

§ 54. **Locutional and elocutional sentence-form. Intonation.** In this chapter the only kind of sentence-form thus far explicitly named is that which is characterized by the employment of particular words (e.g. *fie*) or by the arrangement of its words in a particular way (e.g. *he is well*). The term 'verbal' is ill-adapted to designate sentence-form of this type, since it has the ambiguity of meaning both 'connected with words' and 'connected with verbs'.

Some name must be found, however, as there exists a second type of sentence-form which has in previous chapters been described as 'intonational' (e.g. § 45). A good contrast will be obtained if we adopt **locutional sentence-form** for the variety which depends solely upon words, and **elocutional sentence-form** for that which depends principally on intonation. As we shall see, the two are quite distinct, and may even contradict one another within the limits of a single utterance.

Under the rubric of 'elocutional sentence-form' must be included all those variations of pitch, rhythm, and stress which differentiate one class of sentence from another; also, in case they should some day be scientifically studied, those peculiarities of manual gesture or facial expression which are characteristic of particular types of sentence. For the present, however, 'elocution' in the technical sense here proposed must be equated with 'intonation', the term usually employed. Many German writers prefer the more picturesque name 'sentence-melody' (*Satzmelodie*). The first thing to point out in connexion with 'intonation' is its essentially formal character. By this I mean that it falls into different types due to similar repetition in similar conditions. For example, ordinary affirmative statement in English has its own appointed mode of intonation. If that intonation be heard without hearing the words, the conclusion is at once drawn that the speaker is affirming something.

I can lay no claim to expert knowledge of this now much-studied subject, so that the following observations may seem amateurish to those better informed. The attempt must be made, however, to assign to intonation something like its true place in linguistic theory.[1] Let it

---

[1] For further details see H. E. Palmer, *English Intonation*, 2nd edition, Cambridge, 1924.

be noted that not only sentences, but individual words as well, possess their own elocutional form. For example, the various syllables of the word *comfortable* have certain relations of stress and quantity which vary little from context to context. But over and above the elocutional form attaching to words there exist differentiated schemes of sentence-intonation (mainly variations of pitch) which do not adhere to the component words of a sentence permanently, but are spread over the whole arbitrarily and as something extraneous, like butter upon bread. Intonation-form of this kind is, indeed, the principal means of indicating special sentence-quality. The different types of sentence-intonation in any language are, of course, infinitely more numerous and more closely specialized than the four classes of sentence which we have elected to distinguish. Beside showing the relation of the speaker to the listener or to the things spoken about, intonation brings to light all manner of emotional attitudes, irony, pathos, argumentativeness, menace, and so forth. While the words themselves are openly proclaiming the nature of the things involved in the complex 'state of things' indicated by the sentence, differences of pitch, stress and tempo are simultaneously infusing into the listener, by the subtler method of 'implication' (p. 195), all kinds of knowledge with regard to the speaker's purpose. Thence the listener learns how he is intended to demean himself, without having his attention lured away from the matter in hand. Intonation is less heard than overheard, and members of a linguistic community are apt to resent the imputation that this weapon of speech plays with them too important a part. Thus the Finlanders maintain that the Swedes sing when they speak, and the Swedes make the same accusation against the Finlanders.[1]

[1] Wegener points out (*Grundfragen*, p. 72) that people are unconscious

§ 54   MANUAL GESTURE, ETC.   203

To turn to the auxiliaries of intonation already mentioned in passing, namely manual gesture, facial expression, and the like. It seems impossible to assign these various non-intellectual elements of speech to watertight compartments, each having its own sphere of semantic influence. Manual gesture is perhaps more adapted to giving spatial indications than to exhibiting emotion, but we are familiar with the movement of the hand which brushes aside an argument, and with that which reinforces a warning. If a specialized function could be assigned to facial expression, it would have to be the indication of a speaker's mood. No mention has yet been made of a particularly important use of intonation, or rather of its subspecies known as **stress**. This serves, not only to show how the words in any at all complicated sentence are grouped, but also to indicate the 'logical predicate', that most important element in any sentence. Pauses too belong to intonation and, as we shall see, play a vital part in separating sentence from sentence. Further accessories of speech are such occasional accompaniments of it as laughter, clicking of the tongue against the teeth, throat-clearings, and the like. All these may be purposely utilized to produce special rhetorical effects.

It is difficult to imagine a sentence completely devoid of elocutional form, whereas locutional form can easily be dispensed with. The moment has not arrived to deal with the numerous short sentences which are entirely formless from the locutional point of view, so I will pass them by and mention only a mode of speech which, paradoxical as it may seem, takes the further step of dispensing with

of their own habits of intonation, and quotes as evidence the peoples of Thüringen and Pomerania, each of whom accuses the other of singing in their speech.

words altogether. Questions may be answered with a nod or a shake of the head, and unpleasant subjects dismissed with a shrug of the shoulders. If these acts are not speech, I do not know where to place them; and it should be observed that the communicative means they employ are good elocutional form. There is, however, such a thing as eloquent silence, where words and gesture are alike absent. I am prepared to extend the term 'sentence' to a length which will scandalize old-fashioned grammarians, but here the line shall be drawn.

A fact of great interest is the decisive character of elocutional form. When locutional and elocutional form are in conflict, it is the latter which dictates how a sentence is to be taken. This may be illustrated by picturing a young man who has gone to his bank to draw money. At a word from the clerk, the manager advances to the counter and tells him that his account is overdrawn. If the young man then exclaims, *My account is overdrawn?* he employs the locutional form of a statement, and the elocutional form of a question. The manager will certainly construe the sentence as a question, and will probably answer, *Yes, I am afraid it is!* Suppose now the young man believed a large cheque to have been paid into his account on the previous day, he might conceivably say *Is my account overdrawn!* with the locutional form of a question and the intonation of an exclamatory statement. This would be exceedingly ill-bred, but might nevertheless happen. The sentence would then have to be taken as the equivalent of a denial. The bank-manager might indeed respond to the locutional form professed by the words and might answer as before, but this does not alter the fact that the young man's implication was, *If you will look again, you will see that my account is* NOT *overdrawn!*

This example shows that elocutional form provides the dominant clue to the special quality of a sentence. In short, *elocutional form always functions congruently.*[1] The reason doubtless is that intonation is much closer akin to natural reaction than is a spoken sentence. A speaker cannot disguise his tone of voice so easily as he can dissimulate with words. Nevertheless, intonation is to a large extent a matter of convention. This is proved by the fact that French and English intonation differs immensely, while among members of the same country and race there is a similarity of intonation often amounting nearly to identity. To elicit how elocutional form has developed in any particular case would be exceedingly difficult, in all probability impossible. But we may be sure that particular attitudes on the part of speakers tend, on repetition, to carry with them the same tone and rhythm. Wherever opportunity of judging occurs, linguistic form is found to have originated in single acts of speech. Elocutional form is unlikely to be an exception.

§ 55. **Utterance the principal quantitative criterion of the sentence.** Just as the choice of a particular type of intonation is decisive for the class to which a sentence should be assigned, so too the bare fact of utterance is, under ordinary conditions, decisive for the presence of a sentence. When an utterance is heard, but the words are not caught, it is always assumed that a sentence has been spoken. A companion is not held to be officious if he

---

[1] It must be noted, however, that when locutional and elocutional sentence-form disagree, there is often some slight modification of the latter in the direction of the former. Thus *Is my account overdrawn!* starts almost like a question, though it clearly ends like a statement. Another reason for the congruence of elocutional form is the multitude of its varieties, making it possible to find the right intonation for every shade of rhetorical effect.

replies *I beg your pardon?* or *What did you say?* Indeed, it may be regarded as very doubtful whether utterance of words can occur without a sentence being spoken. My definition (p. 98) demands that a sentence should reveal an intelligible purpose. The purpose may be extremely tenuous, and there are all manner of border-line cases which it would be tedious to discuss at length. It may, however, be useful to cast a rapid glance at some. The listener need not be a living person, but a dog or a cat; a child may address a doll, and a poet apostrophize nature. Under the term 'utterance' writing must be included; authors address an unknown public, and a diarist may speak to his future self. Even in soliloquy utterance is not bereft of purpose. I have already met the objection that speech is often too mechanical to be called purposeful (p. 147). Consciously intentional utterance, at all events, cannot take place without a sentence being spoken. This may be tested, though perhaps not finally demonstrated, by experiment. Let us try to speak some word or phrase without uttering a sentence. The reader may suggest *house of* or *to the*. But either of these is an implicit statement: '*house of* (or *to the*) [is a phrase which I can utter without uttering a sentence]'. The statement is false, but it is a statement; and being a statement, it is also a sentence.

It is not my contention, of course, that every part of an utterance is a sentence, but only that every finished utterance is a sentence. And here it has to be admitted that a sentence can be incomplete. An example has been quoted already; if James Hawkins had changed his mind, and had stopped short after saying *Look at the* . . ., this would have been an incomplete sentence (§ 30). Aposiopesis[1] is a totally different phenomenon, and has great

---

[1] Jespersen (*Language*, p. 251) points out that particular phrases used in

rhetorical effectiveness. The menace of Neptune in Virgil's *Quos ego——!* leaves to the imagination the awfulness of the punishment to be inflicted on the aggressive winds. Aposiopesis can be combined with incompleteness, as when a person says *But——!* and, on second thoughts, decides that it is better not to formulate his objection. Here, however, the single word *but* has conveyed the information that the speaker had an objection. It is an implicit statement, and having fulfilled its author's intention to raise an objection, must be regarded as a complete sentence.

A pause after utterance is the mark of the finished sentence, and indeed there exists no more conclusive testimony that a sentence has come to an end. As a rule, spoken words are run together so closely that mere hearing will not reveal their division; hence those misconceptions which arise in childhood, and for which Jespersen quotes the instance of a child who asked her nurse why she always spoke of *new ralgia*, when it was such an old complaint of hers.[1] The division of a sentence into its component words is further impeded by the fact that these are often clipped. Though the end of every sentence is marked by a pause, not all pauses have this effect or intention. Shorter pauses are frequently used to show how the words of complicated sentences are grouped, and there are also unintentional pauses due to hesitation, failure to find the right word, and so forth. However, human beings have such great experience in speaking and listening that they can readily judge what pauses are to be interpreted as evidence of the speaker's desire to conclude a sentence. Turning now to

this way have become so stereotyped as to be real language-forms, e.g. *Well, I never! I must say!* Most curious of all is *I say!* with nothing following. [1] *Language*, p. 122.

the inner or semantic aspect of this 'outer general elocutional form' constituted by the alternation of utterance and pause, we see that it consists in the effort to divide up whatever has to be said into lengths which will suit the convenience of the parties concerned. Both the speaker's breathing and the listener's powers of interpretative digestion have to be taken into consideration. In written speech, the second of these is of little account, and the first of none, so that longer sentences are permissible there. Both in speaking and in writing it is found practical to split up every long communication into sections of greater or less length. Books are divided into volumes, chapters, paragraphs, and sentences, just as a walking expedition may involve several halts for meals, occasional rests by the roadside, as well as single paces. The separate dishes and mouthfuls belonging to a meal are another parallel. The smallest section or unit of speech is the sentence, marked outwardly by a pause of suitable duration, and inwardly by evincing a communicative purpose recognizable as such —perhaps not the entire purpose of the speaker, but precisely that amount or portion which he thinks fit to accomplish before giving himself and his listener a rest. Thus the sentence is governed by purpose alike in its qualitative and in its quantitative aspect; and if a quantitative definition of the sentence should be demanded, the following would perhaps prove acceptable: *A sentence is an utterance which makes just as long a communication as the speaker has intended to make before giving himself a rest.*

§ 56. **Sentences without locutional sentence-form.** In his recent book on the sentence,[1] John Ries takes to task those grammarians who have, as he asserts, extended the name of sentence to utterances which are not sentences at

[1] *Was ist ein Satz?* pp. 21 foll.

all. He admits the existence of a few cases where decision is difficult, but maintains as a general truth that everyone knows in practice what a sentence is, and can distinguish it from other linguistic phenomena unworthy of the name. The opinion that exclamatory utterances like *Rain! Yes! Alas! No smoking!* are sentences is anathema to him, and he accuses those who hold it, as I unhesitatingly do, of adding heterogeneous matter to that to be defined, and then serving up as the definition of the sentence a definition of what has been added. But such is not the true position. Ries appears to me to refuse the name of 'sentence' to the utterances in question for no better reason than that it has not been accorded to them in the past. I am reminded of a singing-master who sat near me at an early performance of Debussy's *Pelleas et Mélisande* and who, while evidently admiring the beauty of the work, complained bitterly that it was called an opera. Scientific terms cannot be cribbed and confined in this way. Ries himself points out how greatly appreciation of the true nature of the sentence has been impeded by too exclusive attention to 'statements'; 'questions' and 'requests' used barely to be considered sentences at all. I find myself in agreement with Ries at least as regards the method of investigation to be adopted. The first task is to discover the character possessed in common by those utterances which everybody recognizes as sentences, and not possessed by those to which the name is universally refused. This done, any further words or combinations of words possessing the said character must perforce be admitted as sentences.

Here, however, our agreement ends. Ries's own definition is complex and obscure,[1] though he cannot be denied

[1] See Additional Note E, below, pp. 238–9.

the merit of having realized the difference between speech and language, and of having declared the sentence to be the unit of speech. The criterion of purposiveness emphasized by myself is completely overlooked by him, though its presence in statements, requests, and questions leaps to the eye. In a few exclamations there might be a doubt, so close are they to spontaneous natural reaction. But in most exclamations purposiveness is evident, so that this character must be admitted to belong to all four classes of sentence in common. It is absent, on the contrary, from clauses and mere phrases, if taken by themselves without regard to the wholes of which they are parts. Accordingly, intelligible purpose is the real differentiating attribute of the sentence, and we have now to consider whether that attribute can be justifiably applied to the various categories of utterances described by Ries as doubtful.[1] In my judgement, it can be applied to one and all. What is more, there is hardly an example falling under these categories but may be allotted without hesitation to one or other of the four classes distinguished above in § 51.

Some of Ries's categories of doubt will be exemplified in later sections. Here I will deal only with various short utterances in which locutional sentence-form is indisputably lacking. Such are independent nouns like *Rain! Rain?* in the situation of § 26, answers like *Of course! Perhaps!*, requests like *Silence! Hands up!*, labels and notices like *Fragile! To let!*, titles of books like *Ivanhoe*, advertisements like *Bovril*. In all such examples the word or combination of words possesses in itself no sentence-form, and may be employed in lengthier contexts where it is only part of the sentence. But—and here I come to the point of real importance—if these words be pronounced aloud

[1] See the tabulation, *Was ist ein Satz?* p. 112.

in the way suggested by their employment as above indicated, they will all be found possessed of unmistakable elocutional form. Some are statements, namely *Rain! Of course! Perhaps! Fragile! To let! Ivanhoe* (= *This book is about Ivanhoe*), *Bovril* (= *This advertisement is about Bovril*). Two are requests, viz. *Silence! Hands up!* One is a question, viz. *Rain?* And all, by reason of their brevity, partake of a certain exclamatory quality not found in longer utterances. Ries lays great stress on outer form, and one is perplexed and baffled at his seeming inability to recognize it here where it is so patent. *Silence!* spoken as a command is a very different thing from *silence* as a word slumbering in the mind. Further, the *Silence!* spoken by a schoolmaster's stentorian voice is a far more compelling request than a timid young prefect's *Do please keep silence!* Ries would at once admit the latter as a sentence. Can he refuse to do the same with the former? If not, a home has undeniably been found for all those short and undistinguished utterances which he suffers to wander about unhoused like a legion of lost souls.

I append a number of additional examples chosen almost at random, and doubt whether a more minute classification would have any scientific utility. But thus much is certain. Every grammar ought to state unambiguously that, in theory at least, any word or combination of words may serve as a sentence, provided that it makes sense and, when pronounced, is fortified with the appropriate elocutional sentence-form.

EXCLAMATIONS: *Heavens! Dear me! Woe! Bother! I who believed in him!*

STATEMENTS: (1) spontaneous and exclamatory: *Murder! Glorious! Someone!* (= *Someone is coming!*). *Your* health! (= *I drink to your health!*). *The King's Arms* (= *This inn is named The King's Arms*). *Paradise Lost* (title of a poem).

(2) comments: *Nonsense! True! Quite so!*

(3) replies to questions: (*When are you leaving?*) *Tomorrow!* (*Will you take tea or coffee?*) *Tea, please!* (*Are you ready?*) *In a moment!*

(4) replies to requests: (*Come here!*) *No!* (*Give me your word!*) *If you really insist! At your service!*

QUESTIONS: (1) *Headache? Hungry? Why so sad?*

(2) comments or replies: *Yes? Really? Have you, indeed? At what o'clock?*

REQUESTS: *Hush! Careful! Quickly! As you were! Hats off! One more penny, please!*

Why is it that grammarians are so reluctant to accord the rank of sentence to utterances such as these? I believe the reason is that syntax still labours under the domination of formal logic, despite all efforts to free itself. I shall deal later (§ 58) with the claim that every sentence must possess both subject and predicate. Meanwhile let it be noted that some of the utterances above-quoted really betray a certain incongruence. Brevity is perfectly normal and congruent in replies to questions, titles of books, and so forth. But laconic statements like *Glorious! Someone!* and abbreviated questions like *Headache? Hungry?* leave the impression of being substitutes for fuller utterances. The one-word sentence, as we saw, belongs to the childhood of speech. Such incongruence as these sentences show must belong, accordingly, to the type briefly discussed in § 46 (pp. 163–4), where it has arisen through the displacement of an old mode of speech by one more modern. In polite conversation too great terseness is considered barely courteous. Locutionally longer form is socially good form.

§ 57. **Sentence-form in the main elocutional.** The lesson to be learnt from the last two sections is that in audible speech sentence-form is in the main dependent on intonation. No spoken sentence is without a particular elocutional form declaring its special sentence-quality, and it is to this source, rather than to the words themselves, that the grammarian must primarily look to find the outer character which distinguishes the sentence from the spoken word or phrase. The inconsistency and variety of locutional sentence-form have often been the subject of comment, and this peculiarity is certainly not due merely to the way in which the four classes of sentence shade into one another. The reason is, rather, that the proper task of words is to indicate as objectively as possible the things to which the speaker desires to direct the listener's attention, at the same time illumining their nature. The function of informing the listener how he is to take the words lies outside the special province of the latter, and being only of derivative importance, may be left to the less deliberate method of speech known as intonation. Nevertheless, the objective reference of sentences and the speaker's aim in speaking them are often so much entangled that they cannot be kept strictly apart. And so we find all kinds of implication concerning that aim creeping into verbal expression itself, thereby creating what I have termed 'locutional sentence-form'.[1]

Elocutional sentence-form is eliminated when audible

[1] Ries has seen clearly that no particular locutional criterion, such as the presence of a finite verb, is universal enough to constitute a *conditio sine quâ non* of the sentence. But he insists, in my opinion wrongly, that *some* locutional form must be present, and that without this there can be no sentence. See *Was ist ein Satz?* pp. 92 foll.

speech is converted into writing. There it finds an inadequate substitute in punctuation—the full stop, colon, and semi-colon for statements, the exclamation mark for exclamations and commands, the note of interrogation for questions. Minor groupings of words are marked by the comma. But even these imperfect elocutional instruments were absent from early writings, and the consistent employment of them, largely fostered by Aldus Manutius in the sixteenth century, is indeed quite a recent development. Nevertheless, Phoenician inscriptions make themselves understood in spite of the lack of word-division and sentence-division, though there the duties of the interpreter are far more arduous than elsewhere. This being so, the help rendered by locutional sentence-form must not be underrated, even though we recognize that, of the two, elocutional sentence-form is the more important.

§ 58. **The claim that every sentence must consist of subject and predicate.** It is clear that so well-established and passionately held a faith as that which asserts that every sentence 'consists of' or 'can be analysed into' subject and predicate cannot be wholly without foundation.[1] The topic demands fuller treatment than I can give it at this juncture, but it must obviously be placed in the foreground of any discussion of locutional sentence-form. Consequently I shall devote to it now just as much consideration as is required for my immediate purpose, reserving closer investigation for my next chapter. To begin with, it is not by any means clear what the assertions above alluded to are really trying to say. If they mean that the sentence must comprise separate words representing subject and predicate respectively, this contention fails in

[1] On this belief, not shared by Jespersen, see his book *Philosophy*, pp. 305–6.

sentences like Latin *Vixit* or French *Partons!* If it be answered that the predicate resides in the stems *vic-*, *part-*, and the subject in the ending *-it*, *-ons*, then not only would we appear to have been mistaken in considering *vixit* and *partons* as single words, but also we can now refute the contention by quoting *Dic!* ἄγε, *Komm!* as negative instances. These imperatives are devoid of inflexion expressing the second person,[1] so that we here have sentences containing a predicate but no subject. My grammarian now shifts his ground and argues that *Dic!* stands for *Dic tu!* But it is not legitimate, when defeated in an argument over something, to substitute something else claimed as an equivalent and to pretend that this proves the case. It is true that *Dic tu!* can be analysed into predicate *plus* subject, but the same is not true of *Dic!* so long as we are considering outer form only. The line is now taken that in every sentence subject and predicate are present in thought. This restatement of the thesis I believe to be true in fact, as we shall see hereafter. But the interpretation which would be put upon it by orthodox grammarians I hold to be quite wrong. They would maintain, I suppose, that in thought *Dic!* is to be dichotomized into *the words* 'thou' and 'say'. But in the first place such an analysis leaves out an essential feature in the thought underlying this one-word sentence, namely the command or desire of the speaker; in any case, therefore, the analysis into subject + predicate would be incomplete. The second objection I have to make is far more serious. The dichotomy to be assumed is not of words, but of things, and of these only one is referred to verbally. *Dic!* signifies that

[1] Philologists are agreed that singular imperatives (as also vocatives) in Indo-European languages present the bare stems without any inflexion. The same holds good in Semitic and Egyptian.

the person addressed is to perform the action indicated by *dicere*. Two things can be extracted from the utterance, but not two words.

Thus far I have discussed only such single-word sentences as every grammarian admits to be sentences. I hope to have shown that in some case or other of an undisputed sentence the analysis into subject + predicate distinguishes either too much or too little. I venture, therefore, to maintain that, though the great majority of sentences can and must be analysed into subject + predicate, nevertheless as against these, *Vixit, Partons! Dic!* and their congeners must all, on one ground or another, be excepted from that analysis. And since no grammarian will consent to *Vixit, Partons! Dic!* being deprived of sentence-quality, the analysability of utterances into subject + predicate cannot be made the touchstone of the sentence. Thus this criterion no longer affords any reason for refusing the name of sentence to utterances like *Yes! Alas!* and *Balbe!*

What, then, is the source of the almost universally held conviction that every genuine sentence must consist of subject and predicate? In my belief, this conviction springs from a dim consciousness possessed by every user of language that the act of speech involves the two factors, apart from speaker and listener, of a thing spoken about and of something said about it. In my own technical phraseology, speech involves both (1) words having a meaning and (2) a thing-meant. Or again, speech consists in using words to put meanings upon things standing outside speech. Now when speech is quite explicit, it presents to the listener something corresponding to each of the two factors in question. The subject-word places before the listener a thing to which he is to direct his attention, and the predicate-word tells him what he is to perceive or think about it. No sentence can do more,^m and there attaches to sentences with both subject-word and predicate-word a completeness and finality which are absent from sentences not thus equipped.

The greater satisfactoriness of sentences possessing words for both subject and predicate may be illustrated by an incident which sometimes occurs when a third person intervenes in a conversation. Someone may have said *Dreadfully ill, I am afraid!* and on hearing the new-comer's *What's that?* does not reply with his previous words, but substitutes *I was just saying, Sarah's dreadfully ill*. In this form the speaker's sentence leaves nothing to be desired. He proffers the information that he is saying or stating something, names the person whom it is about, and finally specifies what it is.

In highly developed speech, and particularly in speech of a literary description, the presence of subject and predicate is so frequent that some excuse can be made for those who have regarded them as characteristic of all sentences. But even had that belief proved true, the possession of subject and predicate would still have been no infallible test by which a sentence could be recognized as such. For as we saw in § 50, there are some mere parts of sentences which possess both subject and predicate. These are subordinate clauses, and such a clause is rightly defined as '*part of a sentence equivalent to a noun, adjective, or adverb, and having a subject and predicate of its own*'.[1] It is undeniable, moreover, that by virtue of this possession all subordinate clauses have sentence-form, whether that of a statement, e.g. *I hope* HE IS WELL, or that of a question, e.g. HAD HE ARRIVED EARLIER, *I should have invited him to*

[1] This is the definition recommended by the Joint Committee on Grammatical Terminology, see *On the Terminology of Grammar*, p. 13.

the concert. But if the possession of subject and predicate is an essential and differentiating attribute of subordinate clauses, the same is not true of sentences. Many sentences possess them, but many do not. This must be our final verdict.

§ 59. **The claim that every sentence must contain a finite verb.** Equally untenable is the claim of some grammarians that every sentence must contain a finite verb. In discussing this new claim I shall follow the procedure of the last section, first demonstrating that the contention is not true in fact, and then seeking to discover the partial truth which gives it a certain plausibility. It is easy to prove that there are some undisputed sentences which lack a finite verb. For that purpose it would be necessary to quote only the evidence adduced by Paul[1] and Ries,[2] quite candidly by the former, but by the latter very grudgingly and without full admission of its bearing on the theory of the sentence. Often cited examples of sentences with subject and predicate, but without finite verb, are the Homeric Οὐκ ἀγαθὸν πολυκοιρανίη and the Latin *Omnia praeclara rara.* Such sentences without copula are known as nominal sentences, and the theory has been affirmed, though equally emphatically contradicted, that in Indo-European they represent an earlier type than the corresponding sentences with copula. It is not for a stranger to Indo-European philology like myself to pronounce judgement in this controversy, but Ries seems to me to have done good service in pointing out that, so far as Greek and Latin are concerned, such sentences are restricted to proverbs and the like, and by no means constitute a normal and generally employed type. But whatever the facts as regards the Indo-European languages, I

[1] *Prinzipien,* p. 125.   [2] *Was ist ein Satz?* pp. 158 foll.

can aver with the utmost assurance that Old Egyptian dispensed with the copula in more than one common subclass of nominal or, as I prefer to call them, non-verbal sentences. Throughout the whole of the Old and Middle Egyptian periods sentences with a noun as predicative word regularly dispensed with the copula. In Old Egyptian 'His sister is Sothis' would be rendered by *santef Sapdet*, literally 'His sister Sothis', while Middle Egyptian develops a new form which admits of the inversion of subject and predicate thus, *Sapdet pu santef*, literally 'Sothis it, (namely) his sister'. Sentences with adjectival predicate are likewise without copula, e.g. *nāfr eḥras*, 'Beautiful her face', i.e. 'Her face is beautiful'. When the predicate is an adverb or adverb-equivalent, usage varied: *sash em paref*, 'Scribe in his house', is common enough, but appears to have been felt as more abrupt than *yew sash em paref*, 'Is scribe in his house' for English 'The scribe is in his house'. Similar evidence could be produced from Hebrew and Arabic, but I have preferred to quote from a province about which I can speak from long experience.

However, it is needless to look so far afield. The observation that sentences like Οὐκ ἀγαθὸν πολυκοιρανίη and *Omnia praeclara rara* are found only in a rather special case does not ban them from the ranks of true sentences. Indeed, even a single instance of a sentence without copula or other finite verb, however rare and specialized, would be sufficient to demolish the thesis that every sentence must possess a finite verb. And since the examples just quoted are accepted as sentences by everyone, Ries himself included, that thesis is actually demolished. Certainly it cannot be saved by maintaining that the copula is to be 'supplied' or 'understood'. Ries undermines any such defence by his admission that the absence of the copula confers a gnomic character. Since the speakers presumably intended that gnomic character to be recognized, it would seem to follow that they did not wish the copula to be understood. In point of fact, the omission of the copula or other finite verb lends a peculiarly pictorial quality to sentences, assimilating them to exclamations:

> *Twilight and evening star,*
> *And one clear call for me,—*

Ries collects much evidence of the kind, rightly distinguishing many of the types in question from the nominal sentence proper. Thus he quotes from English, French, and German such cases as *A wonderful man, your father! Inutile d'insister! Ein schöner Spass, das!* Or again: *Ars longa, vita brevis; Tel maître, tel valet; Least said, soonest mended.* But instead of admitting that these, as they stand without alteration, are sentences, Ries takes up the strange and arbitrary position that they are 'pre-grammatical, or better still extra-grammatical phrases'.[1] For my part, I wish for no more cogent evidence that sentences can exist without a finite verb, and that this criterion, therefore, cannot be employed to castigate those one-word or simple phrase sentences of which I have given a selection in § 56.

What is the foundation of the false belief that every sentence must contain a finite verb? Traditional logic is in part responsible, the sentence having been confounded with the proposition, of which the copula was deemed a

[1] 'Ich erkenne in ihnen vielmehr vorgrammatische oder besser aussergrammatische Fügungen, d. h. solche, die (noch) nicht zu einer vollkommenen grammatischen Formung gelangt sind', *Was ist ein Satz?* p. 181. But the mere fact that Ries is able to distinguish a large number of types among the verbless sentences so stigmatized is the clearest proof that they have attained full grammatical form. I fear that Ries, despite his protestations to the contrary (op. cit., pp. 95–7), is really under the influence of the old superstition that every sentence must contain a finite verb.

necessary constituent. But grammar could not for ever remain dependent upon a discipline which analyses *gives* as *is a giver* and *gave* as *is one-having-given*. I will not discuss further a standpoint now universally recognized to be obsolete, even though it may still linger on as an unacknowledged source of prejudice in the minds of some grammarians. But formal logic is by no means the only cause that the presence of a finite verb is considered essential to the sentence. Grammar has, in the past, paid exaggerated attention to written speech, and particularly to that of Greek and Latin authors. And among them, it is less the writers of comedy who have been taken as the models of correct parlance, than poets and forensic orators. But in the writings of these, exclamations are rare, so that the only class of sentence which regularly dispenses with finite verbs is well-nigh eliminated. We have still, however, to inquire why the three other classes so persistently demand their use. This seems due to the complementary facts that most speech is concerned with actual, imagined, or desired changes in things, and that the finite verb is precisely that type of word which has been evolved for such purposes. Thus most sentences would naturally possess a verb of this kind, and I shall show how the remainder, which described what things are or should be, ultimately followed their lead, and adopted the copula as the variety of finite verb exactly suited to their requirements.

Whatever may be thought of this attempt to account for the prevalence of finite verbs throughout speech generally, certain it is that all such verbs have a large element of inherent sentence-form. Indicatives profess to state, subjunctives do the same in a more tentative and petitory spirit, imperatives command. There can be no doubt that those words which present things as actions and which we call verbs have picked up this inherent sentence-form in the same way that nouns have acquired noun-form, adjectives adjective-form, and so forth. Constant employment in contexts where the speaker was stating, seeking concessions, or making demands is the source of the qualification of verbs known as **mood**. And out of this, together with the cognate qualification of **tense**—both to be discussed in my second volume—arises the copula, that peculiar phenomenon which in the modern languages of western Europe has become the concomitant of all non-exclamatory sentences not possessing any other finite verb.

Much abuse has been heaped upon this unique element of language, the name of which ought, it is said, to be banished altogether from the vocabulary of grammar. It is true that the copula has been misused by logicians, but that is no reason for placing a taboo upon so excellently named a species of word. For the 'copula' is, in fact, a sign that two things of which one, at least, must be explicitly referred to by a word or words, are to be 'linked' together in thought. These two things are presented by the copula as standing to one another in the relation of subject and attribute respectively; and the word or words indicating the thing to be regarded as the attribute are known as 'predicative' or, if the copula be taken with them, as the 'predicate'. But beside this function of indicating the relation of a subject and its attribute, the copula has the office of attracting a superior degree of attention to the latter, and also of instructing the listener as to the manner in which he is mentally to entertain this relation of attribution. If the indicative be employed, the listener is merely to accept the attribution, though the situation must show exactly the mode of acceptance intended. If the subjunctive be employed, the attribution is to be envisaged as a possibility, desired or otherwise. If the copula be in the imperative, the listener is to act in such a manner as himself to become the subject of the attribution. Thus the authority and responsibility of the speaker lie behind the use of the copula, which accordingly is an effective instrument for shadowing forth his purpose. In statement, of course, this function is latent and normally unobserved, since statements are the most objective examples of speech, having as their purpose to make the listener look at some 'state of things' so far as possible without attending to the person who refers to them. Hence the force of the copula is here apt to manifest itself as a sort of inherent cogency, the source of which lies in the actual matter in hand. But that this cogency is in fact no more than the *ipse dixit* of the speaker, or in the case of scientific formulae, of a consensus of authoritative speakers, comes to light in disputed or palpably false assertions like *Two and two are five*. The function of the copula as backing an utterance by the speaker's authority and purpose may be seen if we compare sets of words containing the copula with others omitting it. Let us take the exclamation *Lovely, that song!* pronounce it as much like a statement as possible, and compare it with *That song is lovely*. In the latter case the speaker definitely declares, or gives as his opinion, that the song is lovely, in the former case his exclamation of enthusiasm merely implies it. To be strictly accurate, *That song is lovely* itself only 'implies' the judgement of the speaker, for we have seen (§ 52, beginning) that no sentence can actually state its purpose, but conveys it only by the method of implication, as opposed to that of description. But it is no vain paradox to say that, as a statement, *That song is lovely* is explicit in its implication. Relatively, and as compared with *Lovely, that song!* the statement *That song is lovely* does declare the speaker's purpose to impose that view.

Similarly, *Be careful!* is more explicit than *Careful!* without the copula. But conveyance of the speaker's desires as to the listener's attitude is not the only service rendered by this peculiar verb. It serves also to convey notions of time, person, and number, without the necessity of modifying any of the other words in the sentence. One or more of these notions is shown by the outer inflexions of the copula, which has become in fact a purely instrumental word. Derived from various stems once having a definite descriptive force of their own,[1] the copula, when used as such, has dropped this force entirely, and now serves merely as a carrier of the subsidiary notions above specified. Vendryès has given an admirable account of the gradual penetration of the copula, and I will translate a short extract from it:[2] '... the introduction of the copula into the nominal sentence is easily explained. There is, indeed, one notion that the simple juxtaposition of subject and predicate is unable to express; this is the notion of time. A verb, inasmuch as this is the symbol of time, thus becomes necessary. To render "the sky was blue" the Hungarian is forced to say *az ég kék vala*, adding the imperfect of the substantive verb, which serves to mark the past, while at the same time playing the part of the copula. So too Homer employs the future εσται in το δε τοι ξεινήιον ἔσται.' Vendryes goes on to quote Homer's εἶς δέ τις ἀρχὸς ἀνὴρ βουλήφορος εστω as an example of the use of the

---

[1] English *be* comes from a stem meaning 'to grow'; Latin *fuit* is to be compared with Greek φύειν; French *etant* is derived from Latin *stantem*, 'standing'; and so forth.   [2] *Le langage*, p. 146.

copula to convey mood. All this agrees admirably with the evidence afforded by Old Egyptian. I have noted above (p. 219) how often the copula was there omitted when the time intended was the present. But as soon as future time had to be indicated, or any notion like that of a wish, use was made of a verb *ꜥwnon* which elsewhere signifies 'to exist'.[1] Similar testimony could be quoted from the Semitic tongues, and doubtless other languages are in the same case. However, Vendryes offers no explanation for the general employment of the copula in reference to present time, an employment which has become invariable in all modern languages of Western Europe. The true explanation seems to emerge from the argument in which I pointed to the superior objectivity of statements inserting *is* or *are*. We saw that the omission of the copula gives a more pictorial or exclamatory turn to statements. Conversely, its insertion marks their greater detachment. The propositions affirmed seem abstracted from speaker and listener, and stand forth as though they were independent of personal judgement or prejudice.

The copula is the only verb from which the stem-meaning has wholly faded out, enabling it to devote itself entirely to the functions indicated by its inflexions. But in *become* and *grow*, for example, this has occurred in part; upon somewhat similar lines, *do* serves to convey particularly urgent requests, e.g. *Do come!* while it performs more intricate functions in negative and interrogative sentences, e.g. *He did not come, When does he arrive?* To conclude this section, I will add that the finite verb does not stand quite alone as a class of words having acquired through their associations an element of special sentence-form. Interjections (e.g. *alas*, *fie*) have inherent exclamatory

[1] See my *Egyptian Grammar*, § 118, 2.

form, and so have vocatives in Latin (e.g. *Balbe*), though both, when employed, need the appropriate intonation of exclamations to give them that quality. Without such intonation they would be mere quoted items of English or Latin vocabulary.

§ 60. **Other words suggesting special sentence-form: Word-order.** Certain other sources of locutional sentence-form have not yet been named. There are many adverbs and adverbial phrases which have no other function than to indicate the degree of assurance with which statements are spoken, and which, consequently, are in themselves indications of statement-form; such are *perhaps, certainly, of course, no doubt*. *Please* is confined to requests, while *pray* is employed in both requests and questions. In Latin *num, nonne* and *-ne*, in Greek οὐκοῦν and μή are marks of questions, but also possess, like the interrogative pronouns, adjectives, and adverbs, more or less decided implications with regard to the answer expected (§ 73). *How* often prefaces an exclamation in English, like *que* in French, *wie* in German, and *·wy* as suffix of adjectival predicates in Old Egyptian. Closely related to these are the prefixed or affixed words with sentence-form which show the activities of speaker or listener in connexion with some particular sentence, e.g. *Spare me*, I PRAY; I TELL YOU, *I will do no such thing; Nothing*, I ASSURE YOU, *was further from my thoughts*. These additions are sentences functioning incongruently as sentence-qualifiers, and are pronounced in such close conjunction with the utterances to which they refer, that they must be regarded as part of the same sentence. Note in this connexion that *pray* and *prithee* are shortenings of *I pray* and *I pray thee*.

Word-order is another mark of special sentence-form. Here the best-known instance is the inversion of subject and verb employed by many modern languages to indicate a question, e.g. *Have you heard? Whom did you see? Viendra-t-il? Pourquoi fais-tu cela? Ist es gut? Wieviel kostet das?* (see below, § 73). Similarly, the position of the adjective in front of its noun in Old Egyptian shows that it is to be taken as a predicate, not as an epithet, e.g. *nāfr eḥras* 'beautiful (is) her face'. This is clearly a development of the exclamatory word-order seen in *Lovely, that song! Beau, ce spectacle! Schön, ihre Stimme!*

§ 61. **Locutional sentence-form in incongruent function.** Having reviewed the various ways in which words have become adapted, through repeated use, to indicate special sentence-quality, I shall go on to show that the locutional sentence-form thus created can be used in incongruent function, unlike its elocutional counterpart. In other terms, the struggle between speech and language, studied in the last chapter in connexion with word-form, is about to be seen re-enacted in connexion with the sentence. Here there are two possibilities, which are best exhibited by means of an example. The words *he is well* have not only sentence-form, but also the particular sentence-form of a statement. When incongruently used, they may serve either (1) not as a sentence at all, or (2) as a sentence, but one of a kind other than a statement.

(1) We saw in § 50 that a set of words having the form of a sentence, but not imbued with the vivifying purposiveness needed to make it into a real sentence, may do the work of a mere word, and is then called a 'subordinate clause'. The example I quoted was *he is well* in *I hope he is well*, where the words *he is well* function, in ordinary grammatical parlance, as a noun-clause object of the verb *hope*. The speaker here makes no affirmation that the person in question is well, but uses *he is well* merely as the

name of the thing he is hoping. Consequently, these words no longer exercise the function which their form might have led us to expect, and to that extent their employment is incongruent. But since nothing unnatural is felt about this use, the degree of incongruence is very slight. Noun-clauses of this type are common, e.g. *I believe* HE WENT, *I think* HE SAID SO, *I fear* THE BOAT WILL BE LATE, *It was proved* HE WAS NOT GUILTY. It would, therefore, be quite correct to regard *he is well* in *I hope he is well* as exhibiting the form of a noun-clause used in congruent function. Regarded as having sentence-form, *he is well* is here incongruent; regarded as having the form of a noun-clause, it is congruent. Thus we have an originally incongruent use of words that by force of continual repetition has grown into a new form—the form of a noun-clause—betraying its origin from statement-form and carrying with it a tinge of incongruence only because the use of the same form of words as a statement is even more typical of it, even more central in our feeling. It is probable, if not certain, that the use as a sentence is more frequent than the use as a noun-clause, but statistics being in the nature of the case impossible, we are thrown back on history and linguistic feeling for our verdict of incongruence. As a matter of history there can be no doubt that the use as a noun-clause is derived from the use as a statement, and not vice versa. The proper course for the writer of a grammar to pursue, in face of such a phenomenon, is to make a double entry in his Syntax. Under the heading of statements he will merely note that the form of a statement can be used as a noun-clause, and in the section devoted to noun-clauses he will deal with the fact in detail.

In a grammar of modern English it would be wrong to accord a similar treatment to those clauses of condition which, in the opinion of most scholars,[1] originated in questions. For in a sentence like HAD HE DONE SO, *I should have been sorry*, both the outer form of the protasis and the time implied in it, show that it has completely lost touch with the interrogative form from which it probably sprang. As a fact of present-day colloquial English the use of a question in place of a protasis is incongruent in the last degree, though one might just conceivably hear ARE YOU PLEASED, *then I'm pleased too*, with question and consequence run so closely together, and an answer so little expected, that *are you pleased* would have to be taken as the equivalent of *if you are pleased*. Accordingly, mention of the supposed origin from questions of clauses like *had he done so* should be left to historical or genetic grammars, and should have no place in a descriptive Modern English Syntax.

A much less incongruent English use is that of requests in the sense of a protasis, as in *Laugh and the world laughs with you*. Here *laugh* has the form of a request, but functions as a clause of condition. The writer did not really ask her readers to laugh, but suggested that if they did so, they would not lack company. That the form is still strongly felt as a command is shown by the *and* introducing the apodosis. Since the latter is presented as a co-ordinated statement, it seems necessary also to take *laugh* as a sentence in its own right. Were I compiling a comprehensive work on English syntax, I should place this example under the heading of 'Requests' rather than that of 'Clauses of Condition', though I should point out that

---

[1] e.g. Jespersen, *Philosophy*, p. 305. In Middle Egyptian, questions for corroboration introduced by *ỉn ỉw*, 'is it (the case that)?' are sometimes employed as clauses of condition, and it is possible, though far from certain, that Coptic has extended this use to unfulfilled conditions.

the sense approximated to that of a protasis; and I should give a cross-reference under the latter head.

I have dealt with these examples more fully than I otherwise should have done, because it is important to emphasize the fact that incongruence can have very many degrees. But on this topic more will be said before the present section is brought to a close.

(2) A sentence having the form of one class may function incongruently as though it belonged to another. In considering this, we must remember that, if my theory be true, every sentence presents the rudiments of all four classes, so that the classification into exclamations, statements, questions, and requests is only a classification *a potiori* (§ 51, end). Here it will be shown that sentences the locutional form of which *clearly* assigns them to one specific class may nevertheless *clearly* function as though they belonged to another. In dealing with the dominating importance of elocutional sentence-form I have already had occasion to quote two examples of locutional sentence-form functioning incongruently; these were the apparent statement *My account is overdrawn?* serving as a question, and the apparent question *Is my account overdrawn!* serving as a statement (p. 204). Both examples belong to well-established types, and their incongruence has a peculiar rhetorical motive and effect in either case. Another instance similar to the first of these two would be *He is well?* Here the speaker does not just perversely use the form of a statement, when he ought to be using that of a question. His device is subtle: he is anxious for true information, and somewhat incredulous; accordingly, he echoes the words of the previous speaker with a tone of doubt in his voice, knowing that his hint of disbelief is bound to evoke a speedy answer. Just as *boy*

in *the boy king* did not lose all its force as a noun, when used as an adjective, so too here both statement and question emerge from the sentence unmistakably. This is incongruent function of the most live and characteristic kind.

In other examples which I shall quote, new locutional sentence-form has already come into being, so that incongruence is on the wane, and indeed in some cases is no longer felt. So well accustomed are we to recognize *Thou shalt not steal!* as a command, that it is none too easy to realize that the actual form employed is that of a statement. The grammarian will naturally classify this under the rubric of 'Requests', though in that case he should explain matters by saying: 'The form of the statement may serve to indicate commands when the verb *shall* is employed. Similarly with the verb *must*, e.g. *You must turn to the left at the post office*.' Much more incongruent are orders in statement-form such as might be addressed to a child, e.g. *You are coming home this very instant!* Here we feel both the injunction and the assertion of the parent's determination to see it fulfilled. Requests in question-form like *Will you pass the salt, please?* or *Would you mind passing the salt?* still sometimes evoke the answer *Certainly!* or *With pleasure!* accompanying the performance of the act. A rhetorical question like *Who cares?* functions as a statement, but the statement-sense *I don't care* is thrown in the shade by the defiant appeal to all and sundry; the sentence has less incongruence as a question than it has when interpreted as a statement. This balance of congruence in favour of the question-form is still more apparent in *Have you lost something?* addressed to a person fidgeting about the room. This is in effect equivalent to the request *Do hurry up and go!*

The last example is one used by Ries[1] to show the absurdity of paying exclusive attention to meaning at the expense of form. Much as I disagree with this scholar in many of his conclusions, in the present issue I think him altogether in the right. Such an irritable question is too much the outcome of a special situation and too much tied down to the speaker's particular thought ever to become the model for a new form of request. The interpretation of it as a request would be a right deduction, but one which could not be made from other sets of words having the same form. The concern of grammar is with linguistic form, and particularly with that of the 'outer' kind, though not, as some grammarians seem to think, without reference to the semantic aspect; grammar is not interested in purely individual and exceptional function. We may now make an important generalization: *Grammar is, in the main, concerned with linguistic form in congruent function, and treats of incongruent function only in so far as this is building up new form in which such function will be congruent.* This is equivalent to saying that grammar is concerned solely with language, not with speech; but that, of course, does not mean that the grammarian must shut his eyes to speech, for speech is as necessary to language as language to speech. Every science must take a broad view of its subject-matter, and not exclude any extraneous fact or condition which may throw light upon it.

It was seen in § 56 that out of single words and simple phrases lacking locutional sentence-form, sentences can be made by merely pronouncing them with the right intonation. Having sentence-form on their elocutional side, these certainly deserve a mention in every grammar; but since grammars, at least as they are at present written, do

[1] *Was ist ein Satz?* p. 31.

not enter into elocutional details, the mention should be quite summary. Due place ought, on the other hand, to be given to those words and phrases of special types which, without having locutional sentence-form congenitally, have secondarily acquired it. I refer to such constructions as the exclamatory infinitive, e.g. *I* OFFER *mischief to so good a king!* MOURIR *sans tirer ma raison!* Mir DROHEN! or as the infinitive of command, e.g. *Partir! Umsteigen!* or again as the French use of the form of an indirect question for emphatic statements,[1] e.g. *Si je l'ai connu!* In all these cases a certain incongruence is still felt, the use as sentences being obviously less normal and natural than the more literal employments.

§62. **Quoted words.** Thus far no allusion has been made to the peculiar phenomenon of quoted words, and since these on the one hand have an appearance of incongruence, albeit illusory, and on the other may consist of whole sentences, the present seems a suitable opportunity for discussing them. The problem is to determine the exact status of quotations. I will begin by giving a few examples: (1) mere words or phrases: *The Latin 'dic' is an imperative; 'Maison' is French for a house; The mere sound of the word 'asphodel' is beautiful; No passage in Shakespeare is more familiar than that beginning 'To be or not to be'*; (2) entire sentences: *'Come in!' he said; Everyone knows the proverb 'A rolling stone gathers no moss'; 'Tantum religio potuit suadere malorum' is a Latin hexameter.*

In all these examples the quotation functions as a noun.[2] But it is evident also that this function does not annihilate or in any way exclude the morphological or syntactic

---

[1] For a similar use in other languages see Jespersen, *Philosophy*, p. 304.
[2] Quotations may, however, on occasion be used as adjectives, e.g. *his go-and-be-hanged look; a devil-may-care appearance.*

status of the words concerned. *Dic!* remains an imperative, *Come in!* continues to be a request, *gathers* does not cease to have *a rolling stone* as its subject and *no moss* as its object. All feeling of incongruence is absent from the quoted words themselves. And yet they are somehow wrested from their normal employment. How is this puzzle to be solved? The truth is that, in relation to the sentences of which they form part, the quoted words are not word-signs at all, but very nearly the actual things-meant which the speaker intends to communicate. It is as though I were to forget the name of someone whom I am introducing, and were to complete my introduction with a gesture towards him: *Allow me to introduce Mr. . . . .* In this case, Mr. Stewart, or Sampson, or whatever his name might be, would himself stand in apposition to my word *Mr.* But the strange predicament in which he would thus find himself would not deprive him of whatever rank or status he possessed before. So too it is with quotations, only here the words are not precisely the things-meant to which the speaker is referring, but faithful copies. They had life and being only in their original situation, and it is mere counterfeits which are resuscitated in the new one. To put the matter in a different way: when words are quoted, they are given to the listener as things interesting in themselves and worth attending to on their intrinsic merits. In order to evaluate their linguistic status, the context or place from which they are taken has to be considered. Thus *Dic, maison,* and *asphodel* are mere words, not, as they are here quoted, specimens of speech at all. The quotations from Shakespeare and Lucretius are to be regarded as real speech, as though their authors were themselves speaking them.

Words quoted are thus exterior to, and independent of,

the speech of their quoter, and in this respect resemble anything else to which he may refer.[1] They differ from such a thing only in the manner in which they are brought to the listener's attention. Instead of being described by class-names, they are directly reproduced, even as a picture is reproduced by photography. But the speaker presents them, like anything else he may speak about, in a particular aspect. Sometimes he may point to the sense, at other times, as in *asphodel* and in the hexameter from Lucretius, to the mere sound or rhythm. This observation enables us to estimate the status of the sentences found in grammars and manuals of composition. When instances are there quoted from original sources they are live samples of speech, and there can be no suspicion of their genuineness. Made-up examples, on the other hand, are barely actual sentences, since their words have relevance neither to real things nor to a specific listener. But they are as good as actual sentences, since they conform to the rules which the grammarian meant them to exemplify, and since imaginary situations could be invented for them, if this were demanded. Though sentences merely in form, they will serve their purpose; for if they were impugned on this score, an act of the imagination could easily convert them into full-blooded, meaningful sentences functioning congruently.

§ 63. **Conclusion.** This chapter has been mainly devoted to showing how a speaker's purpose in referring to his subject-matter makes itself felt. But irrespective of the

---

[1] In course of time quotations often repeated may become new elements in a language. See the examples, p. 233, n. 2; and such Latin quotations as *verb. sap.*, *vice versa*. Egyptian is fond of these uses, particularly for forming proper names, cf. *Whenever-he-will-he-does* as a designation of the great god of primordial times. Other examples in my *Egyptian Grammar*, § 194.

extent to which that purpose is betrayed by the intonation or the words, an utterance *is* a sentence when the speaker can be recognized as having put into it, taken as a whole, all that is necessary for conveying an intelligible purpose. It differs from any sequence of words that is not a sentence by the sense of relevance and appositeness which it leaves in its train. A mere phrase is either unapplied language or else simply a fragment of a sentence. A genuine sentence is a unit of actual speech, i.e. language meaningfully applied to some state of things, and purposefully addressed to some listener.

It might, on first hearing, perhaps seem a strange contention to assert, as I have done, that it is the *function* of a sentence which declares it to be such and fixes its kind, whereas the nature of a word is fixed by its *form*. But the explanation lies in the correlated truths (1) that the word is the unit of language, while the sentence is the unit of speech, and (2) that form is a fact of language and function a fact of speech. Naturally the unit of language must be judged by the facts of language, and the unit of speech by the facts of speech. To make form (in the linguistic sense) the criterion of the sentence is really to deny that this is the unit of speech, and Ries's fundamental error seems to me his attempt to tie down the sentence to certain external forms of utterance, and to refuse the name to others. For my part, I do not deny that every sentence must have some element of form, but it is not the form which makes it into a sentence. To speak and to pause when the utterance is ended is, indeed, a certain minimal indication of sentence-form, and one which occurs in all speech.

ADDITIONAL NOTE TO CHAPTER IV

Note E (on p. 182). *Remarks on some definitions of the sentence, mostly recent.*

Ries is so admirable as a destructive critic that he has left but little work to be done in the way of demolishing those theories of the sentence which we are at one in condemning. I shall therefore devote these notes to the views of the few scholars with whom I am in partial agreement. Among the many definitions of the sentence quoted by Ries, *Was ist ein Satz?*, pp. 208 foll., the purposiveness which for me constitutes its essence is hardly ever alluded to. A notable exception is Georg Fränklin, a scholar who lived at the end of the eighteenth century. His definition may be rendered: 'Speech [by this Fränklin clearly means the sentence] is a notification, consisting in words, of the speaker's feelings (Gesinnung) towards the object denoted by those words.' 'Feelings' are not 'purposive attitude', but this definition was a good start. Wegener gives no formal definition, but his opinion is indicated in the statement that 'the purpose of our speech is always to influence the will or the perception of someone in a way which the speaker considers to be of importance' (*Grundfragen*, p. 67). My own former definition ran upon the same lines: 'A sentence is an articulate sound-symbol in its aspect of embodying some volitional attitude of the speaker towards the listener,' *Word and Sentence*, p. 355. Though this resembles Wegener's formula, it was reached by a different method, namely by the effort to find a principle common to all four classes of sentence. The like holds good of Kretschmer's revised definition (*Sprache*, p. 60): 'The sentence is a linguistic utterance through which an emotion or volitional impulse is discharged' ('eine sprachliche Ausserung, durch die ein Affekt oder Willensvorgang ausgelöst wird'). This formulation is so close to my own, that it seems almost cantankerous to quarrel with it. Nevertheless, I feel it necessary to point out how near Kretschmer comes to identifying all sentences with exclamations; one cannot guess from his definition that sentences describe anything. My own attempt (which Kretschmer wrongly criticizes on the ground that it takes the listener into account) eluded this objection by being juxtaposed to a definition of the word, which ran, 'A word is an articulate sound-symbol in its aspect of denoting something which is spoken about.' When my article was written, I had not yet perceived the difference between language and speech, or realized that the word is the unit of the former, so that I defined only the spoken word. That was a mistake. Another difficulty about Kretschmer's standpoint is that in 'questions' and 'requests' the speaker's intention is not fully discharged until the listener has done what is demanded of him. But this I do not press, since 'ausgelöst' should perhaps be rendered 'released' rather than 'discharged'.

The great merits of Bühler's view are not well seen from his final definition, which reads: 'Sentences are the simple, independent, and self-contained functional units of speech, or briefly, the sense-units of speech' ('die einfachen selbständigen, in sich abgeschlossenen Leistungseinheiten oder kurz die Sinneinheiten der Rede'), *Theorien des Satzes*, p. 18. These expressions disguise his recognition of the fact that speech comprises the three functions of 'proclamation' (= exclamation), 'evocation' (= demand), and 'depiction' (= statement), a correct analysis (see above, p. 188) which would, however, have gained greatly in clarity and fertility, had it been expressed in terms of the speaker's varying purpose. Bühler shrinks from using the word 'purpose', and though he may have good psychological grounds for this, his linguistic theory has suffered in consequence. Dempe (*Was ist Sprache?* pp. 33 foll.) holds, in my opinion rightly, that no adequate theory of speech can fail to insist upon the speaker's purpose. Unfortunately Bühler never explicitly states (though I have it from him orally that on this point he has been misunderstood) that his three functions are present in every sentence whatsoever. This oversight is pointed out also by Dempe (p. 20), though the latter will not admit the possibility of such a position. In spite of these defects, Bühler's outlook seems to me fundamentally sound, and to require merely a sharpening of focus. Dempe's own definition disarms criticism by purporting to be a merely logical description ('logisch bestimmt' in heavy type, op. cit., p. 108), wherefore I will not discuss it.

This brings me to an end of the theories having any measure of resemblance to my own. The genetic definitions given by Paul and

Wundt will be dealt with in the next chapter (§ 65). Justice demands, however, some further comment on Ries's book *Was ist ein Satz?* assuredly the most learned and methodical treatise on this theme ever published. In its controversial aspects the work is very able, and it is a mine of information with regard to previous hypotheses. Ries's own positive contribution appears to me doomed in advance to failure by the narrow outlook he adopts. He refuses to attend to any factor of speech but the words themselves, the listener being deliberately rejected, the speaker barely glanced at, and the things spoken about entirely ignored. His definition (p. 99) reads thus: 'A sentence is a grammatically formed smallest unit of speech, which brings its content to expression with an eye to this content's relation to reality' ('Ein Satz ist eine grammatisch geformte kleinste Redeeinheit, die ihren Inhalt im Hinblick auf sein Verhältnis zur Wirklichkeit zum Ausdruck bringt'). The one great merit which I find here is the recognition that the sentence is the unit of speech. From the rest I cannot but dissent. For passages in this book where I deal with the criteria advanced by Ries see as follows: 'grammatically formed', above, p. 213; 'smallest', above, p. 208; 'content', above, p. 26, n. 1; 'relation to reality', below, p. 298, n. 1.

V
THE SENTENCE AND ITS LOCUTIONAL CONTENT

§ 64. **The content of the sentence.** The last chapter was concerned almost exclusively with that purposiveness which in my view constitutes the essence of a sentence—the quality which makes sentences out of what would otherwise be mere words or phrases. Our next task is to study the content of the sentence. Given that the speaker has chanced on a topic to speak about, what does he actually say? What words does he choose, and how does he set about choosing them? But before we embark on this problem, the manner in which it has been formulated calls for comment. In the first place let it be noted that no contrast is here drawn between the purposiveness which makes sentences what they are and a lack of purpose in the content of sentences, for clearly the speaker intends and purposes the words which he utters no less than he invests them with a further intention and purpose in the main external to them. Indeed, we shall find as we proceed that the chief defect in previous theories has been the failure to recognize that the sentence is volitional throughout, just as though speech were nothing but perception or thought passively reflected in a new and audible medium. I shall premise, therefore, that every sentence embodies two distinct, though interdependent purposes, the one affecting the thing or things spoken about, and the other affecting the way in which the listener is to receive or react to what is said. In devising his sentences, the speaker has to pay attention alike to the 'why' and to the 'what' of them. The second comment I have to make is that, in now describing the 'what' of the sentence as its content, I am not contradicting my often-repeated thesis that the thing meant by any sentence necessarily lies outside it. I mean by the 'content' of the sentence its component words or, otherwise expressed, the series of appropriately arranged word-meanings which it offers as clues.

These points being settled, we can proceed with our problem. At once we are confronted by two rival hypotheses, associated with the names of Paul and Wundt respectively. Both are concerned only with the content of the sentence, and their difference turns mainly upon the way in which this content comes about. The view favoured by Paul may be characterized as 'the synthesis hypothesis', while that of Wundt may be called 'the analysis hypothesis'. Presented in an English version, Paul's definition of the sentence runs as follows: 'The sentence is the linguistic expression, or symbol, for the fact that several presentations or groups of presentations have become combined in the mind of the speaker, and is the means of producing a like combination of the like presentations in the mind of the listener.'[1] Wundt's definition is later in date, and was framed in conscious opposition to that of Paul: 'A sentence is the linguistic expression for the arbitrary dismemberment of a complex presentation into its component parts, these being placed in logical relations to one another.'[2] Readers of the last chapter will at once

---

[1] 'Der Satz ist der sprachliche Ausdruck, das Symbol dafür, dass sich die Verbindung mehrerer Vorstellungen oder Vorstellungsgruppen in der Seele des Sprechenden vollzogen hat, und das Mittel dazu, die nämliche Verbindung der nämlichen Vorstellungen in der Seele des Hörenden zu erzeugen.' *Prinzipien*, p. 121.

[2] 'Hiernach können wir den Satz nach seinen objektiven wie subjektiven Merkmalen definieren als den sprachlichen Ausdruck für die willkürliche

realize the criticism I am bound to make upon these definitions. While both seek to explain how the sentence takes shape, neither affords the slightest indication of what it actually is, or how it differs from any combination of words which is not a sentence. Each of the two definitions is applicable alike to the phrase *a beautiful sunset* and to the sentence *The sunset is beautiful*.[1] No one could possibly guess from them that sentences may be classified into statements, requests, questions, and exclamations, for they offer no hint of the purposive attitude towards the listener which is the principle of that classification. Wundt does not mention the listener at all, nor for that matter does he mention the speaker. Paul is careful to name both parties to the act of speech, but only in order to make of the listener a partner, for no apparent reason, in some psychic experience of the speaker. Lastly, an obvious defect of both definitions is that they ignore the one-word sentence. Paul and Wundt might perhaps not be expected to include in their purview all the one-word utterances which I insist on classifying as sentences. But it might fairly have been demanded of them not to forget imperative sentences like *Come!* where there is obviously neither 'synthesis' nor 'analysis' in the sense intended by the definitions.

§ 65. **The origination of sentences.** If the definitions of the sentence given by Paul and Wundt are thus inadequate as definitions, at least we may ask how far the one or the other suffices as a description of the way in which sentences come into being. From Paul's answers to Wundt's objections it is clear that he conceives the contro-

---

Gliederung einer Gesamtvorstellung in ihre in logische Beziehungen zueinander gesetzten Bestandteile.' *Die Sprache*, ii, p. 245.

[1] Ries makes the same criticism as regards Wundt, see *Was ist ein Satz?*, p. 4.

versy to turn solely upon whether the sentence emerges in the mind (1) as a complete whole, or (2) piecemeal and in consecutive stages. That in certain cases the latter account may be true he seeks to prove by an episode eventuating in the sentence *The lion roars*. A roaring is heard, and then 'this at first isolated auditory impression awakens the presentation of a lion'; hereupon, says Paul, the speaker 'comes to' the sentence *The lion roars*.[1] But Paul is anxious to do justice to the listener as well as to the speaker, and he rightly reproaches Wundt for neglecting this important factor in the transaction. In the case of the listener, Paul maintains that the sentence clearly originates piecemeal; one word falls after the other and adds, as it falls, a new presentation to those preceding. Now for our present inquiry the behaviour of the listener is entirely irrelevant. I have already explained wherein this behaviour consists. We have seen the listener attending to the intonation, previous experiences of which provide the basis for a correct deduction as to the attitude which the speaker expects of him; we have seen him attending to the clues given by the words, form and meaning alike helping him to his conclusions; and lastly, we have seen him attending to the situation (or perhaps I should say, the rest of the situation), and from all these factors combined drawing his inference concerning the thing meant by the speaker. The interpretation of speech, like all linguistic processes, has become highly mechanized and is, therefore, almost instantaneous. But if we could behold interpretation

[1] 'Jemand weiss, dass sich in der Nähe ein Löwe befindet, den er aber im Augenblick nicht sieht, und an den er auch nicht denkt; da hört er ein Gebrüll; dieser zunächst für sich gegebene Gehörseindruck ruft die Vorstellung des Löwen wach; er kommt zu dem Satz *der Löwe brüllt*; hier ist doch nicht erst die Gesamtvorstellung 'der brüllende Löwe' in ihre Teile zerlegt'. *Prinzipien*, p. 122.

immensely slowed down, as the movements of horses or athletes may often be seen at the cinema, we should undoubtedly recognize it as gradual, and to some extent following the consecutive fall of the words. That, however, is not our problem here. The present investigation turns upon an entirely different question, namely, how the speaker sets about constructing his sentences. Thus at least for our particular purpose, Paul's argument from the standpoint of the listener may be ignored as irrelevant.

Paul's definition is obviously framed to accord with the assumption that every sentence must contain both subject and predicate. The objections to this view have been stated in § 58. Nevertheless, sentences of that bipartite kind are extremely plentiful, and it is interesting to inquire how, in Paul's opinion, they come about. When we scrutinize his account of *The lion roars*, we are surprised to find that the transition from thoughts to words has simply been left out. An auditory impression (*Gehorseindruck*) graves itself upon the speaker's mind, and with it comes the word *roars*. Then follows a presentation of the lion, and this gives the word *lion*. A few pages further on Paul explains that one of the two elements may push itself to the front of the speaker's consciousness before the sentence is uttered, so we must not reproach him with a failure to explain how the word-order *The lion roars*, instead of *Roars lion*, came about.[1] But so far as I can see, he makes no attempt to account for the definite article. It would be difficult to find a more complete identification of thought and speech. According to Paul, a sentence containing subject and predicate is the outcome of two successive thoughts, one for the subject and one for the predicate. And he must somehow conceive of the thought of each

---

[1] *Prinzipien*, p. 127.

thing as simultaneously the meaning of the corresponding word, so that thought and word arise together in consciousness as it were automatically.

If such be an accurate account of Paul's views, they are so naïve that further examination is superfluous. Turning to Wundt, I have little doubt that it was under the influence of his definition that I came by my notion of a complex thing-meant later differentiated into a number of parts, and I take this opportunity of acknowledging my indebtedness. But as regards the exact formulation of his definition all manner of doubts assail me, though it is only with diffidence that I put forward criticisms of a position confessedly not linguistic, but psychological. My first difficulty arises over a presentation which is subsequently divided up into its parts. To me the term 'presentation' suggests something momentarily presented to the mind and being just what it is, either relatively complex or relatively simple, but anyhow unique and indivisible. As I conceive of presentations, one may follow another, but can the second be part of the first? And further, can any presentation be simply the meaning of a word? For when Wundt talks of his part-presentations (*Teilvorstellungen*) 'being placed in logical relations to one another' in the sentence, it is difficult to avoid the impression that he is speaking of words, one being made subject, the next object, and so forth.

Wundt's formulation is so abstract that I return with relief to my own more workaday distinction of 'things' and 'words'. Intermediate between them are, no doubt, 'presentations', the reflections of things within the mind, but it has been seen that linguistic theory has no difficulty in dispensing with these troublesome intervening factors, except when word-form and word-function are under consideration. And even then we may still treat the objects referred to in speech as 'things', merely qualifying the term with epithets like 'presented as a thing', or 'as an attribute', or 'as an action' (§ 42). To revert to Paul's example, *The lion roars*, it seems clear that, when the thing referred to by this sentence first came before the speaker's mind, it was as a relatively undifferentiated whole, not divided up into the three separate things subsequently designated by the words *the*, *lion*, and *roars* respectively. If—as I desiderated above for interpretation—the mental operations leading up to this act of speech could be slowed down and revealed to the speaker introspectively, he would probably become aware of some such events as the following. First of all the unexpected sound has braced his mind to sudden attention and activity, having as immediate result the thought of a lion, possibly already more or less distinctly verbalized as the word *lion*. The sense of danger and the need for action now bring in rapid succession thoughts of this being the particular lion which has worked such havoc in the neighbourhood, of the proximity of a companion, and of the desirability of letting the latter know, not only that the roar is that of the lion in question, but also that he, the speaker, is fully aware of the situation. Speech is decided upon, and various considerations are weighed to determine the exact words to be uttered. If the danger were imminent, brevity would be imperative, and the speaker might either say *Hark!* or *The lion!* his choice depending upon whether it seemed more important to stimulate the listener's attention or to identify for him the cause of the sound. In the latter case, the definite article would be prefixed to *lion*, both because language dictated that use, and also because the particularity of the lion presently heard forbade the alternative *A lion!* The word *roars* would be added only if the occasion were less pressing, the animal being at some distance. And now note that though thus far the chain of thought might well have been the same for an Englishman and a German, the sentence would undoubtedly turn out differently for each. The German would probably choose the form *Der Löwe brüllt* (= *The lion roars*), that being the way in which he was wont to express present momentary occurrences. For the Englishman the natural form would be *That's the lion!* omitting any mention of the roaring, but prefixing a demonstrative indicating its source, and adding to this the copula to give the utterance a more objective and less emotional turn.[1]

Anyone who has ever found himself in circumstances impelling him to utter this particular sentence may at first be inclined to dismiss my description of its genesis as fantastic, but on second thoughts he will probably be prepared to admit that something of the kind actually happened. He will not know for certain, because speech takes place almost spontaneously and at all events unintrospectively. My account will gain in plausibility the longer he reflects upon it. After all, the lion *was* at some distance. And his companion *was* at least as alert and as quick of hearing as himself, so that it would be more important to show that he himself had heard the roar than to bid his companion to hearken. And again, in the circumstances, the form he adopted in the end *did* seem the most appropriate, and the most in harmony with his mother-tongue. But there are other tests by which he

---

[1] In English, so far as I can see, *The lion roars* could only (1) refer to custom, (2) characterize the lion, (3) narrate a present occurrence, not as an isolated occurrence, but as an incident, e.g. in stage-directions, or (4) be the statement of a past event employing the historic present.

might verify the correctness of my analysis. Suppose his companion had been a nervous child, would he not have elected to be silent? Had the roar come from the distant hills, and the listener been a visitor new to the country, might he not have given the utterance some such form as *Did you hear that sound a moment ago, far over there in the hills? Well, that must be the lion we've been trying to get for three weeks or more.* If he himself had been the new arrival, might he not have put the question *Was that a lion?* To sum up, though a small proportion of the things referred to in any sentence may be reached by analysis of the global, undifferentiated thing-meant which was its starting-point, the bulk will have been derived from various other subsidiary things-meant or considerations, both factual and linguistic, which have put in an appearance only after the intention to speak was formed. And above all, the whole utterance is governed by the speaker's needs and caprice. Thus Wundt's analysis hypothesis, although containing an important nucleus of truth, is very far from describing the real genesis of most sentences.

Leaving now Paul's test-case, let us consider the problem in a more general way. Rapid and easy as is most speech, there are nevertheless some circumstances in which we nearly possess the experimental conditions needful to display the motives and hesitations which usually go to the making of a sentence. Writing is much more laborious than uttered speech. Do not I, in penning this very paragraph, often stop in the middle of my work, search for a word, cross out one and substitute another, wonder whether what I have written is good English, and perhaps remould the entire passage? How far removed are such proceedings from the dismemberment of a whole into its parts postulated by Wundt! Nor is his thesis saved by the word 'arbitrary' (*willkürlich*), with which he hints that the analysis of a sentence may not always turn out alike. For firstly the notion of 'analysis' seems to imply a more or less complete resolving of something into its ingredients, whereas some of the most important of these, as we have seen, may be entirely left out, e.g. *roaring* in *That's the lion!* And secondly, much may be added which was not present when the sentence was first conceived. To take a fresh instance. A child is seen to dash across the road right in front of an oncoming taxicab. Someone cries out: *Look at that stupid little girl!* The exclamation is almost spontaneous, and yet its gradual development is scarcely open to doubt. Are we to imagine that the notions of the child's stupidity, its size, and its sex were already present when the word *look* was decided upon? As I see this utterance, it reflects a *crescendo* of indignation at the child's folly gradually welling up out of a first impulse of sympathetic fear. *Stupid* qualifies that folly directly, *little* is partly a sign of contempt derived from the ill-judged scorn which is habitually cast upon the undersized, and *girl* has a classificatory identifying aim. Unless I am mistaken, this rapid utterance thus contains a whole sequence of expressive inventions, admirably contrived and planned to exhibit the speaker's purpose and feeling.

My quarrel with Wundt is twofold: firstly, that he has overlooked the purposeful, calculating character of speech; and secondly, that he takes far too static a view of thought. He seems to ignore the fact that the mind is as volatile and as restless as a flowing river. His definition cannot be saved by the contention that, before a sentence is spoken, a new complex presentation has arisen out of a multitude of previous presentations, and that it is this new presentation which is analysed into words. The difference between our standpoints seems due to Wundt's failure to look at, or at least to mention, the objective world to which speakers actually refer. My own conception is rather that of a mental eye ranging over an ever-widening field: an eye whose activity does not stop short an instant before utterance, but which continues to explore new ground right down to the end of the sentence, when its doings cease to have immediate interest. And concurrently with this process, I seem to see the mind busily fitting word-clues to the things upon which its eye has momentarily rested. Of the two, mind and eye, it is the former, in my conception, which supplies the controlling force, permitting the latter to travel only in such directions as will suit the sentence's general trend and objective. Inexact psychology this, no doubt; but the imagery will serve to counteract Wundt's rigid and static view of sentence-formation.

But on this conception of yours, I may be asked, what becomes of the complex thing-meant of which you have talked so much? This, I reply, obtains its final shape only as the last word of the sentence is uttered. Perhaps the speaker himself never quite realizes it as a whole, having lost sight of the beginning by the time he reaches the end. But the mind of the listener, if rightly attuned, catches it up in passing, though promptly proceeding to convert it into something new; for the listener's mind, like that of the speaker, is for ever on the move, actively creating and transforming. I will add nothing to what I have written about the thing-meant in § 27. As we saw there, a certain fixity and definiteness are given to it by the speaker's depth of intention.

To conclude, my verdict that previous writers have treated speech as though it were nothing but perception

§ 65   THE GENESIS OF SENTENCES   251

or thought passively reflected in a new and audible medium (p. 240) seems amply justified by the examination to which the views of Paul and Wundt have here been subjected. Wundt regards the gist of a sentence as something definite presented to the mind which later is simply reproduced in analytic linguistic form. Paul regards the sentence as taking shape by successive steps, but merely as the result of perception, the part of the speaker being nothing more than that of a sounding-board. In opposition to such views, my conception emphasizes the intensely purposive character of every sentence. Not only is this the outcome of a speaker's decision to speak and of his choice of the manner in which he desires to influence the listener, but also it is he who selects the things to be referred to, and who actively devises the precise form in which they shall be presented. Speech is, in fact, at once a reproductive and a creative activity. The element of truth in Wundt's analysis hypothesis is that no speech takes place without an external stimulus, data arising from which are analysed in the sense of being classified under their kinds. And the element of truth in Paul's synthesis hypothesis is that the construction of sentences undoubtedly takes place by consecutive steps. This, indeed, is practically implied by Wundt's own definition. Bühler agrees that the two standpoints are not irreconcilable, and that each has its share of truth and falsity.[1] Jespersen adduces evidence to show how gradually many sentences come about, additions being made down to the very end.[2] One example that he quotes is *There I saw Tom Brown, and Miss Hart, and Miss Johnstone, and Colonel Dutton*, which is both arrived at and pronounced differently from *There I saw Tom Brown, Miss Hart, Miss Johnstone, and Colonel Dutton*, where the main

[1] *Theorien des Satzes*, pp. 13–15.   [2] *Philosophy*, pp. 27–8.

lines of the sentence were foreseen from the start. And he makes the further correct observation that all cases of *anacoluthon* are due to imperfect prognostication of the finished sentence at the moment of its inception.

§ 66. **Concessions to the expressionistic hypothesis.** Among those who hold that the purpose of speech is the expression of thought (§ 1) we may perhaps distinguish two schools. Firstly, there are some who, like Wundt, regard the spoken sentence merely as an analysed reproduction of a previously conceived thought, a point of view which has been criticized in the preceding paragraph. But there are others, like Croce, Vossler, and J. A. Smith,[1] who equate speech with the aesthetic impulse, and look upon speaker or writer as the arbitrary author of all he says. It would be unfair to these thinkers if I failed to point out how near I have come to admitting their contention, though in reality dissenting from it fundamentally. I have chosen to represent one and the same thing, namely the heard roaring of a lion, as the gist of a number of different sentences formulated under slightly different conditions. But from a shifted standpoint it is obviously absurd to contend that *Hark!* can ever mean the same thing as *Was that a lion?* even though one and the same perceived circumstance served as the point of departure for both utterances, and was intended as the goal for the listener's attention. The fact seems to be that the speaker always creates a considerable proportion of his things-meant as he proceeds with his speech. Without a stimulus impinging upon the speaker from a more or less objective source speech does not arise. This holds good, I think, whether the stimulus be an external event, as in the case here envisaged, or whether it be, as

---

[1] See the quotation from the latter above, p. 57.

often happens, the culmination of inner reflections or emotions. Speech, to put it briefly, is always of the nature of a reaction. But when once the determination to speak has emerged, an enlivened sense of reality brings all manner of new things into view, and these provide stimuli for further linguistic reactions. The term 'reaction' here must not give rise to misunderstandings on account of its chemical or biological associations. The reactions of which I speak are, if not wholly, at least to a large extent volitional. The speaker chooses the things to be spoken about, though, viewed from another angle, those things are borne in upon his consciousness from outside to serve as the stimuli evoking his speech.

I maintain that speech is inexplicable without the twofold assumption of (1) stimulating circumstance, and (2) volitional reaction. Assuming only the first, the same circumstances would always, as it seems, lead to the same speech, and the erroneous implication of both Paul's and Wundt's theories, namely that speech is the passive replica of presentations, here comes into view. Assuming only the volitional character of speech, we fall into the fallacy of the Crocian expressionists, whose statements seem to imply that at any moment we may say whatsoever we choose, without reference to the situation or to conditioning circumstances.

To do full justice to realities, equal stress must be laid upon the liberty of speech and upon its dependence. No pressure from without can compel a man to open his lips, if he is determined to keep them closed. But when he does speak, what he says is a matter of his individual choice; *le style c'est l'homme*. On the other hand, only the words of a raving lunatic fail to have relevance to the situation wherein speech arises. Out of that situation the speaker extracts those things-meant which appeal to his personal caprice and particular purpose. Taciturn and loquacious alike are restricted by a dependence upon the situation. Seeing a shooting star, I should find it extremely difficult to bring any of the words *discipline*, *oxygen*, or *pig* into my comment; in fact, I am not free, or at least as a practical man I am not free, to say what I like. The things to which I am entitled to refer must in a sense be dug out of the situation.

To what things, then, may a sentence refer, whilst remaining within the bounds of proper relevance and conforming to ordinary habits of speech? The answer must be as follows. No word is legitimate unless it refers, directly or indirectly, to one or other of the factors with which the sentence was concerned at the outset. Far more often than not the originating stimulus, e.g. the roaring lion, supplies the finished utterance with ingredients. Descriptions of these ingredients are common, e.g. (*a*) *dangerous* (*lion*), and descriptions of those descriptions may also occur, e.g. *very* (*dangerous*). The speaker often alludes to himself, or to actions or attributes of his, e.g. *I thought I heard* . . ., and these again may lead to descriptive ramifications. The listener likewise may be brought into the picture, together with his doings and attributes, or anything which may hitch on to these, e.g. *Did you hear* . . . ? *Hush! Get back!* And lastly, a great many words belong solely to the outer linguistic structure into which the more significant words have to be fitted, e.g. *whether*, *was*, *the*, and *which* in *I wonder whether that was the lion which* . . . These last instrumental and auxiliary words are by no means without semantic relevance, and if we look deep enough, will always be found to have some real connexion with the matter in hand. But their employment is barely subject to the speaker's choice. They are a legacy from his ancestral habits of speech, and from these he cannot escape without giving a perverted aspect to the thing he seeks to convey. Thus the whole of speech and sentence-making arises out of the four factors enumerated in my first chapter, however complex the sentence, and however remote from the originating nucleus some of the words employed may at first sight seem. Apart from this stipulation, however, the speaker is at liberty to choose as he will, and his temperament, attitude to the listener, emotional or aesthetic reactions to his theme, and finally linguistic preferences all give him wide scope for the assertion of personality.

§ 67. **Predication as a process involved in all speech.** The argument of the last two sections has pointed ever more insistently to the conclusion that all formulation in words necessarily constitutes an addition to the thing formulated. I wish to indicate my hat, and in course of doing so linguistically with the words *That is my hat* I am compelled to indicate also the yonderness of my hat (*that*), its 'being' yonder (*is*), and its belonging to me (*my*). The thing-meant, however simply or vaguely conceived of by the speaker before he makes up his mind to speak, becomes much more complicated and distinct as the result of that decision. This thought leads on, by a natural transition, to the topic of **predication.** For predication, in its shortest and pithiest definition, *consists in saying something about something*, and this very way of describing the operation implies an act of adding. Now our main concern with predication in the next few sections will be in connexion with the division of many sentences into two parts, (1) the part referring to the thing spoken about, which is called the **subject,** and (2) what is said of the subject,[1] namely the **predicate**. In the present section, however, I wish to dwell upon the fact that predication is involved in all use of words whatsoever.

In considering predication from this point of view, we shall find that our attitude towards words as employed in speech must be enlarged to embrace a wider perspective. Hitherto we have looked upon the meanings of words solely as instruments, as clues to certain things that are meant by them. In doing so we have been too ready to forget that we mean our meanings as well as the things which we mean by their help. When I point at a tree and call it a *tree*, not only do I indicate the tree, but I also imply the fact that it *is* a tree, that it belongs to the class 'tree'. If I do not assert, at least I assume, that there is something about the thing so described which justifies me in attaching to it the label *tree*.[2] For me as speaker this character in the thing is identical with a character in the meaning of the word I employ (C = χ in Fig. 6 above, p. 151), and if all goes well, the listener will take the same view. Thus in choosing my word, although in intention I refer to something outside speech, actually I refer to part of the meaning of that word. The neglect to recognize that in speaking the word *tree* I am adding to the object signified a comparison with other trees previously seen and recognized as such is a neglect of too common a kind. A

---

[1] This is an abbreviation for 'what is said of the thing meant by the subject'.

[2] 'Sagen wir, z. B., *diese Birne ist hart*, so müssen wir erst den Gegenstand, von dem wir etwas aussagen wollen, unter die allgemeine Kategorie *Birne*, die Eigenschaft, die wir an ihm bemerkt haben, unter die allgemeine Kategorie *hart* gebracht haben. Wir müssen also um unser Urteil auszusprechen noch zwei Hilfsurteile gebildet haben,' Paul, *Prinzipien*, p. 132. The position could hardly have been better put. It is a pity that Paul has not kept it in view more consistently, see above, p. 58.

parallel is the insensibility of some people to war itself in their excitement over war-causes and war-aims. And yet for the proper accomplishment of a purpose the instrument must, as a rule, be fairly and squarely envisaged, as well as the purpose itself. Nay more, the instrument must be willed; he who wills the end wills also the means.

Let us admit, therefore, that whenever we employ a word we at least implicitly intend, purpose, or mean *two* things: not the thing-meant alone, but also as much of the word-meaning as is applicable to the thing-meant. But in adopting this new position precautions must be taken against making certain assumptions which here easily arise. Firstly, it must be recognized that in the application of some words meaning and thing-meant are so nearly juxtaposed that only in a limited degree can they be regarded as separate objectives; they may be compared to the nearer and remoter stations of one and the same town, some trains stopping at the hither station, while others run on to the terminus; the town itself is reached by both kinds of train. A meaning is said of a thing-meant; but the listener may be induced to stop at the meaning, in which case the thing-meant, though still there, fades into momentary insignificance; or else he may have his attention drawn on to the thing-meant, passing clean through the meaning, which is then merely a station upon the way.

Our new standpoint still regards words as instruments or clues, and their extensive areas of meaning as fields within which the listener's keen selective intelligence has to identify the objective intended by the speaker. But that objective presents alternative possibilities. Either it is the **ultimate thing-meant**; or else it is 'as much of the (total) word-meaning as is applicable to the (ultimate) thing meant', and this second alternative may be called the **proximate thing-meant**. In more commonplace parlance, the proximate thing-meant is the aspect in which the ultimate thing-meant is seen. Here we come to the second of the possible assumptions to which our new standpoint may give rise, and against which special precautions must be taken. The two things-meant are not on the same footing. Our previous example *tree* in *yonder tree* will illustrate this fact more convincingly than abstract statement could do. The ultimate thing-meant belongs outside both speech and language. The proximate thing-meant, on the other hand, holds together closely with the word and with the previous experiences associated with the word. If this proximate thing-meant be described as a thing, i.e. by a noun, the description will take the form of an abstract, e.g. 'the treeness' or 'the being-tree' of yonder tree. When I say *Let us run to that tree* my objective is the ultimate thing-meant, the tree itself as the goal of our race. When I say *The thing you imagined was a signpost is only a tree* my objective is the proximate thing-meant, the fact that the thing mistakenly classified by the listener is really a tree, the being-tree or treeness of the-thing-you-imagined-was-a-signpost.

Now in some spoken words, and especially in those which play a subsidiary part in the sentence, the balance is held so evenly between proximate and ultimate thing-meant that it is impossible to say which of the two was the more intended. Take the preposition *over* in *She looked over the wall*; what exactly is meant by *over*? If it makes us see the place where, in relation to the wall, Mary looked, the word has evidently fulfilled its office. If, on the other hand, this preposition has made us realize that the place in respect of the wall where Mary looked was *over* it, clearly it has again fulfilled its office. A slight deflexion of interest in connexion with the word *over* has removed our attention from the place in question and directed it to the fact of this place 'being-over' the wall. If the proximate thing-meant is to be emphasized at the expense of the ultimate thing-meant, a vocal stress will achieve that end. We are hardly likely to stress *over* in *She looked over the wall* since, if the wall be a good example of its kind, Mary will be unable to look under it. There is more point, however, in stressing *over* in *She looked óver her spectacles*, since as a rule people look *through* spectacles, and the preposition here seeks to enforce the fact of the place where Mary looked 'being-over' (not 'being-through' or 'being-under') her spectacles. Such a stressed use of a word is in grammar called a **predicative** use, and this technical term shows us where the importance of predication as a concept in linguistic theory lies. Predication is the act of saying one thing about another, but the fact that this mode of action is involved in every use of a word whatsoever may be ignored with impunity whenever the ultimate thing-meant is the sole objective. When I say *Let us run to yonder tree* or *This tree is going to be felled*, it is true enough that being-a-tree is here predicated of the tree in question. But the listener's selective attention is not called upon to focus that point, and in such cases predication belongs merely to the machinery of the linguistic drama, and takes no place among the stage effects. Predication is of importance to linguistic theory only as a technical term for what happens when, as is extremely often the case, the proximate thing-meant is of greater moment than the ultimate thing-meant.

In the sentences *She looked óver her spectacles; Mind you come eárly; I called Jóhn, not Émily; Vénice is my favourite among the Italian towns*, the words *over, early, John, Emily,* and *Venice* are all used predicatively, since it is the nature, quality, or, in the case of the proper names (§ 13), simply the differentiating label, which is here brought into prominence. But these words merely 'function' predicatively, there being nothing about their locutional form to favour the meaning (proximate thing-meant) at the expense of the (ultimate) thing-meant. There are, however, certain kinds of word or, as they are commonly called, parts of speech the form of which is essentially predicative from the very start. The adjective is a word congenitally so constituted as to exhibit its meaning and to hide its thing-meant; *beautiful* displays 'beauty' as an attribute of something, but leaves that something to be revealed by the situation or by another word. A finite verb is not quite so simply characterized, since among its implications, as I have already observed (§ 59), is the suggestion of an assertive or some such attitude on the part of the speaker. But if this character be disregarded, the finite verb resembles the participle in exhibiting the verb-meaning as exerted by something mentally imaged as a personal being; *lovest* displays 'loving' as enacted by some person or thing addressed. I am encroaching, however, upon the topic of my second volume and will, therefore, now turn to the discussion of subject and predicate as distinct parts of the sentence.

§ 68. **Subject and predicate.** From the broadest point of view all speech is a meaning put upon things, or in other terms, every sentence is a predicate, the subject of which, in the very nature of the case, must remain unexpressed. In admitting this truth, we do not deny the various other subject-predicate relations which scholars have discovered in speech. A relation which holds between a given whole and something outside that whole

§ 68 SUBJECT AND PREDICATE

may equally, and without contradiction, hold also of parts of that whole and other similarly correlated lesser things. In the minds of some philologists there has been real confusion on this score, it being thought that, on the one hand, the fact of entire sentences serving as predicates to the states of affairs underlying them, and on the other, the recognition of predication as involved in the use of single words (§ 67), are incompatible with the grammatical concept of subject and predicate with which we have next to deal.[1] I shall now show that the dichotomy of subject and predicate visible in many sentences, e.g. *Pussy | is beautiful, John | has come*, as well as in various sentence-like parts of sentences, e.g. (*the man*) *who | called yesterday*, (*I know*) *Ralph | to be brave, viribus | unitis*, exemplifies exactly the same principle of predication as was discussed in the last section. In these cases there are, however, the differences (1) that the word or group of words called the **predicate** is presented as *in course of being said* of the underlying subject-matter, and (2) that this subject-matter, instead of remaining unexpressed outside speech, is brought conveniently to the listener's notice in a locutional description which is known as the **subject**.

Jespersen has given to this subject-predicate relation, as exhibited in whole sentences or parts thereof, the name of 'nexus', and he rightly insists on the fundamental duality of the relation. *The dog | barks furiously* is an example of nexus, while *a furiously barking dog* is not.[2] Jespersen admirably illustrates the numerous constructions in which this relation comes to light, and as regards

---

[1] For this mistake see (e.g.) Kalepky, *Neuaufbau*, pp. 19 foll. On Jespersen's standpoint see below, p. 274. In summing up, below, p. 292, I recognize five kinds of predicate, all compatible with one another.

[2] *Philosophy*, pp. 114 foll.

the actual material to be studied one could wish for no better guide. But while stressing the duality which distinguishes *The dog | barks furiously* from *a furiously barking dog*, he is at a loss to explain it. I think we may well retain the term 'nexus', though it will be clearer to extend it into 'predicational nexus'; the relation seen in *a furiously barking dog* Jespersen calls 'junction', and 'furiously barking' is in his terminology an 'adjunct'. He seems reluctant[1] to give the names 'subject' and 'predicate' to the correlated parts of a nexus like *(I know) Ralph | to be brave*, but to this there is little objection so long as it is realized that in one and the same sentence subordinate subjects and predicates can coexist with a main subject and predicate. Take, for example, the sentence *Joan having asked her mother, the latter advised her to persevere in the course she had adopted*. Here the main subject is *the latter* and the main predicate *advised her . . . adopted*. But side by side with these are no less than three subordinate predicational nexuses, namely (1) *Joan* (S) *having asked her mother* (P), (2) *her* (S) *to persevere . . . adopted* (P), and (3) *she* (S) *had adopted* (P). In all four nexuses the predicate is felt as being presently said of its subject, and the warm-blooded vitality evidenced by all grammatical predicates contrasts markedly with the lifelessness which distinguishes their subjects. Each predicational nexus, whether main or subordinate, seems to reflect a separate act of speech assuming its characteristic aspect of saying something about something. And this aspect persists, notwithstanding the fact that all four nexuses are linked together both formally and functionally as each playing its respective part in the achievement of a common purpose.

After this brief summary of the facts our next task is to

[1] *Philosophy*, p. 145.

seek for their explanation. We have noted that all speech is a meaning put upon things or, from a rather different point of view, the speaker's reaction to a stimulus. But in adopting in reference to speech the metaphorical term 'reaction' I must again warn the reader against certain implications which that term has derived from chemistry and physical science. Blue litmus-paper, if dipped in an acid solution, turns red; if dipped in an alkali, it shows no reaction. Some human reactions are doubtless almost as automatic and invariable as that of litmus-paper; a man writhes or flinches when he feels intense pain. But speech, at all events, is neither automatic nor invariable, and in regarding it as reaction to a stimulus we merely recall the facts that some relatively objective thing must impinge upon the mind before speech arises, and that, when speech does arise, it both stands in a causal relation to the stimulus and is of a lively and purposive quality. Above all, it must be observed that human beings can react to one and the same thing in many different ways. This is true, indeed, even of perception; man has five senses, and each sense provides him with a different way of perceiving an identical presented object; a cigar can be seen, touched, smelt, tasted, and its crackling heard. But the higher reaches of thought enable human beings to react to things in a well-nigh innumerable variety of ways. A given house can be looked upon, not merely as being-a-house, but as being high, or empty, or far away, or as having been built, or as tumbling down, or as costing too much. Now all these different potential reactions are strictly parallel to the kind of predications described in the foregoing section. Something (an ultimate thing-meant) is assigned to a class of previous experiences on account of a factual similarity which we called the proximate thing-meant, and when such a reaction occurs the proximate thing-meant or meaning, as it may equally well be called, comes very prominently into view. This is true of mere thinking, and if so, still more must it be true of speech, for we do not speak unless something interests us or has meaning for us, and apart from those portions of speech which are completely mechanized and not specifically willed, every word spoken necessarily insists with greater or less emphasis upon the proximate thing-meant. But here, as we shall soon see, there are differences of degree. Now the reactions to things which are, as a rule, of the greatest interest to human beings, those reactions in fact which incite to speech, are the more fortuitous and less obvious aspects in which things present themselves. In the course of a country walk we see many trees, but the fact of their being trees does not strike us on each occasion, nor do we feel called upon to say *tree* about every specimen that meets the eye. In Patagonia, where the men are said to be exceptionally tall, not every tall man encountered would evoke the utterance *tall*. Suppose, however, that here in England a very tall woman presents herself to our notice, this is a case of 'tallness' which may well call for speech. The predication springs to our minds, and also to our lips if we decide that it shall. Such predications are not, of course, restricted to adjectives. Along the same lines we may say of something that it is *gold* (a case of being-gold), *there* (a case of being-there), that it *fell to the ground* (is a case of having-fallen-to-the-ground), or whatever may be our reaction or the category which has chanced to impress us.

Now in solitary thought this is often the way in which predications present themselves. The kind or class-label or proximate thing-meant or however else we may choose to describe it claims conscious attention, and the stimulus (the ultimate thing-meant) which has evoked it may only dimly be descried in a sort of demonstrative ('that') or pronominal ('it', 'he') way. Speech likewise is often mere predication. *Wonderful!* I exclaim, without saying what is wonderful; *Here!* I call out, without mentioning that what I want is for a ball to be thrown to me here; *Fire!* may be heard at dead of night, without indication as to which house is on fire. From the speaker's standpoint such utterances are wholly satisfying. He knows, or at least knows well enough, to what stimuli these reactions refer. The listener, however, receives only the speaker's reaction. All that is vouchsafed to him is that something immediately interesting the speaker belongs to the class *wonderful*, is wanted *here*, or involves *fire*. Whether he can or cannot guess what this something is depends upon circumstances. That part of the sentence which is called the subject is the word or group of words designed to help the listener in his quest for the ultimate thing-meant.

This simple explanation of predicational nexus is due to Wegener.[1] It is so simple that it has made no visible impression upon many scholars who have read and quote his book. Wegener prefers for 'subject' the term 'exposition' to describe the words which disclose to the listener what any utterance is about. Whether a 'subject' or 'exposition' is really indispensable depends on the situation. Suppose two friends, John and Henry let us call them, are watching some athletic sports. One of the athletes wins a race and breaks the record, whereupon John ejaculates *Splendid!*

---

[1] *Grundfragen*, pp. 19 foll. Curiously enough, Wegener does not mention the listener, but the latter is clearly implied in his formulation, which reads as follows (p. 21): 'Die Exposition dient dazu, die Situation klar zu stellen, damit das logische Prädikat verständlich wird.'

Henry, the listener, can see without difficulty to what this ejaculation applies; no mention of the actual feat is necessary. The predication *Splendid!* itself is at least comparatively indispensable, since it reveals that the speaker is attending and interested, and aims at creating or reinforcing the same effect in the listener. Suppose again that the two friends are sitting at breakfast, and one of them says *Splendid, wasn't it?* The addition *wasn't it* leads the listener to infer that he himself was in the situation to which reference is made, and for that reason he will now have but little trouble in identifying the ultimate thing-meant as the concert attended by both on the previous night. But if, in the same situation, only *Splendid!* were said, it would be excusable if Henry scolded John with the irritated query *What is splendid?* To this John would have to reply *The concert which we heard last night.*

The 'subject' or 'exposition' is thus for Wegener a word or set of words which aims at explaining to the listener exactly what thing is being exhibited in the aspect of the predicate. Just as a sentence cannot be successful unless the listener is able to infer how he is meant to take it, so too it cannot be successful unless the subject to which the predicate is applied be made accessible to him. The predicate *Splendid!* alone does indeed reveal the fact that the speaker is assigning something to the class 'splendid' and wishes this to be known; but the listener, being no passive automaton, will not enter into his friend's enthusiasm without knowing what it is all about. Let us see exactly how the word or words known as the 'subject' operate. I have already insisted that human beings have the power of reacting to the same thing in different ways, and that the predicate is ordinarily some mode of reaction which is fortuitous, exceptional, or surprising. This latter condition carries with it the consequence that the predicate is seldom the simplest and most direct way of designating the ultimate thing-meant. A child learning to speak may certainly practise that art, or exhibit his cunning, by saying *mo'car!* [motor-car] concerning every example of the kind he sees, and then such utterance is truly self-sufficient. *Splendid!* refers, on the contrary, to a multitude of disparate objects, persons, acts, and what not; the word points indeed to an attribute, a proximate thing-meant, but not directly to any definitely located stimulus or ultimate thing-meant. Now language has created certain words which travel as directly to their ultimate thing-meant as an arrow to its mark. The words employed as subjects should be of this kind. The most effective among them are proper names like *John* or *London*, or demonstratives like *this, that*. If no proper name be available, and no demonstrative be sufficient, the speaker may reach the ultimate thing-meant by successive stages; what is *splendid* is not merely a *concert*, it is *the concert which we heard*; but again not merely *the concert which we heard*, but *the concert which we heard yesterday*. Each of the really essential words in the subject is a class-name and a clue helping the listener to see the ultimate thing-meant. The 'subject' cannot fail to be predication in the sense of § 67, for all use of words is this. But it differs from the 'predicate' of the sentence wherein it occurs in having a purely instrumental purpose, in not exhibiting, or seeming intended to exhibit, more of the proximate thing-meant than is absolutely necessary, and in being felt as merely a concession to the listener, not part of the real aim of the speaker.[1]

[1] Here I am referring to predicational nexus in its original form. In highly developed speech the subject can be an integral part of the speaker's communicative purpose, and can convey information of an important kind,

To put my argument somewhat differently, both subject and predicate are in a sense names of one and the same thing, reactions to the same stimulus, but the predicate embodies the speaker's interest and principal aim, while the subject is vouchsafed merely as a help to the listener. No doubt the speaker purposes the subject as well as the predicate, but a marked difference in his personal interest is always felt between the two. No better *a posteriori* proof of the essentially communicative character of speech could be adduced than the division of most sentences into subject and predicate, if, as I hope is now clear, the predicate exists for the sake of the speaker, and the subject for the sake of the listener.

The following definition of 'subject' and 'predicate' will be found roughly adequate: *Whenever a sentence or other set of words can be divided into two parts of which the one part is felt to convey something as in course of being said about the thing meant by the other part, the former part is called the predicate, and the latter the subject.* This definition takes into account subordinate as well as main predicational nexuses, and by stressing the different feeling awakened by the two parts clearly distinguishes *a furiously barking dog* from *the dog barks furiously*. The predicate makes itself felt as alive, the subject as relatively dead. In comparison with the subject, the predicate is what the speaker really wishes to say. And just for that reason its meaning must be carefully attended to, whereas the mean-

---

see the discussion of *The steep climb up the other bank was very tiring*, below, p. 278. The addition of epithets to the subject is a favourite way of making implicit statements, e.g. the word *steep* in the sentence quoted above. Non-defining relative clauses are, indeed, explicit statements couched in the grammatical form of an epithet, this form functioning incongruently as a parenthetic sentence; for example, *Your brother, whom I met in the street yesterday, told me* . . .'.

ing of the subject is, or may be, merely a clue to the thing-meant lying behind it.

The terms 'subject' and 'predicate' are derived from Aristotelian doctrine, and accordingly date from a time when grammar and logic were inseparable. As used in linguistic theory, they are to be regarded as designations of words or groups of words, though not of course without regard to the things meant by these. Primarily they belong to speech, not to language, i.e. they refer primarily to function, not to form. To give an illustration: however the word *London* be employed, it is always a noun, but in *London is a very great city* it is the subject and in *This is London* it is the predicate, or best part thereof, while in *I live in London* it is only a fragment of the predicate. Thus 'subject' and 'predicate' are merely temporary qualifications of words as they occur in some particular sentence, in opposition to those designations, like 'noun', 'adjective', and so on, which adhere to words permanently. The contention that the terms 'subject' and 'predicate' belong to speech is not contradicted by the fact that finite verbs are words of a kind constitutionally adapted to serve as predicates. As such, of course, they are facts of language, but they do not become actual predicates until so employed in particular sentences.

Are there any 'parts of speech' beside 'subject' and 'predicate'? This dichotomy affords no place for **sentence-qualifiers**, i.e. words which either qualify the purport of the sentence as a whole, like *doubtless* and *perhaps*, or else describe its relation to the gist of some other sentence, like *accordingly*, *moreover*. Apart from 'subject', 'predicate', and 'sentence-qualifiers', there are, so far as I can see, no further parts of speech.[1]

[1] Under the heading of sentence-qualifiers we must include words in anticipatory emphasis, see below, p. 290.

Are we entitled to use the term 'predicate' when the subject is not expressed? This seems necessary in some cases of real ellipse, like *Thank you kindly, Sir!*[1] It is certainly also legitimate in others where the predicate is of a form which presupposes a subject in thought; I should not find it a heinous crime to call *Wonderful!* a predicate when it stands alone. The same applies to the Latin imperative *Dic!* and of course also to those cases in which the inflexion of a finite verb points to the subject, as in Latin *Vixi*. Obviously the term 'predicate' should not be used of exclamations like *Yes! No! Alas! James! Truly?* though all these are predications in the sense indicated at the beginning of this section. That certain cases of 'predicate' cannot be brought strictly within the scope of my definition does not invalidate the latter, but merely confirms what I have had to say about the infirmities of definition in general. Jespersen gives an excellent conspectus of the various possibilities of a predicate without any expressed subject.[2]

The above account of predicational nexus will be found to have much in common with the logical doctrine that the subject of a proposition is used in extension, and the predicate in intension. This formula will stand, provided it is understood to emphasize only the greater prominence of ultimate thing-meant over proximate thing-meant or vice versa; for every use of a word carries with it a reference to both things-meant (§ 67). But Wegener's genetic account puts the matter on a much more human footing,

---

[1] I take the term 'ellipse' in a wide sense to embrace all those types of incongruent function where the feeling of an omission is awakened. A very complete attempt to classify such types will be found in E. Wellander, *Studien zum Bedeutungswandel im Deutschen*, second part, Upsala, 1923. This author restricts the term to a much narrower field.

[2] *Philosophy*, pp. 141–4.

and we also cannot dispense with some explanation of the vital warmth so apparent in the predicate as compared with the cold rigidity of the subject.

§ 69. **Grammatical and logical subject and predicate.** Fixed linguistic habits, have, as elsewhere, grown up in connexion with predicational nexus, 'subject' and 'predicate' having each its own appropriate form in particular languages. These forms are both elocutional and locutional, and as in sentence-form (§ 54), so too in predicational nexus the elocutional criteria are more decisive than the locutional. It is probably true of most languages that a vocal stress is laid on the word or words which function as predicate, while the subject is correspondingly unstressed. As regards the locutional form, languages differ both in the word-order and in other respects. Statements in English are normally of the form X *is* Y or X *does* Y, and in any sentence of the kind, simple inspection arouses the expectation that the information which the speaker really wishes to convey will lie in the words *is* Y or *does* Y, while the remaining element X will merely instruct the listener as to whom or what the information is about. Formally, therefore, *is* Y or *does* Y is the predicate and X the subject.[1] When the expectations aroused by the form are fulfilled, and *is* Y or *does* Y actually is the predicate in the functional sense explained in the last section, a slight vocal stress is placed on the most important word in it, e.g. *John is my friend* or *Henry has arrived*. In that case form and function agree, and there is complete congruence of employment. But this does not always occur. For

---

[1] It is now usual, and on the whole satisfactory, to take the copula as part of the predicate. Nevertheless it is often convenient and, where there can be no confusion, also legitimate, to use the term 'predicate' of the word or words serving as complement to the copula.

reasons to be discussed later, the locutional form of predicational nexus may sometimes be used incongruently, the formal subject functioning as the real predicate. Whenever this happens, the vocal stress is transferred to the formal subject, so that we have now the sentences *Jóhn is my friend* and *Hénry has arrived*, the sense being 'The one who is my friend is John' and 'The one who has arrived is Henry'. But though the point which the speaker particularly wishes to emphasize here lies in the proper names, the locutional form nevertheless continues to exert a certain force, as it was found to do in other examples of incongruence studied above (§§ 45, 61). It is as though the speaker had said 'I have a friend, and that friend is John' or again 'Someone has arrived, and that someone is Henry'. Form will never brook complete eclipse, but its force is always much impaired when function is incongruent.

To Paul belongs the merit of having recognized the distinction between 'formal' and 'functional' subject and predicate, and of having stated explicitly that the first of these is gradually built up on the basis of the second.[1] But though the interaction of language and speech is thus not unknown to him in practice, it has not assumed in his eyes the importance of a guiding principle, nor has he recognized that 'form' is the character of language which corresponds to 'function' in speech. Consequently the terms employed by him are different from mine. Where I have hitherto written 'formal subject' and 'formal predicate', he has **grammatical subject** and **grammatical predicate**; and for my 'functional subject' and 'functional predicate' he has 'psychological subject' and 'psychological predicate'. His former pair should be retained, being perfectly clear and also having acquired a certain

[1] *Prinzipien*, § 87, beginning.

measure of general acceptance. His latter pair rest, however, upon a view which I shall refute below (pp. 280-1), and must therefore give place to the terms **logical subject** and **logical predicate** in common use among grammarians and logicians alike. We may now settle upon the following as our final definitions:

A word or phrase which functions in speech as subject is called the Logical Subject.

A word or phrase which functions in speech as predicate is called the Logical Predicate.

A word or phrase which has the locutional form of the subject is called the Grammatical Subject.

A word or phrase which has the locutional form of the predicate is called the Grammatical Predicate.

To these definitions we can add a terminological rule: *When 'subject' and 'predicate' are used without further qualification* (as above in § 68) *it must be understood that grammar and logic, or what amounts to the same, form and function, are here in agreement, and that the terms refer to congruent function.*

An easy way of discovering the logical predicate is to cast the sentence into the form of a question, when the words corresponding to the interrogative pronoun will be found to yield the required result. Thus *Henry has arrived* answers the question *Whát has Henry done?* and therefore *has arrived* must be the logical predicate. The question answered by *Hénry has arrived* is *Whó has arrived?* and consequently *Henry* is here the logical predicate. In questions themselves the logical predicate is always the interrogative word or the phrase in which it occurs, as the strong stress laid upon it bears witness.

So many different notions have been attached by scholars to the terms 'grammatical', 'psychological', and 'logical' predicate, that Jespersen appears at first sight to be taking the only sensible course in refusing to recognize any kind of subject and predicate except the grammatical. As to the latter, says Jespersen, every one is able to tell them at sight.[1] But concurrence in this view is not possible for those who draw a distinction between language and speech, and who have attained to the conviction that all forms created by language are nothing but well-tried and standardized methods of fulfilling certain semantic functions. To recognize 'grammatical' or 'formal' subject and predicate, while rejecting those of the 'logical' or 'functional' variety, is to ignore the very reason for which the first-named exist. The evil which comes of attaching over-great importance to mere outer form is here glaringly illustrated. Even if there were no sentences in which 'grammatical' and 'logical' predicate clash, the concept of the logical predicate would nevertheless be necessary to explain the purpose of the grammatical predicate. Nor is it true that the grammatical predicate can always be discerned at sight. For the most part it can be, especially in modern languages like English, French, and German, where in ordinary statement-form the grammatical predicate is regularly announced by a finite verb or by the copula, the grammatical subject having the form of a noun or noun-equivalent, e.g. *Cain slew Abel*, *To-day is Tuesday*. But how are we to tell which is the subject and which the predicate in exclamatory statements like *A good fellow, Charles! Ein vorzüglicher Wein, dieser! Des mensonges, tout cela*? Here two nouns or noun-equivalents are simply juxtaposed, so that the rule just mentioned avails us no longer. Examination of a number of sentences of this kind proves that the first member is always logical

[1] *Philosophy*, pp. 149–50.

predicate, since it regularly contains the information which the speaker wishes to drive home. Having established this fact in individual cases, we can go on to the generalization that in such exclamatory statements the word-order is (1) grammatical predicate, (2) grammatical subject, or more briefly (1) predicate, (2) subject, since unless the contrary is said, we must always assume congruence, i.e. coincidence of the grammatical and logical elements. It is true that if we heard these sentences pronounced we should note a vocal stress on the first member, and could thus answer our question on the evidence of outer elocutional form alone. But frequently the grammarian has to work on texts that are merely written, and there the elocutional criterion fails him. On similar lines we come to the conclusion that in proverbial utterances like *No cure, no pay; Araignée au soir, espoir; Lange Haare, kurzer Sinn*, the first member is the subject and the second the predicate. In dealing with some Oriental languages the criterion of logical function is of special importance, since here the copula is regularly omitted. What are we to make of a sentence in Old Egyptian like *r·k r n bḥs*, literally 'thy mouth the mouth of a calf'? A wide survey shows that the second member of an Egyptian sentence having a noun or noun-equivalent in both positions is generally the logical predicate and contains the real point, so that the rule can be established that in this type of sentence the normal word-order was (1) subject, (2) predicate. None the less, contrary examples are sometimes found, and unless these belong to definitely established types we conclude that they are incongruent, and conjecture that their import was made clear to the listener by means of a special stress on the first member, as in the English *Jóhn is my friend*.[1]

[1] For examples of grammatical subject as logical predicate in Middle

The outer characters marking grammatical subject and predicate as such differ in different languages, and no rules of universal application can be given. The broadest generalization that can be made concerns the subject, which is nearly always a noun or some recognized equivalent of a noun. The reason is clear. Predication as exhibited in predicational nexus consists in putting a meaning upon something. The thing upon which the meaning is put is naturally regarded as a thing; every operation of attribution assumes something solid and substantial which may serve as its base. It is for just such uses that the noun-form has been evolved. Nevertheless the generalization that the subjects of sentences must be nouns is not completely immune from exceptions. If we agree with Paul,[1] as I think we must, that proverbs such as *Safe bind, safe find; First come, first served; Like master, like man*, exemplify predicational nexus, then here we have instances where the subject is not a noun. Next in order of widespread validity comes the generalization that the predicate should be introduced by a finite verb. I have dealt with this contention above in § 59, where it was seen to have many exceptions.

Great interest attaches to the question whether the subject should come before the predicate or vice versa. Wegener has seen that two opposing tendencies have been at work, some languages representing the one, and some the other.[2] Primitive, emotional man was doubtless prone to blurt out his reaction to things without reflecting that the listener could not understand him unless he knew what was being reacted to. Not until a look of incomprehension

Egyptian see my *Egyptian Grammar*, §§ 126, 130, end. For cases where the inversion has stabilized itself as congruent see § 127.

[1] *Prinzipien*, p. 125.   [2] *Grundfragen*, pp. 33–4, 107–8, 181.

was seen on the listener's face would such a speaker add the subject as a corrective. This state of affairs must be the ultimate source of such exclamatory statements as *A good fellow, Charles!* which have become a recognized form in many languages. It is a far more sophisticated and intellectual method to name the subject first, and to add the predicate afterwards. This procedure has some title to be held superior to the other, both because it ostensibly gives the actual order in which the event narrated occurred to the speaker, i.e. (1) stimulus, (2) reaction, and also because it manifests more consideration of the listener's convenience. In point of fact, however, it is of little moment which word-order is adopted, for the listener's interpretation will be based upon the sentence as a whole, and is barely influenced by the sequence of the words. Whenever the speaker has liberty of choice, as in English, the word-order (1) predicate, (2) subject, e.g. *A good fellow, Charles!*, is symptomatic of an emotional attitude towards the statement, whereas the reverse order, (1) subject, (2) predicate, e.g. *Charles is a good fellow*, produces the effect of calm, unimpassioned judgement. These inferences do not hold good, however, of languages like Hebrew, Arabic, and Old Egyptian, where the predicate, if a verb, regularly precedes the subject. Here the more primitive word-order has become congruent as regular statement-form, and having once acquired that status is bereft of its former emotional quality.

§ 70. **The subject becomes a matter of choice.** Sentences of the kind which provided Wegener with his explanation of subject and predicate are still sometimes heard. On issuing from a theatre where a lurid melodrama is being given one might easily catch the utterance *Horrible—that play!* with a perceptible pause after the first word. The speaker has voiced an almost spontaneous reaction to the piece still obsessing him, and it is only as an afterthought that the subject is added through a semi-conscious realization that by this time his companion's mind may be otherwise occupied. In ultimate analysis such an utterance consists of two predicates, each without a subject: *Horrible* [it was; the thing I refer to is] *that play!*[1] Of these two predicates the first vibrates with emotion, and is ejaculated almost involuntarily; the second is due to deliberate design, and its less impulsive character is marked by a lesser intensity of stress. But if we select a random example among the sentences which occur by thousands in our books or daily newspapers, probably this will be found to have travelled very far from the model just analysed. The following is taken from this morning's paper: *The steep climb up the other bank was very tiring.* Most of the things said about subject and predicate in the last two sections still apply here. The dichotomy is still evident. *Very tiring* is both logical and grammatical predicate, and is affirmed of the thing directly denoted by *the steep climb*, the phrase which constitutes the subject. And yet there is an unmistakable air of artificiality about the structure of the sentence as a whole. We feel that the central point in what the lady-artist who wrote it wished to convey was the fatigue she experienced as the result of a climb up a certain bank, this being steep, but she has chosen to depict her own physical condition in terms of an action producing it, this action being predicated of another action of which the performer is unnamed, and which, to crown all, is qualified by an attribute appropriate, not to itself, but only to the object affected by it. I am not criticizing the writer adversely. It is an excellent sentence,

---

[1] On this sentence see further below, p. 291.

clear and concise; indeed, it would be impossible to better it. The deduction which I wish to be drawn is that the evolution of speech has brought about a complete transformation in the character of predicational nexus. This originated in nearly spontaneous linguistic reactions which proved ineffective because only the character of the reaction (i.e. the speaker's meaning) was named, so that a description of the (ultimate) thing-meant had later to be added for the listener's enlightenment. In modern speech, however, predicational nexus has become no more than a sentence-form having the two advantages (1) that it conveys an immediate impression of completeness (§ 58), and (2) that the dominant notion can be suitably stressed, without being overstressed. There is only a slight vocal stress on the predicate of ordinary English statements, so that, although the predicate normally indicates the high-water mark of interest in a given sentence, the possibility of interesting information being given by the subject is not excluded. The writer of the sentence quoted had not previously said anything about the other bank or about her climbing of it. Thus in one pithy sentence she contrives to include four implicit predications: *I came to the other bank and climbed it; it was steep, and at the end of my climb I was very tired.*

How has the transformation of predicational nexus come about? Faced with this question, I must recall that my book is not a history, but a diagnosis of speech, and that though it has been impossible to exclude all genetic problems, I am under no obligation to go further with them than inclination prompts me. Paul has used great skill and learning in dealing with the later developments of predicational nexus.[1] He shows how both subject and

[1] *Prinzipien,* §§ 96 foll., 197 foll.

predicate came to be multiplied and enlarged, so that an abundance of information could, in developed speech, be conveniently housed within the structure of a single sentence. And he proves that objects and adverbial qualifications of verbs, epithets of the subject, and so forth are nothing but degraded predicates rendered subservient to a fundamental and planned dichotomy.

I shall content myself with discussing one important point not emphasized by Paul—a point, indeed, wherein he has gone grievously astray. The point in question touches the very origin of predicational nexus, and Paul's error is intimately connected with his fallacious conception of the sentence, examined at length in a previous section (§ 65). He contends that the logical subject (I substitute 'logical' for his 'psychological', see pp. 272-3) is always that notion which arises first in the mind of the speaker, and to which the predicate is later added.[1] He ignores the fact that, between the emergence in consciousness of a topic to speak about and the actual utterance, a whole series of psychical events has usually taken place. Chief among these is the decision to speak, and this may bring in its train a number of considerations which are the main determinants both of the form ultimately given to the sentence and also of the things chosen to be described to the listener. Above all, it is upon these considerations that depends what constituent of the total thing-meant shall be taken by the speaker as his starting-point or subject. In disproof of Paul's contention let us examine a simple

[1] 'Der Subjektsbegriff ist zwar immer früher im Bewusstsein des Sprechenden,' *Prinzipien*, p. 127. In a footnote Paul explains that he is referring to the psychological subject, and the whole trend of his argument shows that by this term he means what is here meant by 'logical subject'. Indeed, at the beginning of § 198 he substitutes the latter term, evidently by an oversight.

statement, namely *Mary has toothache*. Since *Mary*, besides being the grammatical subject, is here also the logical subject, the thought of her ought, on Paul's hypothesis, to have preceded the thought of her toothache. In given circumstances this may actually be the case. Mary may have been bustling about the room, collecting the breakfast things, making up the fire, and all the while inspiring her employer with a drowsy satisfaction at possessing the advantage of her services. Suddenly he notices her swollen cheek, and in due course may make the remark that *Mary has toothache*. In this case the sight of Mary has preceded the sight of her toothache. But that selfsame remark might well be the outcome of different conditions. Imagine an employer usually so absorbed in his newspaper at breakfast-time that Mary's ministrations are wont to pass unobserved. To-day, by way of exception, her swollen cheek attracts his attention. Waiting until she has left the room, he says to his wife, *Mary has toothache*. In this case, if we can fairly say that either Mary or the toothache first attracted his attention, assuredly it must be the toothache. We thus see that the order in which the constituents of a complex thing-meant emerge in the mind has no necessary connexion with the order in which they are subsequently referred to linguistically. In sum, Paul's notion of psychological subject and predicate rests upon a misconception, and this nomenclature should disappear.

In the great majority of cases, before a speaker proceeds to determine the exact structure of a statement, he has present to his mind the general drift of the whole which he intends to communicate. Exceptions certainly occur, as might happen if a timid visitor found himself under the necessity of complimenting a young mother upon her baby. In this predicament he might start off with the subject *Your baby* . . . or *Really, your baby* . . . without having any clear idea how to finish his sentence. Usually, however, when a statement is projected, there is an appreciable interval between reception of the stimulus and verbal reaction. Herein lies one of the most important differences between statements and exclamations. A corollary of this generalization is that *the subjects of statements are not imposed upon the speaker from outside, but are chosen by him arbitrarily.* In the kingdom of statements the speaker is an absolute monarch, and may dispose of his subjects according to his good pleasure. This does not signify, of course, that he will make his decision regardless of his material. All I am maintaining is that the subject of a statement is not preordained, as is necessarily the case when an exclamatory predicate like *Horrible* . . .*!* has preceded, but that it is the result of intelligent design and considered motives. So far from statements being mirrored replicas of external circumstances, they are perhaps the most purposive of all utterances.

How, then, are the subjects of statements chosen? In literary style there is almost complete freedom of choice, and an author may be swayed by all manner of considerations not at first sight obvious—desire for variety, striving after vividness, euphony, economy of means, to name but a few. In everyday parlance, however, some sort of rule can be discerned. This topic has been already touched upon in connexion with word-form. We there saw that *The horse neighs* is preferred to *The neigh horses*, not without good reason (p. 139). The permanent, substantial, humanly valuable things which man cannot do without, his fellow-men, his animals, his weapons, his property, and his food—these are the predestined subjects of sentences. And correspondingly, the fugitive experiences of life, events and actions, the attributes discerned in things, the relations of one thing to another—these are the predestined predicates. But at this point the reader may discover a difficulty. I have sought to show that it is the predicate of the sentence, not the subject, which communicates what is interesting, and this contention seems borne out by the fact that a vocal stress is laid upon the predicate. But here am I maintaining that the things really important to man are the material objects and the creatures which he takes as his subjects. Is this a contradiction? I think not, and will give a psychological reason which disposes of the apparent inconsistency. Everyone knows that the deepest affection does not call for words. When the beloved is tranquil and happy the lover simply takes her existence for granted; she is rarely named. But the least little thing which affects her, any new aspect in which she may show herself, any action she may perform, assumes at once an importance proportionate to the love that is felt. The like holds good in varying degree about all the things that are valuable to us. We are keenly sensitive to their vicissitudes, while the same vicissitudes, if happening to indifferent subjects, would be lacking in any particular interest. The sight of a dead human being inspires horror, while a dead fly may pass unnoticed. This proves that our interest is not in death, but rather in who dies. And yet if it comes to speech, the predicate *dead* is what will seem important, and its unstressed subject will be given only because this is the accustomed and well-motivated way with purely descriptive sentences.

Plain, straightforward statement thus takes concrete things for its subjects, leaving to become predicates what is transitory, incidental, or too widely diffused for convenient use as subject. However, the advance of civilization shows an ever-increasing range among the things deemed worthy to form the basis of descriptions; even speech and the theory of speech may be made the subjects of whole books. Abstracts like *patriotism, fair-play, unemployment* now become all-absorbing themes, dealt with under every conceivable aspect. Actions like *motoring, golf, divorce* are equally common subjects both of single sentences and of entire conversations. Naturally there are many abstracts and *nomina actionis* which are confined to the talk of the educated, so that the employment of these tends to be felt as a mark of refinement or literary culture. Quite simple sentences such as *This man is very rich* acquire alternatives with an abstract as subject, e.g. *The wealth of this man is stupendous*. The uses and abuses of these new modes of parlance are discussed by Jespersen in some of the most illuminating of his pages. His final conclusions are summed up in the following words: 'When we express by means of nouns what is generally expressed by finite verbs, our language becomes not only more abstract, but more abstruse, owing among other things to the fact that in the verbal substantive some of the life-giving elements of the verb (time, mood, person) disappear. While the nominal style may therefore serve the purposes of philosophy, where, however, it now and then does nothing but disguise simple thoughts in the garb of profound wisdom, it does not lend itself so well to the purposes of everyday life.'[1]

Far less acceptable are certain other remarks which Jespersen has to make about subject and predicate. Since, as we have seen, the act of predication consists in assigning something to a class of past experiences, it follows that the subject of a sentence cannot have greater extension, in

[1] *Philosophy*, p. 139.

the logical sense, than the predicate. But this way of looking at predicational nexus, though true, requires more reasonable handling than it receives from Jespersen. His view is formulated as follows: 'The subject is comparatively definite and special, while the predicate is less definite, and thus applicable to a greater number of things.'[1] This principle, according to Jespersen, will in some difficult cases enable us to decide which is the subject and which the predicate. But on examination we shall find Jespersen's principle a very poor substitute for the time-honoured logical test of asking ourselves what is being spoken about. Had Jespersen contented himself with saying that the subject is always definite, and the predicate less definite, his argument would have been defensible. At all events it would have been unassailable as regards the subject, since, as I have shown (pp. 266-7), the main purpose of the word or phrase known as the subject is to locate and define the thing which the predicate refers to under a non-defining aspect. The objectionable features in Jespersen's view are the additional stipulations that the subject is comparatively special and the predicate applicable to a greater number of things. If these stipulations alone were considered, a strange position would arise in regard to such often heard exaggerations as *All men are hypocrites*. Since in point of fact there are undoubtedly fewer hypocrites than people in the world (whatever the speaker of this sentence may have thought) we should here, if we followed the second half of Jespersen's rule, have to declare that *hypocrites* is the subject, and *All men* the predicate. The truth is that his appeal to reality is entirely irrelevant as a linguistic criterion. It is the same fallacy as displayed itself in the strange contention of his *Modern English Grammar*

[1] *Philosophy*, p. 150.

that a primary word (i.e. a noun) is always more special than a secondary word (i.e. an adjective), in support of which he adduced as illustration the phrase *a very poor widow; widow* is a primary, he maintained, and *poor* a secondary, because there are more poor persons in the world than widows.[1] Jespersen here forgot that speech is as capable of dealing with fiction as with fact, and that if there were not enough widows in the world to make *widow* a secondary word, a few million more imaginary ones (some could be found in novels) could easily be added in order to attain this result.

Again, Jespersen tells us that when two subjects connected by *is* are equally indefinite in form, it depends on the extension of each which is the subject, e.g. *A cat is a mammal*.[2] He then proceeds to affirm that one can say *A spiritualist is a man*, but not *A man is a spiritualist* with *man* as subject. Jespersen loads the argument in his favour by giving an example the original of which is not very probable, and the converted form of which would absolutely never occur outside a book on logic or grammar. Nevertheless, I venture to assert that it is quite possible to say *A man is a spiritualist* with *man* as subject. Many false and even absurd statements are linguistically flawless, and in this case the affirmation might even pass unchallenged and unridiculed in a roomful of people if made more palatable by a few deprecatory qualifications: *Every man is a bit of a spiritualist*. Furthermore, Jespersen's criterion fails altogether when, in a sentence with the copula, subject and predicate are coextensive. With regard to this

---

[1] *A Modern English Grammar*, Part II, Syntax, vol. i, p. 3. See Sonnenschein's valuable criticisms in his paper 'Recent Progress in the Movement for Grammatical Reform', in *Proceedings of the Classical Association*, vol. xx, pp. 41 foll.   [2] *Philosophy*, p. 151.

case, Jespersen says that the two terms may now change places as subject and predicate, and that 'this is what Keats implied in his line: *Beauty is truth; truth, beauty*'.[1] Do I entirely misconstrue Jespersen's point, or is he maintaining, as he appears to do, that Keats was wishing to bring home to his audience a purely grammatical fact? Surely this is to do monstrous injustice to the poet, whose deeply felt aphorism was clearly meant to say that whenever our minds dwell on Truth, we shall always find it revealing itself as Beauty, and that whenever our minds dwell on Beauty, this will always reveal itself as Truth. Which is a wholly different matter.

One concession may be made to Jespersen's standpoint. On rare occasions the fact that the predicate must be a class does seem to determine the choice of the subject. A case in point occurs among the many interesting examples of predicational nexus quoted in Jespersen's book. The word-order *My brother was captain of the vessel* carries with it an implication which is not present in *The captain of the vessel was my brother*. In its first form the statement suggests that the speaker possessed only one brother, unless indeed a particular brother has been mentioned in the preceding context. The second form leaves it open whether the speaker had only one brother or several. The reason for this difference is that the subject seeks to tie down the thing it means to some definite identifiable unit, and if a speaker employs the phrase *my brother* to do this, the suggestion is that there are no other brothers who might have been understood from the words.

To sum up: in the course of its history predicational nexus has undergone a great change. Its origin is revealed not only by certain survivals of the primitive type, but also

[1] *Philosophy*, p. 153.

by the traces left in highly developed speech. The starting-point was an exclamatory predicate to which, since it did not suffice to tell its own tale, a noun had to be added as an afterthought to indicate the subject. At a later stage predicational nexus has become a mere grammatical form. As such, however, it is of so great utility that it provides the regular form of statements and questions, besides having been taken over to serve as a substitute for single words, i.e. as the form of subordinate clauses. In these derivative states, the subject is no longer a mere corrective following automatically from the predicate, but has become a matter of the speaker's choice. The problem before the speaker is transformed; he still has to ask himself, 'Shall I predicate?' but to this question a second is now annexed, namely, 'What shall I take as my subject?' Speech has thereby grown less simple, but it is more effective. The range has become much wider, for the things to which an exclamation is the appropriate reaction are strictly limited in number. Merely impulsive speech has given place to an intellectual mode of utterance. The evolution of predicational nexus is, in fact, the evolution of the statement.

§ 71. **The predicative use of words.** I return now to the consideration of sentences where the grammatical predicate does not fulfil its duty as the logical predicate, where indeed it fails to indicate the real centre of interest in a communication. In such incongruent predicational nexus the part of the logical predicate is played by some other word, e.g. by *Henry* in the previously quoted example *Hénry has arrived*. There is no serious ground in this particular sentence why the grammatical subject should not be called the logical predicate, and indeed to put the position thus yields a striking antithesis. Nevertheless, this nomenclature has the disadvantage of suggesting that *has arrived* is the logical subject, which, of course, the form of the phrase precludes it from being. It will, in point of fact, nearly always be found that, when the logical predicate does not coincide with the grammatical predicate, the words representing the logical subject need to be converted into another form in order to present the aspect suited to a subject. But in grammatical analysis words and phrases must be classified as they stand, and it is not legitimate first to cast them into a different mould. For this reason it is better not to employ the terms 'logical subject' and 'logical predicate' in connexion with incongruent predicational nexus. Happily grammar possesses a term which gives the sense of 'logical predicate' without implying the presence in the sentence of a 'logical subject'; this is the adjective **predicative**, together with its adverb **predicatively**.[1] These names have come before us already in connexion with the twofold possibility of reference involved in all use of words (§ 67), and it was seen that, when a word is used predicatively, it both bears a marked vocal stress and draws attention to its meaning rather than to the thing ultimately meant by it. Among the examples quoted were *She looked óver her spectacles* and *Mind you come eárly*. If the sense of these sentences be rendered in such a manner as to make *over* and *early* not only logical, but also grammatical predicates, very uncouth forms result, namely, *The way in which she looked was óver her spectacles; Mind that the time when you come is eárly*.

The predicative use of words is thus an elocutional

---

[1] From the *Report* of the Joint Committee on Grammatical Terminology, p. 9, Recommendation II, it does not seem likely that they would have assented to so extended a use as is here given to these terms.

trick by which the complete remoulding of a sentence to obtain congruent predicational nexus can be avoided. The predicative word or phrase may occur either in the grammatical subject or in the grammatical predicate. Examples of the former are *The réd pencil belongs to Mary* (= the pencil which belongs to Mary is the one which is réd); *The house over thére belongs to the Murrays* (= the house which belongs to the Murrays is the one which is over thére). Or again, the predicative word may be completely outside the grammatical subject and predicate, e.g. *Cértainly you may tell him* (= that you may tell him is certain). On the same lines as this last example is the very common anticipatory use of nouns, often preceded by *as to* or the like, e.g. *As to your lást argument, it is completely beside the point.* In some languages this employment is so stereotyped that it can barely be called predicative any longer. Thus French questions with a noun as their subject normally take the form *Jean est-il venu?* Particularly interesting is the fact that some sentences may have two or even more predicative words, e.g. *Jámes is múch older than Jóhn and Máry*, where the speaker has contrived to make no less than four points, namely, 'a much older child than John and Mary is James', 'The amount by which James is older than John and Mary is much', 'James is much older than another child whose name is John', 'James is much older than another child whose name is Mary'.

Someone may object that in my last example James and John and Mary are not logical predicates, but logical subjects, and applying our criterion of asking to what question the statement responds this objection seems vindicated at least in the case of James. For it cannot be denied that the statement answers the question *What have you to tell us about James?* In this apparent contradiction we penetrate to the very heart of the mechanism of speech. What is the predicate or linguistic reaction at one instant may become the subject or linguistic stimulus at the next. Indeed, this is the inevitable sequence of events in every many-word sentence. Take *Horrible, that play!*[1] At first *horrible* is the speaker's reaction to the stimulus of which the influence is being exerted upon him. Hardly is the word out of his mouth, however, than it becomes the subject of what follows. 'What are you meaning by *horrible?*' 'The horrible thing I am meaning is that play.' In other terms, the word *horrible*, though not having the form of a subject, provides the clue to what must be taken as the subject or stimulus evoking the succeeding words. Each word as it falls is a predicate rapidly passing into a subject. None the less, in *Horrible, that play!*—I am now envisaging the case that the pause between the two members has become very brief—we are grammatically forced to regard *Horrible* as the predicate, and *that play* as the subject. The reason is that the speaker has contrived to prescribe this analysis by his mode of utterance. A greater stress has been laid upon *horrible* than upon *that play*, and the listener, thereby enabled to gauge the speaker's depth of intention, fastens upon the first word as that which indicates the speaker's point. To return to *Jámes is múch older than Jóhn and Máry*, subsequent reflection might doubtless justify the listener in arguing that something has been said about John and Mary, but primarily and so far as the intention of the speaker was concerned, the words *John* and *Mary* merely mark important factors in what has been said about James. As regards James, the speaker has willed his name to be interpreted in two distinct ways. As

[1] See above, pp. 277-8.

grammatical subject, it is a mere clue to the person about whom the statement is made. As a predicative word, the name insists that the person about whom the statement is made is James and no one else.

James and no one else—this last stipulation of mine calls attention to the fact that a word predicatively employed practically always implies a denial.[1] *Mind you come eárly*, not late; *Hénry has arrived*, not John; *The réd pencil belongs to Mary*, not the blue one; *The house over thére belongs to the Murrays*, not the one you are looking at; *Cértainly you may tell him*; you have no reason to doubt it. This useful implication supplies an additional motive for the predicative employment of words. Note that a congruent grammatical predicate may itself be stressed for this very purpose. *That play is hórrible*, not charming, as you maintain; *He róde*, he did not walk.

I have reached the end of my account of predication. Looking back, the reader will see that the existence of at least five kinds of predicate has been admitted: (1) every word is a predicate in the sense that it declares the nature of the thing to which it refers, the class to which the thing belongs; (2) every sentence as a whole is a predicate or reaction to a state of things which lies outside it; (3) every word as it falls is predicate of a state of things to which the preceding words have provided clues; (4) in all sentences exhibiting the dichotomy of subject and predicate, the grammatical predicate says something about the thing denoted by the grammatical subject; and (5) any given word in a sentence may be used predicatively or in the sense of a logical predicate, i.e. may convey an implicit

---

[1] Inclusion in one class is necessarily exclusion from the contradictory class, but it is only when stress is laid on an inclusion that the corresponding exclusion comes prominently into view.

statement concerning the gist of the sentence as a whole. I must recall the contention with which § 68 began; the existence of one type of subject-predicate does not prohibit the existence of another type. Not all the five kinds of predicate mentioned above are, however, of grammatical importance. How shall we discriminate between them? The answer to be given harmonizes well with the conclusion which the argument of this chapter is bringing into ever-increasing prominence; it is the speaker's purpose which lends to every element of speech its significance and interpretative importance. Among the five kinds of predicate enumerated above, the first three are inherent in the mechanism of speech, and are not specially intended by the speaker. The last two, on the contrary, are definitely meant by him. Accordingly, grammar can dispense neither with the notion of grammatical subject and predicate, nor yet with that of the logical predicate. But the rest can be ignored.

§ 72. **Statements.** No detailed discussion of the four kinds of sentence (§ 51) could be undertaken until predicational nexus had been closely examined, since it is this which gives to statements their characteristic form, and differentiates them from pure types of request and exclamation. I shall now treat of the four classes in turn, but shall deal only with really typical examples of each, since, as we have seen, the classes merge into one another, the rudiments of all being present in every sentence whatsoever. I begin with statements. A few remarks are needful in regard to their external form. The most completely developed specimens exhibit both subject and predicate, the subject being a noun or noun-equivalent. More often than not the predicate is ushered in by a finite verb. If this be merely the copula, it has to be supplemented by some predicative word or phrase, a noun (e.g. *He is king*), an adjective (*good*), an adverb (*here*), or the equivalent of one of these (*the man whom I saw, of noble birth, at home*). The word-order differs in different languages. English, French, and German usually follow the scheme *X is Y*, *X does Y*. Latin is more free, but shows a preference for subject, object, verb, e.g. *Romulus urbem condidit*. The Semitic languages favour the type verb, subject, object, e.g. *katala Zaidun ragulan*, literally 'killed Zaid a man'. In some languages the subject, if merely pronominal, manifests itself as an inflexion of the verb, e.g. *amas* in Latin. At a later stage a pronoun is often added so as to yield forms like *tu aimes*. A very important feature of statements is that they can be negative as well as affirmative. They are negated by means of an adverb (*not, never*) which, though having the force of a logical predicate (*Henry has not arrived* = that-Henry-has-arrived is not-the-case), is often without vocal stress, e.g. *Henry hasn't arrived yet*. The negative word is thus on much the same footing as the sentence-adverbs indicating the degree of assurance with which a statement is made, e.g. *certainly, perhaps* (§ 60). Only passing mention need be made of those forms of statement which approximate to exclamations, e.g. *How well he sings! A good fellow, Charles!* or of those which are elliptical, e.g. *Twopence*, as answer to *How much did that cost?*

It has been seen that the greater degree of prominence accorded to one or other of the three factors of speech apart from the words is the principle underlying the threefold division of sentences into statements, demands, and exclamations (§ 51). The statement is that class of sentence in which 'things' predominate. The function of statements has, accordingly, much in common with that of words. Except for one remarkable peculiarity to be discussed below, statements are simply complex names of things. Their aim is to describe things objectively, and to eliminate speaker and listener as far as possible. Both may, it is true, have a place among the things referred to by statements, being represented by the personal pronouns *I* and *you*. But it is only in objectivated form that they are there presented; the speaker alludes to himself and to the listener just as if they were on the same footing as anything else that might be spoken about. To hark back to the example quoted from Jespersen, the gist of any statement is comparable to the gist of the words *a furiously barking dog*. But those words constitute no statement, whereas *The dog barks furiously* does so. We now see wherein the peculiarity of statements lies; they predicate something of something. Or to use the term customary in this connexion, statements 'assert'. **Assertion** is of two kinds, positive and negative. The positive kind is **affirmation,** and the negative **denial.** Statements say either that something is or does something, or else that it is not, or does not do something.

The recognition of this essential character of statements goes back to Aristotle. 'All speech', he wrote, 'is significant, but not all is declarative, only that in which the telling of truth or falsehood is inherent. However, this is not inherent in all kinds, for example, prayer is indeed speech, but it is neither true nor false.' [1] What Aristotle says here about prayers, i.e. requests, might equally well be said

---

[1] "Ἔστι δὲ λόγος ἅπας μὲν σημαντικός . . . ἀποφαντικὸς δὲ οὐ πᾶς, ἀλλ' ἐν ᾧ τὸ ἀληθεύειν ἢ ψεύδεσθαι ὑπάρχει. οὐκ ἐν ἅπασι δὲ ὑπάρχει, οἷον ἡ εὐχὴ λόγος μέν, ἀλλ' οὔτε ἀληθὴς οὔτε ψευδής, *de Interpretatione*, cap. iv (17ᵃ). I have striven to keep my rendering free from technical terms, but for 'all speech' it might have been preferable to write 'every sentence'.

about exclamations. Questions, on the other hand, not only are directly concerned with truth and falsehood, but also have the outward appearance of affirmations or denials (§ 73). In another sense, however, they clearly neither affirm nor deny. Leaving questions on one side for the moment, we see that the genius of Aristotle has discerned the true differentia of statements. They alone can assert. A more positive turn can, indeed, be given to the generalization; all statements must either affirm or deny. That is their nature, and it always makes itself felt, even in subordinate clauses which are statements only in form. The problem before us is to investigate exactly what assertion is, whence statements derive the power to assert, and to what ends they exercise it.

The generalization that all statements assert should not be confounded with the logical doctrine that statements must be either true or false.[1] That is a very different thesis, and one which, in the light of our previous conclusions, can only signify that the particular things referred to by statements must either be, or not be, in conformity with the facts of the universe. But this conformity of things with reality is a relation lying completely outside speech, which is concerned solely with communication to a listener. We have seen that speech refers to actual and imaginary things with strict impartiality. Language has created no forms to distinguish the real from the unreal. *Nobody* and *everybody* are alike nouns, *non-existent* and *existent* are adjectives with equal title, and we can make absurd and impossible references like *Please jump over the moon* or *if you had jumped over the moon* with exactly the same syntactic constructions as sensible and practical

---

[1] Bühler seems to have made this mistake, see *Theorien des Satzes*, pp. 7–12.

references like *Please lend me five pounds* or *if you had lent me five pounds*. The argument can now be extended to things asserted. *Two and two make four* is a statement referring to the proposition that two and two make four, and this, in most situations, is true or in accord with reality as we know it. But the assertion *Two and two make five*, which refers to a thing which is false or out of accord with reality, has exactly the same linguistic appearance. From this we may conclude that the nature of speech is entirely independent of the truth or falsity of the things referred to by it. Serious confusion has arisen from the ambiguity of the terms 'statement' and 'assertion', which are sometimes used of the words employed, and sometimes of the things referred to by them. If the thesis that statements must be either true or false had to be understood of the words, naturally linguistic theory would be compelled to take cognizance of it. But such is not the case.

The ground will be still more effectually cleared for the analysis of 'assertion', if I first discuss one or two other points in which the activity of speech comes into contact with truth or falsity. Speech and language are as little affected by the belief of the speaker as they are by the truth or falsity of the things spoken about. Lies have precisely the same form as those statements which reflect knowledge or honest belief.[1] Linguistic theory is indeed concerned with all intentions on the part of the speaker which make themselves felt as implications of the sentences or words spoken, but the intention to lie is not among the

---

[1] Surely Bühler is mistaken in finding the function of *Kundgabe* specially prominent in lies (*Theorien des Satzes*, p. 11). The essence of a lie consists in concealing one's desire to misinform the listener, not in proclaiming it. Linguistically it is impossible to 'tell' a lie. So far as the telling is concerned, this is mere description of something asserted, its truth being at most implied. Speech, of itself, is always a fairly innocent proceeding.

number. On the contrary, the speaker of a lie does everything in his power to have it taken as the truth, though the methods he adopts for this purpose may be as diverse as violent protestation and casual, unobtrusive suggestion. Another way in which truth and falsity may be thought of in connexion with speech is in measuring the success or lack of success with which a speaker finds words or forms of expression adapted to his purpose. If he uses a word perfectly suited to the thing which he wishes to convey, or again if he employs the type of sentence calculated to influence the listener in the way desired, then there is a correspondence of truth between aim and result. Here, however, the ethical terms 'right' and 'wrong', or the normative 'correct' and 'incorrect', are more in place (§ 48). I come last of all to a point of the highest importance. In its ultimate origin speech was a natural, automatic reaction, and at this stage the cry of anguish, or whatever it may have been, was the true effect of its cause. Later on the intervention of will and purpose completely transformed this causal relation, but utterances still retain a character of truth inasmuch as the speaker's sincerity and genuineness of purpose are normally taken for granted. No one doubts the truth of an exclamation of enthusiasm, unless it is uttered in a lukewarm manner. Commands are accepted as signs that the speaker really wishes the performance of the action commanded, and questions that he is seeking a true answer.[1] Only if elocu-

---

[1] This does not mean that exclamations and commands assert in the same sense as statements and questions for specification. The latter imply truth, while the former assume it, which is not the same thing. In point of fact, both the implication and the assumption may be wrong. Moreover, a relation of truth between the speaker's intention and reality is clearly distinguishable from a similar relation between the things meant by him and reality. The fact that speech not only is itself a fact of reality, but

tional indications contradict the locutional, as in irony or playful requests, does the listener hesitate to interpret speech literally.

These observations lead on directly to the topic of 'assertion', the definition of which is contained in the following formula: *All statements assert, i.e. present their predicate either as true or else as false of the thing denoted by their subject.* We have seen that, historically, predicational nexus, i.e. statement-form, originated in exclamations. The truthfulness generally attributed to exclamations still adheres to the statements descended from them; whenever the speaker is kept in view, it is habitually assumed that his statements are honestly meant. Nay more, his knowledge of what he states is usually assumed, so that unless there are grounds for suspicion, statements are accepted as true. When I ask the price of a box of cigarettes and am told it costs two shillings, I do not doubt the statement. This implication of truthfulness is obviously due to the fact that, in the overwhelming majority of cases, the things stated have indeed been found factually true. When a particular statement is recognized by the listener as false, it is for him an incongruent use, which awakens in his mind a feeling of deception. We now come to the strangest characteristic of statements, namely, that the objectivity to which allusion was made at the beginning of this discussion should be combined with a compelling force such as is usually attributed to human agency alone. Not only is the thing meant by a statement

also is either assumed or implied to refer to something true, probably accounts for Ries's stipulation that the sentence must have a *Beziehung zur Wirklichkeit*, see for his definition above, p. 239. His own explanations of this phrase appear to me very muddled, and in places self-contradictory. He would have been on safer ground had he stipulated that every sentence must have a relation, not to truth, but to human interest.

taken as true, but its truth seems to find authoritative expression in the sentence itself. That 'statements assert' can be said with much more legitimacy than is usual when human actions are ascribed to things. The probable reason is that statements possess in subject and predicate representatives both of the stimulus which has incited to speech and also of the reaction to that stimulus. Between these a causal relation appears to subsist, and accordingly the act of speech here seems somehow removed from its external environment and enacted within the uttered words themselves. However this may be, in hearing statements, and still more in reading them, their author is often forgotten, attention being fixed on the things spoken about. Only in the case of false or absurd statements, or of those that are provocative in some other way, does the speaker flash into sight, proving that this factor of speech has really been present, though unnoticed, all the time.

Statements may be negative as well as affirmative.[1] The unique character given to speech by its power of negation is well brought out by Raleigh in his essay on Style: 'Other arts can affirm, or seem to affirm, with all due wealth of circumstance and detail; they can heighten their affirmation by the modesty of reserve, the surprises of a studied brevity, and the erasure of all impertinence; literature alone can deny, and honour the denial with the last resources of a power that has the universe for its treasury.'[2] It seems obvious that this peculiarity is due to the coexistence of a listener with the speaker. There seem good grounds for thinking that denial had its origin in contradiction, in the refusal to accept assertions as true. Thought

---

[1] Jespersen has an interesting chapter on negation (*Philosophy*, pp. 322 foll.), but the problems which he treats, and his manner of treating them, are quite different from my own.   [2] W. Raleigh, *Style*, p. 18.

is so much under the influence of linguistic habit that negative propositions now undoubtedly play a considerable part therein; but most people would probably admit that, when alone, they are more apt to think affirmatively than negatively. The derivation of negative words in general is difficult to determine; in Old Egyptian there is a possibility—it is no more—that the word *n* 'not' is connected with the verb *nì* 'to reject', but in that event the verb may well be secondary. It seems a likely hypothesis that the word for *not* everywhere originated in an exclamation of refusal. This likelihood seems borne out by the syntactic form universally shown by denials. Whereas the vast majority of human reactions may be linguistically represented by the predicate of a predicational nexus, this is not true of the non-acceptance of statements; we do not say *That X is Y is not*. Negative statement is managed quite differently. Mere inspection of instances shows that the affirmative statement is reproduced as a whole, and then qualified by an adverb which annihilates the predication. Can it be doubted, then, that negative statement is in essence the affirmation of a real or supposed speaker into which the listener's exclamation of refusal has been insinuated? Thus negative statement is genetically an affirmation, and as such bears the stamp of truthfulness which we found inherent in all statement-form; in sum, denials, no less than affirmations, present their gist as true assertions. Psychologically, however, negative statements have undergone a transformation. They are no longer felt as predications first affirmed, and then subjected to refusal. Language has changed them into attributions rejected from the very start. Hence it comes that we must define assertions as statements which present their predicate either as true or false. All statement is assertion, and to that extent presents what it says as true; but it is also either affirmation or denial, and when considered in that light presents its gist as either true or false.

Since statements keep speaker and listener as far out of sight as possible, the purposes with which this sentence-form is used are less obvious than in the other classes of sentence. Indeed, those purposes are exceedingly various, and no more is here possible than to glance at a few. Information given for practical ends and scientific formulation are perhaps the fields in which the statement reaches its climax of objectivity and apparent truthfulness." Expressions of opinion and valuations of any kind bring the speaker into view much more conspicuously, and in face of these the listener is apt to assume a critical and sceptical attitude from the outset. There are a number of cases where it is irrelevant to introduce the criterion of truth and falsehood. A novel may open with the words *The sun was sinking slowly towards the horizon;* here we do not ask whether the statement is false or true; that it contains an assertion is indubitable, but this is merely a consequence of the linguistic form which the writer has chosen to adopt. The like holds good of playful statements such as *You are a little pig!* Types of statement also exist where the personality of the speaker, so far from remaining hidden, is obtruded with an even painful emphasis. In threats like *You'll rue it!* the intonation dominates over the objective locutional form, and leaves a sinister impression of danger approaching from the speaker. I have previously dealt with commands like *You shall obey me* (p. 231), and have also shown cause for the satisfying sense of completeness arising from the use of statement-form (§ 58).

It is difficult and often even misleading to fight against

the ambiguity inherent in words, and in the course of this section I have used the term 'statement' freely in no less than three senses: (1) a sentence functioning as a statement; (2) a sentence with statement-form; and (3) the proposition referred to by a statement. I make no apology, for in taking this course I have merely employed language as its nature dictates. The reader has cause for complaint only if I have misdirected or mystified him.

§ 73. **Questions.** I now turn to the two kinds of sentence in which the listener may be considered the predominating factor, since it is upon his performance of some action that the success of the utterance depends. In requests some specifically named action is demanded by the speaker, whereas in questions a relevant verbal response is desired. I shall deal with questions first, these being especially closely related to statements both in form and function. The mere fact that a desire for a relevant verbal response is evinced by questions shows that 'things' are there almost as important a factor as the listener, for the purpose of words is always to point to things. On the other hand, there is obviously a very close kinship between questions and exclamations, the speaker's desire being extremely prominent, particularly from the listener's point of view. There is, indeed, no class of sentence in which the interaction of all four factors of speech is more conspicuous, or in which the relationship to the other classes is more apparent. As regards the outer form of questions, intonation is, as always, the principal means of conveying the sentence-quality. The type of intonation adopted varies according to the nature of the particular question that is being asked. Predicational nexus constitutes, as in statements, the main framework of the locutional form. But this, though usual, is not absolutely indispensable, seeing that a single word like *headache* may serve as a question (*Headache?*), no less than as an exclamatory statement (*Headache!*).

Questions fall into two main groups. In the first of these, which I shall call **questions for corroboration**, the entire gist of the predication is submitted to the listener's arbitrament, and the expected answer is either *Yes!* or *No!* In the second group, which may be conveniently termed **questions for specification**, the speaker's inquiry centres upon some special point in connexion with the predication, the general truth of the latter being accepted. Here some interrogative pronoun, adjective, or adverb is necessary to indicate the exact point in respect of which an answer is required. I shall discuss these two groups separately, since both in form and in function they present considerable divergences. But before embarking upon this undertaking, it will be well to call attention to another grouping which cuts across that already mentioned. In questions of the most authentic kind the speaker is really asking for information. He may, it is true, have a shrewd idea what the answer will be, and may even find a way of intimating the fact. None the less, he is not certain, and the purpose of his question is to ascertain what is still unknown to him. In the other variety, called **rhetorical questions**, the speaker knows, or thinks he knows, what the answer will be, and is merely anxious to see the listener's reaction, is trying to make him admit something, or the like. These are also genuine questions, in so far as an answer is really sought, but they tend to become mere statements, as in the case quoted above, p. 204.

(1) In **questions for corroboration** the original locutional form was identical with that of the statement. An assertion was actually contained in them, but was made

only to be called in doubt by means of the intonation. Such questions are really incongruent statements, the incongruence consisting in the fact that the speaker's purpose is not to give information, but to receive it. In *He told you so?* which is not the usual question-form in English, the incongruence is still felt. But many languages have succeeded in obliterating all sense of incongruence by the mere insertion of an interrogative particle, like Greek ἦ, μή, ἄρα, Latin *num*, *-ne*. Modern European languages possess in inverted word-order an equally successful alternative to the use of interrogative particles, e.g. *Vient-il? Ist er da?* So characteristic of questions do such inversions seem to us, that it is by no means easy to realize that this word-order has not been universally felt necessary. We have already seen that such is not the case; historically, indeed, the inversion is demonstrably secondary, having been copied from questions for specification (see below). Nevertheless, there is a good psychological reason why the practice, once inaugurated, should have been retained; as all exclamatory sentences show, a strong tendency exists to start with a word on which special interest hinges or concerning which the speaker feels at all deeply; and such a word, in questions for corroboration, is the finite verb introducing the predicate. I will only mention in passing the fact that, where an auxiliary verb is used, this alone is placed before the subject, so that here both the desire to mark interrogation and the feeling that the subject should precede the predicate can be simultaneously satisfied, e.g. *Est-il venu? Hat er geschrieben?* In English the same arrangement is carried even into the present and past tenses, compare *Does he know? Did he know?* with *Weiss er? Wusste er?* French reaches a similar result by a different road, e.g. *Est-ce que vous l'avez vu?* Negative questions belonging to this group present various subtleties which cannot be discussed in detail. Nevertheless, I will attempt to explain briefly what seems to me the main principle. Whenever a proposition is questioned, the possibility of the opposite being true is *ipso facto* entertained. But denial carries with it a sense of contradiction not ordinarily inherent in affirmation. For instance, *He is rich* merely affirms, but *He is not rich* suggests 'You may have thought he was rich, but he is not'. Consequently, whereas *Is he rich?* implies no expectation with regard to the answer, *Is he not rich?* has the implication 'I thought he was rich; are you going to tell me he is not? If so, I should be surprised.'[1] This may help to explain why tag-questions, as Jespersen calls them, are of different quality from the statement they accompany, e.g. *He is rich, is he not? He is not rich, is he?* No doubt a question like *Are you not going to school to-day?* may actually be answered either way. But the speaker's implication is, 'If you tell me you are not, I should be surprised'. Accordingly, it is on the whole true to say that negative questions for corroboration expect the answer *Yes!* Cf. Latin *nonne*, Hebrew $h^a l\bar{o}$.

(2) Still closer to statements are **questions for specification**, where the interrogation rests on a single word or phrase. For here the remainder of the sentence definitely asserts, and apart from the emphasis laid on the initial interrogation, English questions of this kind have an intonation indistinguishable from that of an ordinary statement. Interrogative stress at the end, as well as at the beginning, occurs only when the speaker, surprised at a preceding assertion, desires its repetition in order to make sure that

---

[1] Jespersen states that *Is John rich?* and *Is John not rich?* are perfectly synonymous, *Philosophy*, p. 323. It will be seen from the text that I hold a different view.

he has not misheard, e.g. *Whén did you cóme?* in the sense of 'When did you say you came?' The utility of interrogative pronouns (e.g. *who? what?*), adjectives (e.g. *which? what?*), and adverbs (e.g. *where? how?*) resides in the fact that they give more or less precise directions to the listener with regard to the thing concerning which the speaker desires information. The result is brought about mainly by their syntactic employment. For example, in *To whom did George give the book?* the dependence of *whom* upon the datival word *to* shows that the query concerns the recipient of George's gift; the answer may or may not repeat the preposition, e.g. *To Mary* or simply *Mary*. But most interrogative pronouns, adjectives, and adverbs also possess in their form a means of suggesting to the listener the kind of thing to be named in his reply; for instance, *who?* assumes that this thing will be a person presented as the source of some action or action-like proceeding. Apart from such implications, the stem-meaning of all these interrogative words is identical; it marks the thing to which they refer as belonging to the class 'things concerning which immediate specification is desired'.

There can be no doubt that questions for specification are derived from questions for corroboration having an indefinite word as a component. A question like *You saw someone?*, though couched in a form which seems to anticipate *Yes!* or *No!* as the reply, is, as a rule, not satisfactorily answered, if the answer be affirmative, unless a name corresponding to *someone* is vouchsafed. Now it is a remarkable fact that in many languages the interrogative and indefinite words are related; well-known cases are those of Greek τίς, 'who?' τις, 'someone', Latin *quis*, 'who?' *quis*, 'anyone', Arabic *măn*, 'who?' 'someone', *mā*, 'what?' 'something'. In the past, however, most scholars have either refrained from discussing the problem of priority, or else have pronounced in favour of the interrogatives. Decisive evidence that the interrogative meaning is secondary and derived from the indefinite is, however, forthcoming from Egyptian. As Sethe has recognized,[1] Coptic ⲟⲩ, ⲟⲩⲏ, 'what?' can be derived only from *waʿ*, 'one', and the Late-Egyptian *iḫ*, 'what?' from *iḫt*, '(some)thing'; an even clearer case is Late-Egyptian *wēr*, 'how much?' from *wēr*, 'much'. Meillet stands almost alone among Indo-European scholars in advocating the view here adopted.[2]

Note in the same connexion a curious rhetorical use to which questions of this category, when negative, are not seldom put: the question *Whom have you not told?* may be intended to mean 'You have told everyone', 'There is no one whom you have not told'. The origin of this use will be clearly seen if we analyse the question as signifying 'I should be surprised if there is anyone you have not told'. Here again the close affinity between the interrogative and indefinite pronouns is apparent.

In nearly all languages the interrogative word or phrase, as being the centre of the speaker's interest, is placed at the beginning of the sentence. This is true, not only of the classical languages and their modern descendants, but also of Hebrew and Arabic, and wherever verifiable, an emphatic intonation is found to rest upon the interrogative word. Old Egyptian is the only language known to me to which the rule that the interrogative word or phrase

[1] *Zeitschrift für ägyptische Sprache*, vol. xlvii (1910), pp. 4–5.
[2] A. Meillet, *Introduction à l'étude comparative des langues indo-européennes*, Paris, 1912, p. 356. Paul discusses the two possibilities, but refuses to pronounce between them, *Prinzipien*, p. 136. C. Brockelmann, *Grundriss der vergleichenden Grammatik der semitischen Sprachen*, Berlin, 1908–13, vol. i, p. 328, § 113, favours the view that the indefinite meaning is derived from the interrogative.

should be placed at the beginning does not apply, and even here a tendency in that direction exists.[1] But the commoner practice of Egyptian is to place such a word in the position which the answer would occupy in a corresponding assertion; for instance 'What shall I do?' shows the form 'I shall do what?' and 'To what god shall I announce thee?' is represented by 'I shall announce thee to whom (being) as a god?' This arrangement adds to the clarity of the question, while subtracting from its interrogative force. Sporadic examples of the same practice occur in Arabic and other Semitic languages (cf. Egyptian Arabic *inta mîn?* literally 'thou (art) who?'), but only by way of exception.[2]

It remains to discuss the inverted word-order (1) verb (or auxiliary), (2) subject, seen in English, French, and German, e.g. *Why do you say so? Pourquoi taisez-vous? Was wollen Sie?* Philologists tell us that this word-order is only one case out of a number where the more recent tendency of the Indo-European languages to place the verb immediately after the opening word has prevailed over the earlier tendency to favour the word-order (1) subject, (2) predicate.[3] A dilemma arose when, out of a desire for emphasis, some word other than the subject was placed at the head of the sentence; in that case one of the two preferences just mentioned had to be sacrificed. In German it is the subject-verb preference which has gone to the wall, e.g. *Hier sind wir, Schön sieht er aus.* In French the inversion verb-subject has prevailed only after *à peine*

---

[1] A. H. Gardiner, *Egyptian Grammar*, § 495.
[2] C. Brockelmann, op. cit., vol. ii, p. 194, § 116.
[3] See a particularly lucid exposition of the facts in F. Sommer, *Vergleichende Syntax der Schulsprachen*, 2nd edition, Leipzig, 1925, pp. 118 foll.; also Jespersen, *Language*, pp. 357–9.

and *peut-être*. In Old English the same use was frequent, but in more recent times only a few survivals are found, e.g. *There is, are* ..., *Here lies* ... Hence it would seem that the inverted word-order *Whom did you see?* for all its present interrogative feeling, is as a historical fact purely accidental.

§ 74. **Requests.** The types of sentence best classified under this head are so multifarious that it is no easy matter to find a formula which will suit them all. Strong feeling on the part of the speaker is almost everywhere present, and at first sight this might tempt us to regard requests as exclamations of a particular kind. On the other hand, the nature of the act desired is carefully specified in all cases except vocatives, which are not usually placed in this category or indeed admitted to be sentences at all; some might feel inclined, therefore, to rank certain subspecies of request, e.g. unfulfilled wishes, under the heading of statements. Neither alternative, however, does justice to the most salient feature of all the sentences here united by a common label, namely, *the speaker's desire for an action not dependent solely upon his own will.* This is the true differentia of requests, and since the listener is either directly appealed to for help, or else at least included among the powers whose assistance is invoked, we are justified in specially connecting requests with the listener, and in treating them as one of the two types of demand (§ 51). The chief varieties of sentence generally accepted as belonging to the class of requests are commands, entreaties, prayers, advice, permission, exhortations, and wishes, beside negative forms like prohibitions, warnings, and so forth. To these I add vocatives, which qualify as sentences because they reveal intelligible purpose complete in itself, and which bring the listener no less prominently to the fore than imperatives, demanding from him an act of attention. Indeed, in the Indo-European languages imperative and vocative possess in common a peculiarity of outer form, namely, the fact that they consist of the bare word-stem, cf. Ζεῦ, Μενέλαε, *Balbe* with παῦσαι, φέρε, *age*. Nevertheless, it must be allowed that the vocative differs from all other requests in that it names the listener and does not specify the action which he is to perform. Imperative and vocative may, of course, be combined in a single sentence, as in *Tu regere imperio populos*, ROMANE, MEMENTO. Apart from vocatives, the only requests which do not name the desired action, or at least its main constituents, appear to be those employing such interjections as *hey, hi*. These, like many brief non-verbal requests, e.g. *Silence! To work! Hats off! All hands on deck!* should find a place in treatises on syntax under both requests and exclamations.

The most indisputable and characteristic type of request is that expressed by the second person of the imperative, with or without supplementary words. The intonation employed by the speaker is usually incisive enough to make unnecessary any mention of the listener, but every nuance is possible, from the imperious tones of the sergeant-major down to the whining prayer of the mendicant. It is probably on account of the highly significant character of their intonation that imperatives and vocatives are able to dispense with significant inflexions, and the same fact accounts for the employment of the infinitive for a like purpose, as is found in a number of languages, e.g. German *Einsteigen!* French *Ralentir!* and regularly in Coptic; in Italian and Old French this use is particularly common in prohibitions, cf. also the Greek οἶς μὴ πελάζειν. Almost everywhere there may be observed a tendency to replace the imperative by other forms, or at least to mitigate its peremptoriness by the addition of some courteous word or phrase, e.g. *pray, if you please, please*. Reference has been made already to the new form of requests which has developed out of questions, e.g. *Would you please pass the salt?* (p. 231). Paraphrases like *I beg you to* . . . have the same effect, though with the appropriate words the identical method may serve to increase the force of a command, e.g. *I insist on your leaving at once*. A curious fact which requires closer psychological investigation is the reluctance displayed by many languages to use the imperative with a negation. In the Semitic languages this use is impossible, forms analogous to Greek μὴ εἴπῃς, Latin *ne dixeris*, being employed. In the Indo-European languages the same position seems to have existed at the beginning, and though modern tongues like English, French, and German take no exception to commands of the types *Go not! Do not wait! Ne viens pas! Spreche nicht!*, Latin is very sparing in their use (*Ne timē* in Plautus), and Greek restricts them to a particular case, e.g. μὴ λέγε, 'do not make a practice of speaking'. Old Egyptian employs a negative verb (*to not*, as it were), using the imperative of this and accompanying it by a special verbal form or else the infinitive, cf. *noli putare* in Latin. I used to think that these avoidances of negative *plus* imperative were due to the inherent positive directive force of the latter, so that the coupling of it with a negation would be practically a contradiction in terms (*Ne timē* = 'don't—do fear!'). However, this supposition no longer seems to me quite convincing.

Surveying the various 'acts' which a speaker may demand of his listener, we find that they put some strain upon the term, since purely negative behaviour has to find a

§ 74 REQUESTS

place among them. For imperatives may be formed not only from verbs signifying physical acts (e.g. *go, take, buy, speak*)[1] and psychical acts (e.g. *think, feel*), but also from others denoting states (e.g. *remain, be, sleep*) and privative notions (e.g. *refrain, schweigen*). Greek and Latin possess passive imperatives, e.g. *accingere*, πέπαυσο, but these are only partly passive in force; cf. also in German *Seid umschlungen, Millionen*. Since speech is concerned with the world of imagination no less than with that of external reality, there is no reason why the commands that may be given should be within the listener's competence. Thus the door is opened to the inclusion, under the head of requests, of many desires where the listener becomes a merely partial or even completely fictive participant. Various languages employ an imperative meaning 'let' or the like to introduce requests where no intervention on the part of the listener is actually expected, e.g. *Let there be light! Lasst ihn sprechen;* so, too, in Egyptian *imi sḏm n·n nb·n nḫt*, literally 'give (thou) hearken to us our powerful lord', with the corresponding passive *m rdi sḏm·n·tw n·sn*, literally 'not (thou) give be hearkened to them', i.e. 'let them not be hearkened to'.

Requests in the first person plural, like Ἴωμεν, Μὴ εἴπωμεν, *Hos latrones* INTERFICIAMUS, GEHEN *wir*, combine an exhortation to the listener with the intimation that the speaker is willing to play his part in joint action. The forms used in the above examples are not termed imperatives, because their origin and their other employments demand that they should be placed in a different category, namely the subjunctive; but their function is closely similar to that of

---

[1] In view of such imperatives as *speak, tell, declare*, it is impossible to distinguish questions from requests by saying that the former call for verbal, and the latter for non-verbal responses.

the imperative. French stands alone in possessing a form which can best be described as first person plural of the imperative, e.g. *marchons*; in Coptic there is a similar, but as yet not quite satisfactorily explained form ⲁⲙⲱⲓⲛⲉ, from Late-Egyptian *mi·n*, 'let us come', apparently imperative *plus* suffix-pronoun, first person plural. At the outset the notion of requests in the third person may seem self-contradictory, since the third person of a finite verb is a device whereby the action is presented as springing from a source different from both speaker and listener. Nevertheless, we cannot do otherwise than treat as requests subjunctive examples like VALEANT *cives mei*, *The Devil* TAKE *the hindmost*, VIVE *la République*, Er LEBE *hoch*, or Greek optatives like Ζώη; indeed, grammarians have always classified as imperatives the active and passive forms found in Ταῦτα μὲν δὴ ταύτῃ εἰρήσθω, *Regio imperio duo* SUNTO, *iique consules* APPELLANTOR, though of other antecedents than the true imperative. The formulation of a request in the third person is sometimes due to the fact that the prospective performer of the desired act cannot be directly addressed, but often such formulation serves merely as a mechanical contrivance to provide a convenient starting-point for the description of that act, in other terms to put the request in the form of a predicational nexus. The source from which the speaker expects help in such a case may vary greatly: sometimes it is the present listener who is thus indirectly given an order, e.g. *Que ce monsieur m'attende un instant*; on other occasions the addressee is quite indeterminate, and the request may be simply a pious wish. When that wish is impossible of fulfilment, the sentence becomes a mere statement of desire. It is not for a theoretical book of this kind to dictate how any practical grammarian shall arrange his facts, so that I shall not discuss whether unfulfilled wishes should be placed under the heading of statements or requests.[1] In point of fact, grammars as now written seldom classify their data in this way at all, preferring rather to approach the different kinds of sentence from the side of morphology and the discussion of the uses of the 'moods' of verbs. Brunot stands almost alone in his advocacy of a semantic outlook in language-teaching.[2] His pedagogic method is extremely interesting, and perhaps has a brighter future than is generally believed. Here I have wished merely to show once again that the different kinds of sentence merge into one another.

§ 75. **Exclamations.** There remains to be discussed that class of sentences in which the speaker looms forth more insistently than any of the other three factors. Not that his person is necessarily indicated; on the contrary, exclamations containing direct references to the speaker, e.g. *How miserable I feel!* are the exception rather than the rule. The essence of exclamations is that, whether by way of description or only through implication, they emphasize to the listener some mood, attitude, or desire of the speaker, in extreme cases to the exclusion of all else. Thus they approximate more closely than any other kind of sentence to the spontaneous emotional cry. From the listener's point of view, indeed, such a cry cannot fail to be regarded as a kind of speech. The quality of the sound awakens in him the memory of past experiences, and points to some present experience of similar quality on the part of the utterer. Emotional cries are speech in so far as they

---

[1] I must plead guilty to having given advice of the kind on several occasions. However, such has not been intended to imply that there is only one way in which good books on syntax may be arranged.

[2] F. Brunot, *La pensée et la langue*.

display both a meaning and a thing-meant; they fall short of speech only to the extent that they are involuntary. Once we are sure that such a cry is intentional, the bridge between the linguistic and the non-linguistic has been crossed. The most primitive of all exclamations are stereotyped vocal performances like the sucking in of the breath (*fff!*) at the sight or smell of some delicious dish. This is true speech, and the sound employed is a real word, even if it chance not to be recorded in the dictionary. Not words, on the other hand, or exclamations in the linguistic sense, are the strange noises which small boys often take pleasure in making. These are intentional, indeed, but fail to qualify as either speech or language because their sound is not fixed and cannot, accordingly, evoke significant recollections; they are but meaningless sounds.

Writers have invented spellings for some of the meaningful cries just alluded to; *ow* is an expression of pain, *pah* one of disgust, *pshaw* one of contempt or impatience. As words or stereotyped units of language, such sounds are called **interjections**, and may be defined as *words having reference to given types of psychic reaction and arousing an expectation of use in reference to a particular mood, attitude, or desire presently experienced by the speaker.*[1] Like other words, interjections may have extended areas of heterogeneous meaning; *oh*, for example, covers a whole range of

[1] It is incomprehensible to me how Bühler (*Theorien des Satzes*, p. 10, n. 1) can maintain 'Überhaupt keine Nennfunktion haben die primären Interjektionen (*au! oh! aha!*)'. Because interjections used as exclamations proclaim the speaker, it does not follow that they do not simultaneously describe something which must be regarded analytically as distinct from him, namely a specific emotion. Moreover, Bühler does not distinguish, as he should, between interjections and the use of them as exclamations. An interjection, as such, does not proclaim or make manifest some single speaker, but all the speakers who have ever used the word. What an interjection names is a specific reaction on the part of *any* speaker.

diverse emotions. Some interjections not only refer to a psychic reaction on the part of the speaker, but also imply a desire for a particular type of response on the part of the listener; thus *sh* asks for silence, *eh?* demands the repetition of a remark, *fie* seeks to excite shame. Though the meaning of words of this class is not less precise than that of other words, it is more complex and less differentiated. *Pah* may be paraphrased by *I am disgusted*, but the speaker and the disgust felt by him are blended in indissoluble fashion. As regards their inner form, interjections derive their particularity from the anticipation they carry with them of employment as exclamations, i.e. as purposeful references to something presently experienced by the speaker. This word-class is swelled by accessions from other classes—by nouns like *rubbish* and *fiddlesticks*, and by verbs like *hark* and *bother*. When such a word has obtained general currency as an exclamation, the rank of an interjection must be conceded to it in addition to its original rank. As we have seen, there is no reason why a word should not belong to more than one word-class; *silver*, for example, is at once noun and adjective and verb. Accordingly, the fact of *rubbish* being a noun does not prevent it from being also an interjection; but to qualify as an interjection, a word must needs be habitually, not merely exceptionally, used as an exclamation.[1] To

---

[1] I am here polemizing against Jespersen, who, in discussing the habit of regarding interjections as a 'part of speech', writes as follows (*Philosophy*, p. 90): 'The only thing that these elements have in common is their ability to stand alone as a complete "utterance", otherwise they may be assigned to various word-classes. They should not therefore be isolated from their ordinary uses. Those interjections which cannot be used except as interjections may most conveniently be classed with other "particles".' But what Jespersen depreciatingly stigmatizes as the 'only thing' distinguishing interjections from other words is so important and so striking that it

conclude, let it be noted that interjectional phrases are very frequent, e.g. *O dear me, woe is me, alackaday, for shame, good heavens.*

Interjections have been discussed at some length because the purest and most thoroughgoing exclamations are those which employ them. But I trust that it has been made perfectly clear that interjections are merely a class of words, while exclamations are sentences. The former are a category of language, while the latter are a category of speech. Speech is applied language, and exclamations always apply to some present experience of the speaker, real or simulated. The last qualification is necessary, since an exclamation like *Alas!* may be insincere or ironical just as easily as it may be honest and uttered with literal intent. In exclamations employing interjections, these generally stand alone, though occasionally they are combined with other words, e.g. *Ah me! Alas, it is quite impossible!* It is only with extreme incongruence that interjections can be used as predicates, e.g. *My present feeling is damn!* Since every sentence possesses something of the quality of all the four classes, exclamations are never completely confined to self-revelation. Even the interjectional forms may be classified as veering more in one direction than in another. *Fie!* and *Hark!* are obviously exclamations of request, *Eh?* is practically a question, and *Pshaw!* may at least be paraphrased as a statement. Similarly, some sentences in the form of statements, requests, or questions are more exclamatory than others, as I have repeatedly had occasion

amply justifies the placing of them in a separate category. Moreover, a noun like *nonsense* habitually used as an exclamation is not on the same footing as a noun like *fire* only exceptionally so used. Jespersen would not have taken this line if he had been clear about the distinction between 'language' and 'speech', and if he had realized that the so-called 'parts of speech' are categories of language.

to note (e.g., p. 274). As regards all sentences intermediate between exclamations and sentences of some other class, the grammarian has necessarily to consider in which category he shall include them. The course to be taken depends upon external form more than upon anything else. For example, the word-order in *How beautiful she is!* and *What a troublesome time you have had!* differs sufficiently from that of statements to warrant separation from them and classification under the head of exclamations; on the contrary, the Egyptian translation of the former sentence, *nfr·wy sy*, can obviously not be kept apart from the corresponding statement *nfr sy*, 'she is beautiful', since the exclamatory quality of the former is indicated simply by the use of the particle ·*wy*, in origin simply the dual ending, cf. *Twice beautiful is she!*

Mention may be made of a few criteria of outer form, elocutional and locutional, which tend to stamp a sentence as an exclamation. All emotionally spoken sentences are *ipso facto* exclamatory, though not every exclamation is emotional. *Yes!* and *No!* are obviously better classed under this head than as statements, though they are often bereft of all eagerness or special emphasis. Concise utterances are usually exclamatory, because social convention favours the more wordy forms of diction, except under stress of emotion. We saw above (pp. 276–7) that the word-order (1) predicate, (2) subject, is more impulsive than the inverse order; accordingly, where there is a choice between the two possibilities, the former tends to indicate exclamatory quality. Lastly, exclamations are often recognizable by some peculiarity of intonation, by strong accentuation or the like.

§76. **Quantitative classifications of the sentence.** Attempts have not been wanting to supplement the classification discussed above with another having quantitative considerations as the principle of division. Thus the Joint Committee on Grammatical Terminology recommends that sentences shall be distinguished as (1) 'simple', (2) 'complex', and (3) 'double' or 'multiple'.[1] Simple sentences are defined as those 'containing only one predication', e.g. *The quality of mercy is not strained*, and complex sentences as those 'containing one main predication and one or more subordinate predications', e.g. *He jests at scars that never felt a wound*. A different mode of quantitative classification is given in a further recommendation which reads as follows: 'That the terms Double or Multiple be used to describe any Sentence or any member of a Sentence which consists of two or more co-ordinate parts.' As examples of a 'double sentence' are quoted *God made the country and man made the town*; *The tale is long, nor have I heard it out*; *Words are like leaves, and where they most abound,* | *Much fruit of sense beneath is rarely found*. Along similar lines, *Veni, vidi, vici* might have been given to exemplify a 'multiple sentence'. For the interpretation of this recommendation it is significant that *Conticuere omnes intentique ora tenebant* is cited, not as a double sentence, but only as having a 'double predicate'; a 'multiple predicate' is contained in *Après quoi, Jean entra dans la maison, se débarrassa de son sabre, remplaça son képi par un vieux chapeau et s'en alla retrouver le curé*. Evidently it has not been thought suitable to apply to these examples the terms 'double' and 'multiple sentence', since the separate predicates have here one and the same subject. It is clearly the opinion of the Committee that to warrant the term 'double' or 'multiple sentence' the combination subject+

---

[1] *On the Terminology of Grammar*, pp. 12–13, Recommendations VI and VII.

§ 76 DOUBLE AND COMPLEX SENTENCES 321

predicate must recur in its entirety at least twice in the body of one and the same sentence.

The distinctions as thus stated bristle with difficulties. The example *Words are like leaves, and where they most abound, | Much fruit of sense beneath is rarely found* is given as a double sentence, and no objection can be raised to this classification. But is it or is it not also a complex sentence? The strict terms of the definition, as formulated in the Committee's pamphlet, leave the point uncertain. Is 'one main predication' to be understood as 'only one main predication'? If so, then the example in question is neither a simple nor yet a complex sentence, despite the similarity in form of its second half to *Quand il reviendra, je le lui dirai*, quoted among the examples of complex sentences. It would be more reasonable to consider this at once a double and a complex sentence. One might then call *If you want me to come, I'll come, but if you don't want me, I won't* at once a double and a doubly complex sentence. Again, the instance *Après quoi, Jean . . . le curé* is left entirely outside this quantitative classification; it is neither a simple nor a complex sentence, nor yet is it a multiple sentence. Moreover, according to the strict terms of the Committee's proposals, *He who hesitates is lost* would be a complex sentence, while *Old Mr. Jones, a school-friend of my late father, went to tea with my mother yesterday afternoon, taking with him a bouquet of magnificent roses as a tribute to her on her eighty-fifth birthday* would be a simple sentence. What is worse, this last example could be turned into a complex sentence by the mere intercalation of *who was* before *a school-friend*.

In my opinion the diversity of possible sentence-forms is too great to be satisfied by any such rigid terminological distinctions. Ought we not to rest content with calling simple those sentences which are obviously simple, and complex those sentences which are obviously complex? In any case a new category will have to be created for the locutionally formless sentences discussed in § 56. Perhaps here we might speak merely of 'formless sentences', though it must be remembered that no sentence can be really elocutionally formless, since utterance itself imposes a certain minimum of form. Every sentence is bounded fore and aft by a silence, and when spoken and not written, also provides by its intonation some inkling of the speaker's specific purpose. It is impossible to lay down strict rules for deciding whether a speaker has uttered a single sentence, or whether he has uttered several. Whenever an utterance is divided in such a way as to display, when written, a full stop in the midst, then doubtless we must agree that more than one sentence has been spoken. But is a pause equivalent to a semi-colon always sufficient to reveal the presence of a plurality of sentences? If, as I have proposed (p. 208), the sentence be quantitatively defined as an utterance 'which makes just as long a communication as the speaker has intended to make before giving himself a rest', clearly the criterion distinguishing, as among sentences, between one and several must be highly subjective. I will only add that for the presence of a single sentence homogeneity of special sentence-quality is not essential. For example, I should regard *You are not angry, James, are you?* as a single sentence, although it consists of a statement *plus* a request for attention *plus* an abbreviated question. It comes to this: on the formal side the quantitative criterion of a sentence is purely elocutional and depends upon whether the continuity and melodic composition suggests a unity or not. Let it not be objected that I am here making form, not function, the criterion of the sentence, and so am contradicting my own point of departure in § 50. I should retort by referring the objector to p. 205, where it was expressly laid down that elocutional form is always congruent, so that as regards the elocutional criterion of sentences, it matters not whether we speak of form or function.

The advantages of a highly complex sentence, like that concerning old Mr. Jones on p. 321, are firstly that it permits a maximum of information to be compressed into a minimum of space, and secondly that to each of the separate predications involved can be meted out exactly the measure of importance to which it is entitled. The disadvantages are that such a sentence imposes a greater intellectual strain on both speaker and listener than either is prepared to accept in ordinary conversation. For this reason sentences of real complexity are found mainly in written speech. It may be of interest to examine a little more closely the working of the example to which allusion was made at the beginning of this paragraph. The core, so to speak, is a compliment paid by Mr. Jones to 'my mother' on her birthday, and it seems likely that the words *Jones*, *my mother*, and *birthday* were among the first linguistic elements to crystallize in the speaker's mind. We have to assume in that speaker a somewhat verbose habit, which causes him to incorporate in his sentence, as it proceeds on its leisurely way, a number of references scarcely likely to have been held in view at the first moment of its conception. Mr. Jones, being the active party concerned, is naturally made the subject. The predicate *old* is thrown in, partly for purposes of identification, and partly from mixed emotional motives difficult to diagnose. *A schoolfriend of my father* is a little excursion into the past of Mr. Jones not originally intended, and due to a vice of reminiscence which we cannot fail to detect in the narrator. However, this new predicate, being presented as an apposition, is thereby indicated to be purely parenthetic. 'My father', a constituent of this parenthetic predicate, is subject of yet another parenthetic predicate *late*, supplying a further unpremeditated piece of information. The main verb *went* is quite unessential to the purport of the sentence as a whole; it introduces a fact necessarily involved in the little drama here described, and merely provides a peg upon which the other incidental news can be hung. It is unnecessary to pursue this analysis further. In the dozen or so words discussed a most complicated structure has already been revealed, and had the analysis been continued down to the end of the sentence, a far more richly coloured and carefully shaded picture would have been disclosed. If all the predications contained in this are set forth in separate sentences, the result is long-winded and monotonous in the extreme. The first part then runs as follows: *There is a certain Mr. Jones. He is old. He was a school-friend of my father. My father is dead. This Mr. Jones went,* &c., &c. One sees how impossible such a narrative becomes when all the predicates are peaks of equal height, and when a pause is inserted between each predicational nexus. Judged by ordinary standards, the complex sentence describing old Mr. Jones's doings is no miracle of art. But when it is examined from the angle of linguistic theory, we can but marvel at the results which a somewhat prosy and commonplace speaker has been able to achieve. Not only is a mass of information imparted, but the less important features are admirably subordinated to the really salient points. Civilized man, imbued with a never-failing purposefulness and his wits sharpened by constant practice, has attained a wellnigh incredible skill in speech. But side by side with the most finished products of oratory, there survive utterances which are almost on a level with the cries of the ape. From the living speech of to-day may be culled evidence of every different stage of linguistic development.

§ 77. **Conclusion.** The final section of this chapter brings me to the end of the present volume, and some general retrospect seems to be called for. The task which I set before myself was to give a roughly adequate account of the mechanism of speech, and I ventured to believe that the performance of this task would incidentally involve the elucidation of the grammatical terms current among philologists. I am not without hope that the first part of my programme has been accomplished, but as regards the second only a beginning has been made. We have learnt to distinguish between language and speech, between sentence and word, and between form and function. Subject and predicate have been investigated, and some preliminary notions have been gathered with regard to the so-called 'parts of speech'. A further volume will be needed to delimitate the concepts of language and word more closely, as well as to explain a host of terms, e.g. object, phrase, clause, pronoun, tense, case, to which hitherto only the briefest of allusions have been possible. The definitions of these terms given by other investigators seldom yield satisfaction, and I must frankly confess that in many instances my own mind is still utterly in the dark. Nevertheless I am confident that, following the path which Wegener opened up and along which I, among others, have made further progress, scholars will have no great difficulty in attaining an acceptable and reasonably detailed linguistic theory. When this end has been accomplished, general books on language will cease to be collections of interesting but relatively uncoordinated facts, as is, I fear, the impression usually left by those written in the past. As regards my own book, I shall feel myself untouched by any criticism which remarks upon the paucity of the phenomena which I have studied. The quarry I have been pursuing is theory, not facts. What I have striven to envisage is speech as an organized functional whole, and exceptional details have been none of my concern.

One unforeseen result has emerged with increasing insistency, and most of all in this final chapter. It is the purposiveness of speech. To speak is to convey meaning, and meaning has tended, in the course of my exposition, to become displayed ever more conspicuously in its original etymological sense of human purpose or intention —purpose to influence a listener in a particular way, and purpose to call attention to specific things. Out of these two purposes has been born a third, which properly speaking does not belong to the subject-matter of my book, but which can only enhance the interest of its problems. I refer to the purpose of comprehension, which the habit of speech has inculcated and has taught us to regard as desirable in itself. In his effort to influence the mind of others, man has learnt to instruct his own. Whilst elaborating a sentence, the speaker does not completely divest himself of the receptive listening attitude which alternates so regularly and easily with his creative role as speaker. He is, in fact, always a fellow-listener, and hence also a fellow-learner. From this necessity arises the possibility of employing language as the instrument of silent thought. When something is obscure, purposeful effort is employed to reduce it to verbal form, and when this has been done, we realize our enrichment and become aware that our intellectual power has increased. Thought is, no doubt, presupposed by speech, but the habit of speech has given us lessons in thinking. And so, by reciprocal action, thought and speech have developed hand in hand. It is no exaggeration to say that the history of speech is also the history of the human understanding.°

RETROSPECT 1951

IT would be over-sanguine to suppose that the distinction of speech and language first proposed by De Saussure and further developed by myself had by now obtained general acceptance and was beginning to bear fruit. The fact cannot be disguised that many scholars are still unaware of the distinction or else ignore it as of no practical utility. There are others of undoubted competence, however, who have earnestly striven to understand and have failed. It is to these that I now address myself, at the risk of repeating things said in the foregoing pages. Possibly the order of exposition which I felt forced to adopt has been responsible for such incomprehension as there has been. So intent was I on exhibiting the interaction of the four factors claimed to be present overtly or otherwise in every example of speech (§ 9) that I was impelled to regard this latter merely as an 'activity' rather than to dwell upon its concrete results; it was only at a later stage, namely in my third and subsequent chapters,[1] that the analysis of actual utterances became the exclusive preoccupation. Nor will it have helped matters that language was simultaneously described as 'a universally possessed science' (p. 62). The antithesis of an 'activity' and a 'science' may to some have seemed a lame one. The remedy is to transport these two abstractions on to concrete ground. Abstractions can always be dealt with thus, and to many minds, though not necessarily the best, this is perhaps the only method by which abstract notions can be made acceptable. The habitual theatregoer is more likely to acquire a real feeling for comedy

[1] See especially p. 181, ll. 18-20.

than the student who remains at home and reads an essay on the subject. If now we apply this principle to language, the Latin language may be said to consist of all the words in Lewis and Short's Latin dictionary *plus* all the declensions, conjugations, and syntactical rules to be found in any good school grammar. If next we seek a concrete example of speech, the *Aeneid* will stand us in good stead. In this sense concrete speech is nothing more than another name for 'text'.[1] It is true that the term 'text' is, in ordinary parlance, confined to what is written or printed, but for the purposes of linguistic theory the term can and should be extended to anything that has been spoken or reported to have been spoken on some particular occasion, like the sentences *Rain!* and *Look at the rain!* which I have put into the mouth of James Hawkins (pp. 71 ff.).

The words in dictionaries and grammars may be displayed visibly upon a printed page, and so too may be the sentences spoken by James Hawkins upon that rainy day. Here, then, we have 'language' and 'speech' made concretely manifest upon a common plane, and the distinction between them ought now to be as clear as daylight. A few more elucidations may, however, here be added for the benefit of those still unconvinced. 'Language' belongs to the speaker's past (§ 29), 'speech' or 'text' to his present. Again, though 'language' has been built up out of millions of separate occasions of speech, the individual speakers and listeners have, as a rule,[2] faded out for the contemporary user, and the particular things referred to have mostly passed into oblivion. In 'speech' or 'text', on the contrary,

[1] See my paper entitled 'The Distinction of Speech and Language', printed in *Atti del III Congresso internazionale dei Linguisti*, pp. 345-53.
[2] There are, of course, rare exceptions, as with the word *incarnadine*.

we can still discern speaker and listener engaged in a single dramatic situation, the plot of which is what I have termed the thing-meant; or, to change the simile, 'text' presupposes a bowler and a batsman, though what is of greatest importance is the score made. A final consideration: the experts called upon to deal with our contrasted entities differ in the two cases. 'Language' is the task of lexicographer and grammarian, while 'speech', i.e. 'text', calls for the investigations of editor and commentator. It is true that the functions of these four types of scholar cannot, in practice, always be kept apart—the schoolmaster, indeed, exchanges his role with the dexterity of a conjurer, though in the grammar hour his duty as a commentator is temporarily in abeyance, and in parsing the words of *Arma virumque cano* he need not dwell upon the personality of Vergil, nor explain that the martial deeds in question were those of Aeneas.

Nevertheless, even those who are not blind to the distinction of speech and language may still doubt its utility. Such readers I must beg to review my arguments afresh. Is not the distinction indispensable in order to explain all change in 'language' (§ 35)? How else can one interpret incongruent use of word-forms and of both locutional and elocutional sentence-form (§§ 45–6, 61), how else account for positive errors in diction? And is it not plain that the terms 'subject' and 'predicate' find application only in specific samples of 'speech', and do not adhere to words as permanent items of 'language' (p. 269)? But to repeat all this over again is only to aggravate the offence which one otherwise very friendly and favourable critic called my 'damnable iteration'. So I now pass to a theme of which the actuality demands somewhat drastic controversial treatment.

A trend in linguistic theory which appears to be gaining ever new ground in America would reduce to nonsense a very large part of what my book has sought to establish. The trend in question has its roots in the psychological, or perhaps better said anti-psychological, creed known as behaviourism, which condemns as unscientific all data not observable by any investigator whatsoever, and consequently bans everything inaccessible save by self-knowledge and introspection. In the field of linguistic theory the behaviouristic doctrine was until quite recently most prominently represented by Professor L. Bloomfield,[1] though his work entitled *Language* (London, 1935) prefers to contrast the two standpoints with the terms 'mentalistic' and 'mechanistic'.[2] Here, in the late Professor's own words, is a brief statement of the rival theories as he saw them (op. cit., pp. 32–3):

> The *mentalistic* theory, which is by far the older, and still prevails both in the popular view and among men of science, supposes that the variability of human conduct is due to the interference of some non-physical factor, a *spirit* or *will* or *mind* (Greek *psyche*, hence the term *psychology*) that is present in every human being. This spirit, according to the mentalistic view, is entirely different from material things and accordingly follows some other kind of causation or none at all. . . .
> The *materialistic* (or, better, *mechanistic*) theory supposes that

---

[1] The following pages, now only slightly altered, were written and about to be sent to Press when the news of Professor Bloomfield's demise reached this country. It is with some embarrassment and with real regret that I polemize against the behaviouristic views of an in other respects very able scholar so recently defunct, but these views are at the present time so influential that it seemed imperative to follow them back to their fountain-head.

[2] Another book of a similar character is J. R. Kantor's *Objective Psychology of Grammar*, Indiana University, 1936. Upon this I have commented in my article 'Linguistic Theory: Reply to some Critics', in *English Studies*, xix (1917), p. 59.

the variability of human conduct, including speech, is due only to the fact that the human body is a very complex system. Human actions, according to the materialistic view, are part of cause-and-effect sequences exactly like those which we observe, say in the study of physics or chemistry. . . . We could foretell a person's actions (for instance, whether a certain stimulus will lead him to speak, and, if so, the exact words he will utter), only if we knew the exact structure of his body at the moment, or, what comes to the same thing, if we knew the exact make-up of his organism at some early stage—say at birth or before—and then had a record of every change in that organism, including every stimulus that had ever affected the organism.

If my book had chanced to come before the eyes of Professor Bloomfield, he would probably have condemned me as a 'mentalist' of the most reprehensible type. In support of this view he would have pointed to my expressions 'mirrored in the mind' on pp. 28, 142; 'everything spoken of must . . . pass through the mind of the speaker', p. 17; 'purposeful use of articulate utterances', p. 19; 'the ultimate basis of speech is the fact that individual thoughts and feelings are, as such, inalienable', p. 67; and many more dicta of the sort. My defence would have been that at the time when *Speech and Language* was written I had no definite theory of mind at all, and that even had I possessed one I should have kept it sternly in the background, my deliberate intention having been to refer to mental happenings in the terms universally used by novelists, lawyers, nursemaids, and by the man in the street. My sole aim being to elucidate the mechanism of speech, nothing was farther from my thoughts than to link up my explanations with a philosophically impeccable terminology. While the philologist may fairly be expected to understand something about the principles governing his trade, it is too much to ask of him to be a profound philosopher or psychologist as well; and surely he is entitled, in plying this trade, to use the King's English in the way it is used in any other calling. Indeed, I find something self-contradictory in such titles as *Sprachpsychologie*, since *Psychologie* is (if anything) the study of the psychē, while the theoretic study of language would be better called 'Linguistic Theory'. Let not these remarks, however, be read as an attempt to warn off philosophers from dealing with linguistic theory, since this, like every other science and everything else under the sun, is or should belong to the subject-matter of philosophy, while the reverse is not true.

When, accordingly, I employ such expressions as 'mirrored in the mind', this does not imply that I believe, or have ever believed, in the 'mind' as some place or entity external to or contained in the 'body',[1] and any intelligent reader who studies the passages in question with sympathy and a real desire to understand will grasp and, as I venture to hope, will agree with the points I have tried to make.[2] So much in self-defence, which may in truth be something of a tilting against shadows, since I have no evidence of Professor Bloomfield's ever having heard of my book, much less of his having read it. I now turn to his own views. While I have little or no quarrel with Professor Bloomfield's description of his mechanistic theory as set forth above, I deny that this is irreconcilable with every conceivable mentalistic theory. Of course if it be taken that the 'mentalist' *ipso facto* believes in 'mind' as a 'non-physical factor' and as following some wayward chain

[1] Such a belief, which of course goes back much farther than Descartes, since the Ancient Egyptians had it, has recently been wittily described as 'the myth of the Ghost in the Machine' (G. Ryle, *The Concept of Mind*, 1949).

[2] In this connexion I would ask my critics to pay special attention to the contents of my § 17.

of causation of its own,[1] no reconciliation is possible. But do all 'mentalists' take this view? Are there not many who, while admitting that all sensing, thinking, and willing must have each its own physical counterpart, would be very far from endorsing Professor Bloomfield's assertion that '*mental images, feelings* and the like are merely popular terms for various bodily movements'?[2] I must be thankful to others of the same school, however, if they should be willing to concede the existence of such popular equivalents, since those are the equivalents I have preferred to use, and they would be at liberty, if they could, to translate them into the professedly more scientific language alone considered admissible by them.

It is very much to the good that Professor Bloomfield, in his chapter on the 'Use of Language' (ch. ii), attempted to analyse a single specimen of speech-utterance. The example he chose may be reported in his own words.

'Suppose that Jack and Jill are walking down a lane. Jill is hungry. She sees an apple in a tree. She makes a noise with her larynx, tongue, and lips. Jack vaults the fence, climbs the tree, takes the apple, brings it to Jill, and places it in her hand. Jill eats the apple.'

I am encouraged to find speech here viewed as a means of social co-operation, which is exactly my own contention (see above, § 7). Due importance is also attached to both speaker and listener. Laudable attention is likewise paid to the thing meant, of which the central feature is, of course, the apple. The weak point in the sequence of events as above presented is that it leaves the fourth factor, namely the words and their meaning, in utter obscurity. Indeed, it seems to have been overlooked (in

[1] See Prof. Bloomfield's statement above.
[2] Bloomfield, op. cit., p. 143.

this chapter at least) that words have any meaning at all apart from the things meant by them, since the *meaning* of a linguistic form is defined 'as the situation in which the speaker utters it and the response which it calls forth in the hearer' (p. 139). The uttered words are, in fact, thought of as though they were the shot of a gun which by some mysterious virtue in the sportsman's constitution brings down its appointed quarry.[1] By thus confining the account of Jill's successful performance to 'A. Practical events preceding the act of speech, B. Speech, and C. Practical events following the act of speech' (p. 23), Professor Bloomfield renounced any attempt to explain what should surely be the centre of interest in the whole proceeding; he ignored the fact that the words used have a meaning conferred upon them neither by Jill's stimulus nor by Jack's reaction, but by a linguistic community that existed before either of these young persons was born.

The truth is that linguistic theory cannot make any headway without utilization of the mentalistic concepts the validity of which the Chicago Professor disputed. Without these, speech becomes the product of ingeniously constructed robots. 'Purpose', 'deliberation', 'perception' —all these were for him unscientific terms; the utterance of the speaker and the response of the listener are merely the predestined movements of cogs in the universal machine. It may be so, but that is not what I and others want to know about speech.[2]

At this point I take leave of this a regrettable, but necessary, controversy which can hardly be carried on without use of the terms which one of the parties to it fundamentally rejects.

[1] Cf. 'The nervous system is evidently a trigger-mechanism', op. cit., p. 33.   [2] See, further, my p. 263, ll. 3 ff.

The remainder of this Retrospect will be devoted to discussing passages in my book where I have expressed myself wrongly or badly, or where I have felt that something ought to be added.

(*a*) Pp. 13–14. I find to my dismay that some have interpreted the reference here to 'three other books, more objective in their manner, to be written from a similar standpoint at perhaps no very remote date' as the expression of an intention on my part to write those books. But since, according to p. 14, ll. 8–10, the author of the third of them is to be 'not only a consummate grammarian, but also a man of great intellect and wide humanity' I can hardly have been meaning myself! The vision of these much-needed works still remains with me, though it is becoming rather dim and desperate.

(*b*) P. 25, ll. 2–4, '. . . one and the same sentence may, on separate occasions, refer to various different things.' In some correspondence that passed between myself and the late Dr. G. Stern of Gothenburg, he rightly pointed out that here and a number of times below[1] I have used the term 'sentence' in the sense of 'a set of words displaying sentence-form' (§§ 53–4) and not in the technical sense which I attribute to the term in my definition on p. 98 and elsewhere; regarded as the unit of speech, i.e. as a sufficiently complete utterance to be found in some 'text' (above, p. 329), a sentence can properly only be something that has occurred once on some definite historical occasion. Dr. Stern's objection is absolutely correct; furthermore, I confess to not having myself noticed the inconsistency. This I might have avoided by writing 'one and the same set of words' and by carefully eschewing any employment of the term 'sentence'. None the less, I do not regard my

[1] e.g. p. 25, ll. 7, 19; p. 53, l. 5.

offence as a heinous one. It must not be overlooked that the word *sentence* has, like almost every other word, a fairly wide 'area of meaning' (§ 12). Is it not a fundamental principle of the art of speech that advantage should be taken of the suppleness belonging to words, and that the attempt to confine their applications within the strait-jacket of a strict consistency is neither possible nor even desirable? It is to the context that the reader must always look in order to discover in what exact sense a word has been employed. The use of language, as every good writer knows, is a very delicate matter, and to attempt an over-great precision may often lead astray rather than help comprehension. This is perhaps the besetting sin of philosophers. Instead of looking sympathetically for the gist of what another thinker has been seeking to make clear, are they not all too apt to catch him up over what they deem a loose application of words? I may be met with the retort that to advocate the inconsistent use of words is a highly dangerous doctrine. So it is; nevertheless I believe that such inconsistency is often the better of two alternatives. I would beg students to pay serious attention to what I have written on this score at the top of p. 71 and again at the top of p. 303.

(c) P. 32, ll. 16–17. 'Things must occur to our minds before they can be clothed in words.' Here and in my whole account (§ 26) of the gradual emergence of an act of speech, objection may possibly be taken to my representation of this as occurring in successive stages. My preposition 'before' must be read in the sense that any reaction must necessarily be preceded by the stimulus; in the typical act of speech which I have used as an illustration (ibid.), the sight of rain was a precedent condition of James's utterance of the word *rain*. In this particular case there could have been no objection to interpreting the word 'before' temporally, as the publicly observable movements of James's head (Fig. 2) show.

(*d*) P. 36. Had I been able to carry out my project of a second volume, I should have supplemented my conception of 'an area of meaning' with that of 'an area of sound'. Within the latter all the identifiable variations would have been grouped, the recognized 'best' pronunciation occupying the centre, while pronunciations which did not allow of the word's identification would have been banished outside the periphery.

(*e*) P. 41, 'proper names', see, too, p. 267. This highly interesting, but extremely difficult, subject has been dealt with at length in my essay 'The Theory of Proper Names', Oxford, 1940. The only detail on the present page which I now believe to be entirely wrong is my statement that a proper name 'is a word which refers only to one individual thing, usually a person or place'. That this is not true is shown by such examples as *the Plantagenets*, *Veneti*, *Μῆδος*, to quote three examples of different types, cf. op. cit., pp. 21–8. It may be of interest here to reproduce my final definition (p. 43): *A proper name is a word or group of words recognized as indicating, or tending to indicate, the object or objects to which it refers by virtue of its distinctive sound alone, without regard to any meaning possessed by that sound from the start, or acquired by it through association with the said object or objects.*[1]

(*f*) P. 53, l. 5, 'the sentence'. See my remarks on p. 25, ll. 2–4.

---

[1] Since one scholar to whom I showed this definition has misunderstood me, I now ask the reader to note that 'by virtue of its distinctive ... objects' is to be taken with the words 'indicating or tending to indicate', and not with the verb 'refers'.

(*g*) P. 69, § 25. 'Words not really objects of sense, but psychical entities.' So already De Saussure, *Cours de linguistique générale* (1916), p. 32. Those who have paid due attention to earlier pages of this Retrospect will not accuse me of self-contradiction because in p. 68, ll. 12–13, I use the expression 'the sound-signs which we call "words"'; see p. 71, top. More dangerous, at first sight, would be an objection to the epithet 'psychical' here on the ground that the members of a linguistic community are in many cases nearly, if not entirely, unconscious of the words which they employ so readily. This objection may, however, be met partly by remembering that the concept of 'unconscious mind' has now become familiar, so that a 'word' may not need to be the object of consciousness in order to be psychical. Further, words in a foreign language have to be learned, and in order to be learned have to be consciously entertained. The same is true of many words even in one's own language.

(*h*) P. 73, Fig. 2. Alterations have had to be made in the captions in order to meet the objection that according to p. 72 the visible aspects of the act of speech were five in number, not six. I am indebted for this suggestion to the reviewer in the *Times Literary Supplement*. Possibly, however, allowance ought to have been made for six stages, since James's interest in his own utterance would not have been exhausted until Mary's reply had satisfied him of its having been understood.

(*i*) P. 117, ll. 15 ff. Here I have regrettably lost sight of one of the most vital of my contentions: 'speech' in the sense of an 'item of text' can never be identical with 'language', even if 'language' be conceded to mean only as much of language as went into the item in question. If any significance at all be attached to the concept 'an item of text' this must be viewed as embracing, not only the uttered sound, but also all else that adhered inseparably to the occasion of it, viz. the animal that uttered the sound and the stimulus which called forth that sound (part of the thing-meant). I can only hope that the lapse here acknowledged has not been repeated by me elsewhere.

(*j*) P. 138, ll. 7–9. In my definition of 'word-form' I formerly wrote *the listener may expect the speaker to have intended*. The formulation here substituted is desirable, since I make a great point of 'word-form' belonging to language, and the definition in my first edition might easily have been misconstrued to imply that 'word-form' belongs to speech, seeing that the terms 'listener' and 'speaker' are mentioned.

(*k*) P. 172, ll. 19–20. There is more to be said about the infinitival phrase, tending rather to favour the view of those who would prohibit the insertion of an adverb between *to* and the infinitive. The salient points are: (1) that *to* is the only preposition which can thus in English be placed before the infinitive—we cannot (e.g.) say *in dig* or *by dig*; (2) *to* here has no recognizable meaning of its own that would link it up with other uses of the preposition. Accordingly, *to dig* is more of a unity than my argument seems to allow, and that fact might be stressed by grammarians who hold the insertion of an adverb to be a solecism.

(*l*) P. 173, top. Dr. Armbruster, the author of the well-known Amharic grammar, pointed out in a letter that the use of *from* in *different from* is or should be governed by the use of the same preposition in *differing from*. Hence *different to* can hardly be defended until popular usage decides (which it is hardly likely to do) also in favour of *differing to*.

(*m*) P. 217, l. 1. 'No sentence can do more.' This is an exaggeration, since a sentence can also suggest by its form how the listener should take it, see §§ 54 ff.

(*n*) P. 302, ll. 9–11. 'Information given for practical ends and scientific formulation are perhaps the fields in which the statement reaches its climax of objectivity and apparent truthfulness.' The three last words should be omitted; the rest is probably true of statements made in the pages of history books and teaching manuals, where the reader at the moment is not remembering, nor being intended to remember, the author's purpose in supplying the information. I venture to add a few words on 'propositions'. If somebody says *This summer has been exceptionally wet* or *Henry II came to the throne in 1154* the gists of those statements are not, in the contexts in which they occur, propositions. The term 'proposition' is properly applied only where the alternatives of truth or falsehood are being consciously canvassed, and the earnest propounder of a proposition is almost as much putting a question as making an assertion.[1] The factors of speaker and listener (author and reader) are never far distant when 'propositions' are being mooted, and it is difficult to conceive of the existence of a proposition without someone to propound it. This is a matter upon which, I am bold enough to think, philosophers might have something to learn from linguistic theory. In any case, this Retrospect must not end without expression of my conviction that linguistic theory constitutes the necessary prolegomena to philosophy, though admittedly making no direct contribution to it. I would venture, in accordance with the conclusion to my Foreword (p. 14), to put forward a plea for

[1] Indeed, the word 'question' is often used as a synonym for 'proposition'.

closer collaboration[1] between philosophers and those whose business it has been to ponder deeply on the nature of speech. Is not academic syndicalism carried a bit too far?

(o) Pp. 326–7. The late Mr. G. Cookson quoted to me the following from Shelley's *Prometheus Unbound*:

> He gave men speech, and speech created thought,
> Which is the measure of the Universe.

ADDITIONAL NOTE TO THE RETROSPECT

Note F (to p. 341). '*Tweak*' or '*Twinge*'?

HAVING ventured to suggest that philosophy would benefit by the possession of a sound and comprehensive linguistic theory, it seems incumbent upon me to justify my contention. Several examples will be found in my essay 'The Theory of Proper Names'; here a single addition must suffice. In his *Concept of Mind*, p. 205, Professor Ryle disputes 'the hallowed antithesis between the public, physical world and the private, mental world, between the things and events which anyone may witness and the things and events which only their possessor may witness'. He claims that the antithesis is spurious. 'It is true that the cobbler cannot witness the tweaks that I feel when the shoe pinches. But it is false that I witness them.' And this because 'they (tweaks) are not the sorts of things of which it makes sense to say that they are witnessed or unwitnessed at all, even by me. I feel or have the tweaks, but I do not discover or peer at them', &c.

However, the sufferer might, like Professor Ryle, *call* them 'tweaks'. Why does he not call them 'twinges',[2] which are pains of a very similar kind, but coming from within (as of rheumatism) instead of from without? Surely because he recognizes, cognizes, or knows—'witnesses' would hardly be English—them to be caused

---

[1] Not necessarily, however, in oral discussion, where the linguistic theorist is, as a rule, likely to get the worst of it, having had less practice in dialectics than the philosopher.

[2] In point of fact Professor Ryle does once in the same paragraph (quoted below) employ the word *twinge*, but not quite clearly in reference to the pinching shoe. The distinction between *tweak* and *twinge* here made will, I think, be accepted by most English readers, though it is not unambiguously stated in O.E.D.

ADDITIONAL NOTE TO THE RETROSPECT

by the pinching shoe, and knows from previous experiences (above, pp. 74 ff.) that pain from this kind of source may be called a 'tweak'; implicitly, in fact, he classifies the present experience under the heading 'tweak', not under the heading 'twinge' (above, § 11). I see no way of avoiding the conclusion that a good element of cognition enters into the identification of a pain as due to a pinching shoe. If all that Professor Ryle would seek to deny is the consciousness of what I should describe as an implicit act of classification, we ought, I think, to agree with him. But would not he, in his turn, agree that it makes sense to talk of an implicit act of classification? To me it seems no more nonsense than to admit that the intention of walking to Sandford is implicit in every step I take in that direction. It is clear, as Professor Ryle teaches, that consciousness of what we are doing or experiencing plays a much smaller part in our actions or experience than we often imagine; but to reject the notion of what perforce we must think of as unconscious or semi-conscious cerebration seems to land us back in the unfruitful mechanistic speculations of Professor Bloomfield and his followers.

I cannot agree with Professor Ryle's further statement (ibid.) that 'in the sense in which a person may be said to have had a robin under observation, it would be nonsense to say that he has had a twinge [*lege* tweak] under observation'. Except as regards the different organs of sense involved, I see no difference of status here. James's observation of rain pattering upon the window-pane (p. 71) differed in no essential from the sudden unpleasant sensations in his big toe experienced on the previous Thursday. These had awakened in him an attentive observant attitude. To test the cause, he removed his shoe. How great his relief to find the pain subsiding and not repeating itself; it was only a tweak from the shoe. But oh horrors, if the nipping sensation had kept on returning undiminished; previous experience would then have made it dreadfully probable that he was feeling a twinge of the gout.

For my particular purpose it was sufficient to seize upon one petty detail in Professor Ryle's most interesting and stimulating book. Concerning his wider views I comment only very briefly, since, frankly, I do not understand them. He has certainly demolished the crude mentalistic theory likewise imputed by Professor Bloomfield to his opponents (see above, pp. 331–2); the belief in distinct, unconnected worlds of mind and body is indisputably mythical. Professor Ryle authorizes the use of mentalistic terms like 'think', 'feel', 'intention', see his first chapter. On the other hand, he appears to have one foot in the Behaviourist camp, at least as far as method of psychological investigation is concerned, see op. cit., pp. 327 ff. In this he is possibly right, but I still cannot believe that the method of introspection is completely defunct. At all events I maintain that for the purpose of explaining the nature of speech and language the use of 'inner-life' terms is not merely legitimate, but also imperative. On a previous page I asserted that, when writing this book, I had no personal theory of mind. Nor, indeed, have I now, but I discern in myself the rudiments of one in course of emergence. Here are its main lines in all their naked *naïveté*. I feel sure that all consciousness has as its supporting background inner physical happenings of which many, but not all, are accessible to outside observers from their outer effects. On this view consciousness is neither a world nor an entity, but rather one of the functions of living organisms, the complementary group consisting of unconscious bodily processes. Between the two there is definite continuity. For example, the digestion is normally carried on unobserved; a stomach-ache leads the sufferer to ponder the cause and to seek a remedy. Consciousness seems thus to have been evolved in order to help its possessors to cope with the more troublesome situations of life. I cannot believe that consciousness is itself purposeless and, as the Behaviourists appear to think, explicable, if at all, wholly in terms of physical movements. For the Behaviourists, if I understand their standpoint aright, physical events are the only verifiable links in that chain of inner occurrences which connects stimulating circumstances with appropriate human action. I believe, on the contrary, that at the conscious stage such physical happenings cease to be of primary importance, the consciousness which belongs to them now taking over its possessor's problem and mediating the next steps, these explicable for the psychologist partly from observation of his object's physical movements and partly from his own power of reasoning and introspected knowledge. On this hypothesis sensation, perception, purpose, and the rest are themselves indispensable links in the above-mentioned chain of occurrences, and no mere appendages dangling uselessly from certain uncontested, but altogether mysteriously working, inner physical links.

INDEX

The references are to the pages—The letter n. *means footnote*

abstraction 48 n.
abstractions, as things-meant 26; words not, 94, 120.
abstracts as subject 284.
adjectives 39, 260; nouns functioning as, 142, 152, 153; quotations functioning as, 233 n.
adverbs 226.
affirmation 295.
Aktionsarten 147 n.
allegory 167, 168.
anacoluthon 252.
analysis hypothesis 241.
animal cries 19, 116-18, 123.
aposiopesis 206-7.
area of meaning 36, 37, 44, 127.
Aristotle 295, 296.
Armbruster, C. H., 340.
article 46, 47, 244, 246.
aspects 23, 258, 264.
assertion 295-7, 299, 300.

behaviourism 331.
Bloomfield, L., 331-5.
Brockelmann, C., 308 n., 309 n.
Brugmann, K., 117 n.
Brunot, F., 2, 315.
Bühler, K., 4, 7, 63 n., 182, 188, 189, 195, 237, 238, 251, 296 n., 297 n., 316 n.
Butler, S., 57, 67, 104-5.

cases in English 134.
children, speech of, 63, 111, 124, 125.
clauses, *see* subordinate clauses.
clues, words as, 34, 80, 115, 122, 127, 195, 257.
commands 231, 311.
commentator, task of, 330.
concord 157.
congruent function 142, 145, 205.
connotation 60.

constructio ad sensum 158.
content, fallacy involved in term, 26 n., 102; locutional, of sentence, 241.
Cookson, G., 342.
copula 218-26.
corroboration, questions for, 304-6.
Croce, B., 21, 252.

Delbrück, B., 3.
demands 189.
Dempe, H., 195, 196 n., 238.
denial 295, 300, 301.
denotation 60.
depth of intention 25 n., 52, 53, 82, 250.
description 195.
Dionysius Thrax 99.
double sentences 320-2.

editor, task of, 330.
ellipse 50, 51, 270.
elocutional sentence-form 201, 213.
Erdmann, K. O., 4, 36 n., 44 n., 60.
exclamations 188-9, 315-19.
exclamatory statements 190, 277, 294.

fact and fiction, equality of, in speech, 31, 32, 142, 286, 296.
factors of speech 7, 48, 49, 83, 189, 190.
faulty speech 170-4.
finite verbs 218-22, 260.
form 132, 133, 236. *See too* elocutional sentence-form, inner word-form, intonational form, locutional sentence-form, outer word-form, sentence-form, syntactic form.
formless sentences, 322.
formulas, stereotyped, 45, 46.
Fowler, H. W., 165 n., 169, 172 n.
Fränklin, G., 237.
function, notion of, 141; as criterion of the sentence, 181, 236. *See too*

congruent function, incongruent function.

gender 156.
general sentence-quality 185.
genitives 146.
gesture 203, 204.
grammar, subject-matter of, 232; *versus* sense, 158.
grammarian, task of, 330.
grammatical subject and predicate 271–7.
Gunn, B., 74 n.

hieroglyphic writing 121, 122.
homophones 43 n., 77, 120.
Husserl, E., 60, 61.

ideas 44.
idiom 46.
images 37 n.
imperatives 215 n., 311–14.
implication 195, 196, 223.
incongruent function 142, 152, 155, 160–5, 212, 227–33.
infinitive, in commands, 233, 311; exclamatory, 233; split, 172.
infinitival phrase 340.
inner word-form 131.
interjections 311, 316–18.
interpretation, mode of, 113, 114, 198, 199.
interrogative words 226, 305, 307.
intonation 200–5.
intonational form 92, 160.
introspection, condemned, 331; defended, 344.
inversion of subject and predicate 227, 277, 305, 309, 310.

James, W., 117 n.
Jespersen, O., 2, 43 n., 58, 124, 131 n., 141 n., 146 n., 163, 206 n., 207, 214 n., 229 n., 233 n., 251, 261, 262, 270, 274, 284–7, 300 n., 306 n., 309 n., 317 n., 318 n.

Joint Committee on Grammatical Terminology 144 n., 183 n., 187, 189, 217 n., 289 n., 320–2.

Kalepky, Th., 4, 6, 154 n., 183 n., 261 n.
Kantor, J. R., 331 n. 2.
Kretschmer, P., 182, 188, 189, 237.

language, contrasted with speech, 62, 86, 88, 91–3, 106–9, 175, 328–30; as product of speech, 110–12; word the unit of, 63, 88, 103; what is a, 170. And *passim*.
lexicographer, task of, 330.
lies 297.
linguistic theory 4, 5, 85, 333.
listener 18–22, 57, 58, 64, 65, 250, 257; role of the, 76–8, 143–5, 193, 198, 199, 243; subject exists for the sake of the, 265–8. And *passim*.
Locke, J., 119 n., 176, 177.
locutional sentence-form 201, 208, 213, 226, 227.
logical subject and predicate 271–7, 280.

Malinowski, B., 46 n.
Manly, J. M., 111 n.
meaning 33–7; ambiguity of term, 99, 100; and thing-meant, 29–33, 256, 257; as defined by L. Bloomfield 335.
mechanistic standpoint 331–4.
metaphor 165–70.
mechanization of speech 44–7, 125, 155.
Meillet, A., 9, 10, 111 n., 141 n., 308.
mentalistic standpoint 331–4.
Mill, J. S., 42.
mind, guess about, 344.
mood 222.
morphology 132.
mot juste 174.
multiple sentences 320–2.

Nebensatz 183, 185 n.

INDEX

negative questions 305, 306.
negative statements 300, 301.
negative words 301.
nexus, *see* predicational nexus.
nominal sentences 218.
noun-clause 185, 228.
nouns, defined, 9, 10; how formed, 138, 139.

object 154; affected and effected, 102.
Ogden, C. K., and Richards, I. A., 83 n., 101 n.
outer sentence-form 200.
outer word-form 131, 140.

parts of speech, so-called, 9, 39, 106, 138; real, 106, 269.
Paul, H., 3, 58, 218, 238, 241–8, 251, 253, 256 n., 272, 276, 279, 280, 281, 308 n.
pauses 207.
Pavlovitch, M., 124, 125.
Pearsall Smith, L., 111 n.
perception 72.
phrases, set, 46.
predicate 33, 214–18, 222, 256, 260–88.
predication 255, 292, 293.
predicational nexus 261, 262–5, 278–90, 324.
predicative use of words 222, 259, 288–92.
presentations 245, 246.
prohibitions 311, 312.
proper names 41, 42; definition of, 338.
proposition 341.
proximate thing-meant 258, 263, 264.
psychological subject and predicate 272, 273, 280, 281.
punctuation 110, 214.
purposiveness 96, 97, 181, 210, 236, 240, 326.

quantitative criteria of sentence 98, 205–8, 319–25.
questions 188, 189, 303–10.
quotations 233–5.

Raleigh, W., 174, 300.
reaction 32, 253, 255, 263, 277.
requests 189, 229, 231, 310–15.
rhetorical questions 231, 304.
Ribot, Th., 37 n., 48 n., 67 n., 69 n.
Richards, I. A., *see under* Ogden, C. K.
Ries, J., 2, 57, 58, 95, 120 n., 158 n., 185 n., 208–11, 213 n., 218–20, 232, 236, 238, 239, 299 n.
Ryle, G., 333 n. 1, 342–3.

Sachverhalt 26, 78.
Sapir, E. 121, 130 n.
Saussure, F. de, 59, 60, 90, 107 n.
selective attention 48, 49, 77, 113–15.
semantics 85.
sentence, definition of, 98, 207, 208; unit of speech, 63, 88, 103. See Chapters IV, V *passim*.
sentence-form 184, 199. *See too* elocutional, locutional.
sentence-function 184, 198, 236.
sentence-qualifiers 226, 269.
sentence-quality 185, 192, 193.
Sethe, K., 308.
Sheffield, A. D., 4, 188.
signs 67, 68, 101 n.
silence 63. *See too* pauses.
similes 167.
simple sentences 320–2.
situation 49–52, 82, 114, 115, 122, 126, 127, 193, 194.
Smith, J. A., 57, 252.
soliloquy 206.
Sommer, F., 309 n.
Sonnenschein, E. A., 2, 286 n.
sound, area of, in words 338.
sound-signs 339.
special sentence-quality 186, 197.
specification, questions for, 304, 306–8.
speech 62, 87, 106–9, 328–30. And *passim*. *See too* parts of speech.
split infinitive 172.
Sprachpsychologie 104.
statements 188, 189, 293–303.
Stern, G., 336.

stimulus 32, 253, 254, 263, 277.
stress 203.
style 55, 56, 253.
subject 33, 214–18, 255, 260–88.
subordinate clauses 183, 217, 227–9.
substantive 144 n.
suppositio 32, 60.
symbol 101 n.
symptom 101 n.
syntactic form 92, 158, 159, 161.
syntax 158.
synthesis hypothesis 241.

tense 222.
'text' as synonym of 'concrete' speech 330.
theorist of speech 85, 86.
thing-meant 29–33, 78–82, 256–60.
things as subject-matter of speech 22–8, 37–44, 143.
thinking 27, 64, 326, 327.
thoughts 26, 27, 249.
truth and falsity 296–300.
'tweak' distinguished from 'twinge' 342.

ultimate thing-meant 257, 263.

undifferentiated word-sentence 116–19.

Vendryès, J., 135 n., 156 n., 224, 225.
verbs, defined, 9, 10. *See too* finite verbs.
vocatives 215 n., 310, 311.

Ward, J., 69 n., 117 n.
Wegener, Ph., 3, 12, 60, 68 n., 123, 124, 154 n., 182, 198, 202 n., 237, 265, 266, 270, 276, 277.
Wellander, E., 60, 120 n., 270 n.
word-consciousness 53–5.
word-form 130–41, 148–53.
word-function 141, 144, 148–53.
word-meaning 33–7.
word-order 226, 227, 244, 277, 305, 306, 308–10.
words 119–29; as class-names, 38, 43, 74, 256; as psychical entities, 69, 70; as units of language, 63, 88, 103. And *passim*.
writing 109, 110.
Wundt, W., 3, 10, 11, 58, 134, 135, 165 n., 238, 241–3, 245, 248–53.

PRINTED IN GREAT BRITAIN AT THE UNIVERSITY PRESS, OXFORD
BY VIVIAN RIDLER, PRINTER TO THE UNIVERSITY